•Bartholomew•
GLASGOW
Streetfinder
COLOUR ATLAS

Contents

Bartholomew
A Division of HarperCollins*Publishers*

Key to map symbols

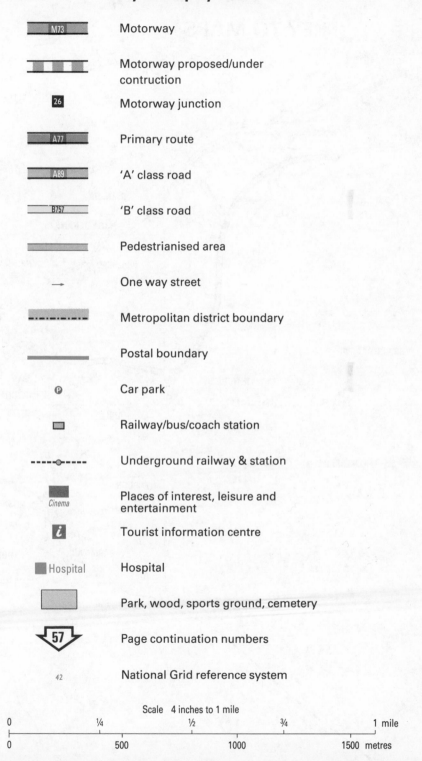

M73	Motorway
	Motorway proposed/under contruction
26	Motorway junction
A77	Primary route
A89	'A' class road
B757	'B' class road
	Pedestrianised area
→	One way street
	Metropolitan district boundary
	Postal boundary
Ⓟ	Car park
	Railway/bus/coach station
	Underground railway & station
Cinema	Places of interest, leisure and entertainment
i	Tourist information centre
Hospital	Hospital
	Park, wood, sports ground, cemetery
57	Page continuation numbers
42	National Grid reference system

Scale 4 inches to 1 mile

0 ¼ ½ ¾ 1 mile
0 500 1000 1500 metres

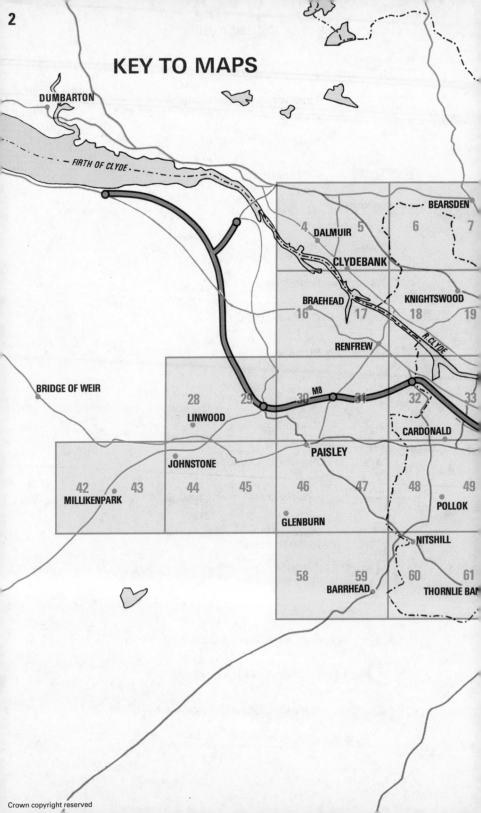

2

KEY TO MAPS

DUMBARTON

FIRTH OF CLYDE

BEARSDEN

4 DALMUIR

5

6

7

CLYDEBANK

BRAEHEAD

KNIGHTSWOOD

16

17

18

19

RENFREW

R CLYDE

BRIDGE OF WEIR

28

29

30 M8

31

32

33

LINWOOD

CARDONALD

JOHNSTONE

PAISLEY

42

43

44

45

46

47

48

49

MILLIKENPARK

POLLOK

GLENBURN

NITSHILL

58

59

60

61

BARRHEAD

THORNLIE BAI

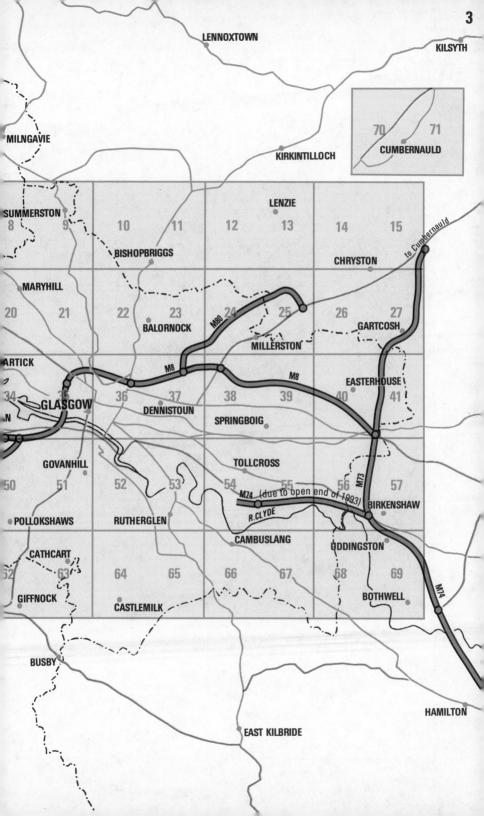

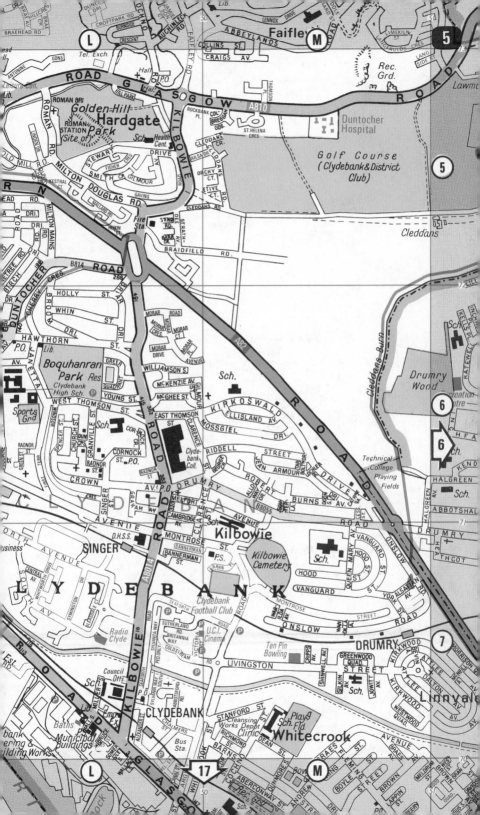

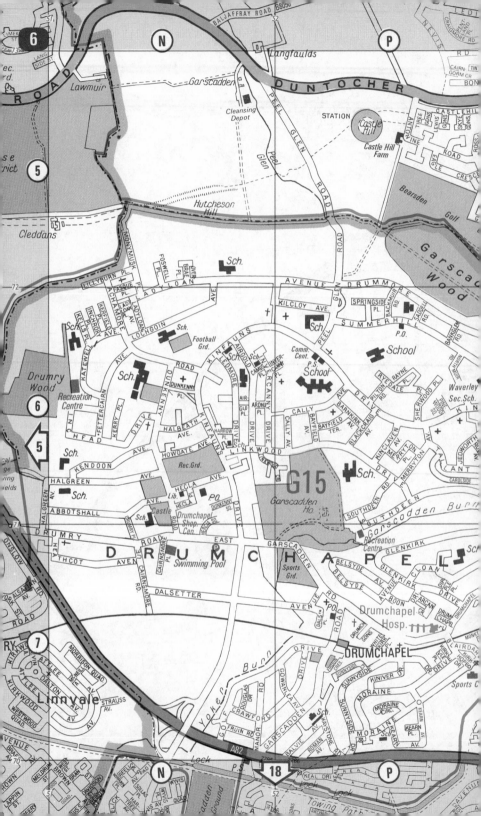

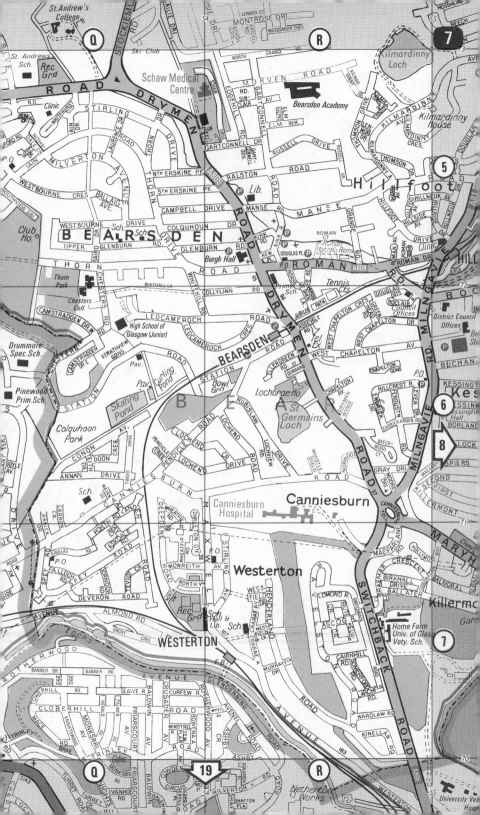

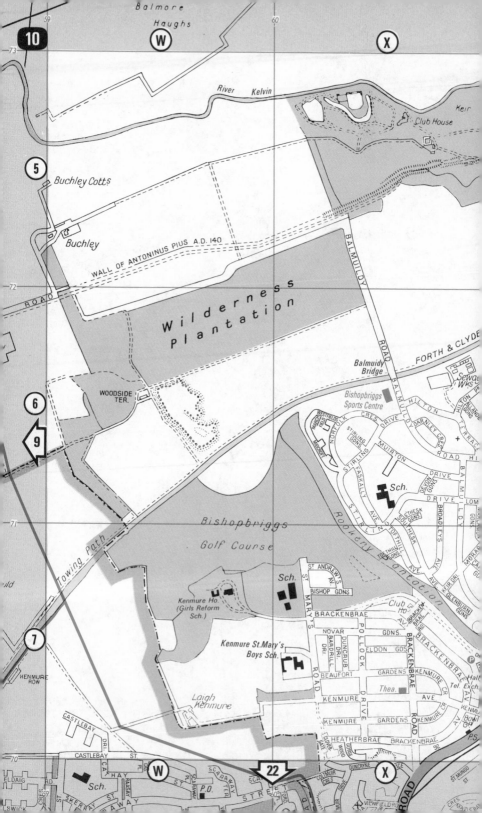

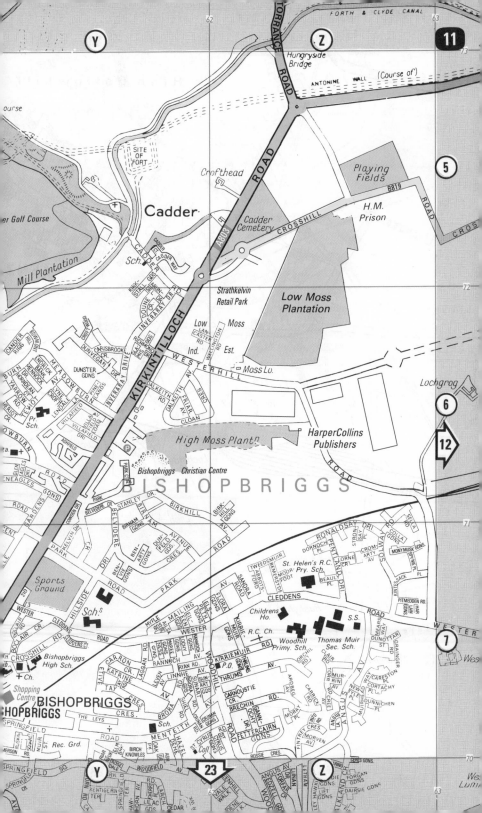

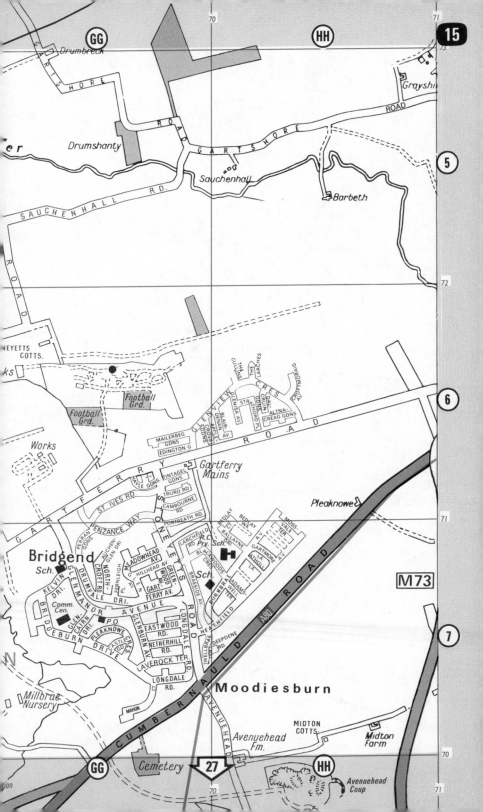

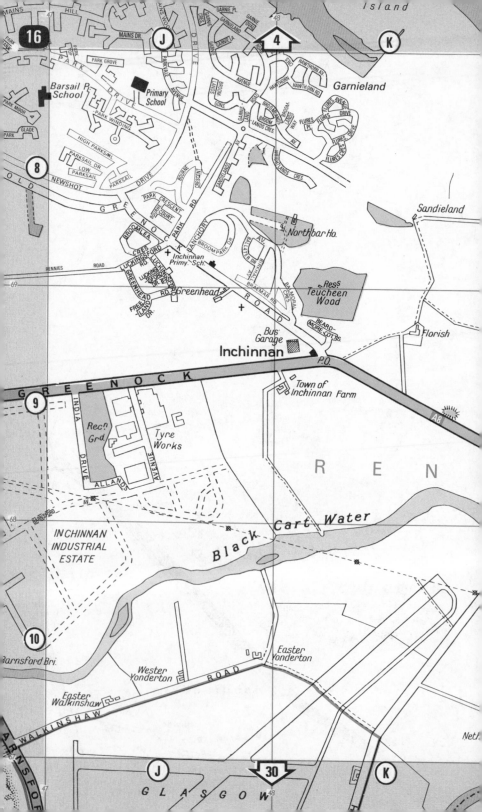

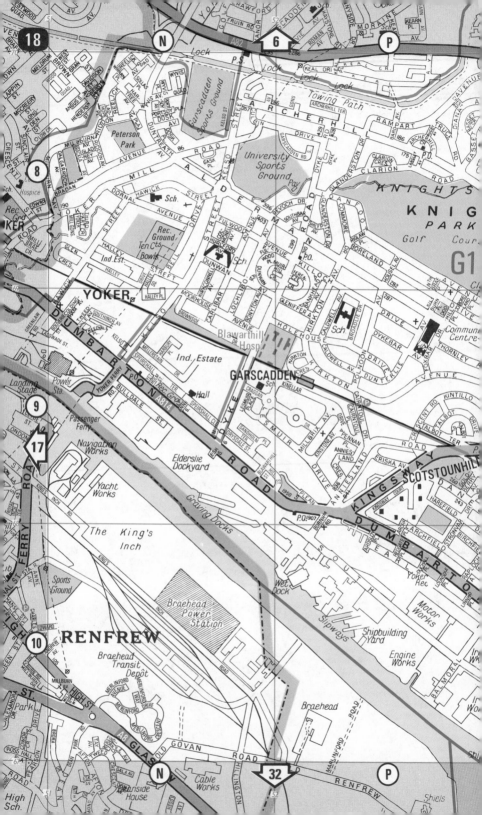

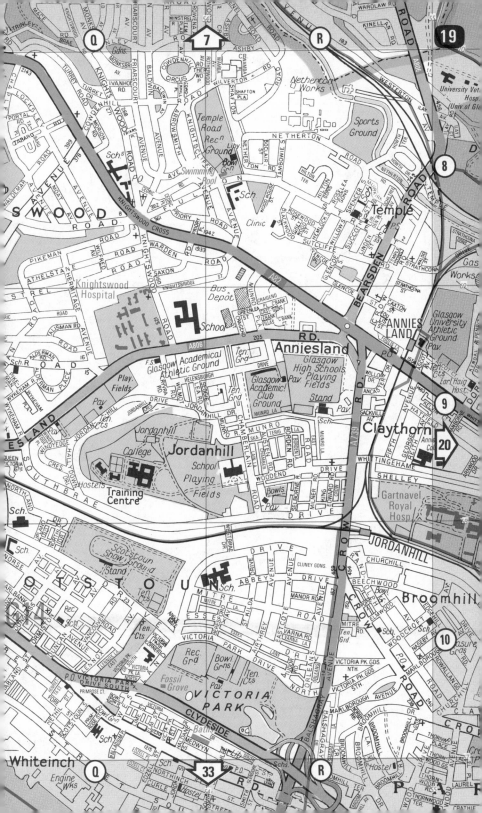

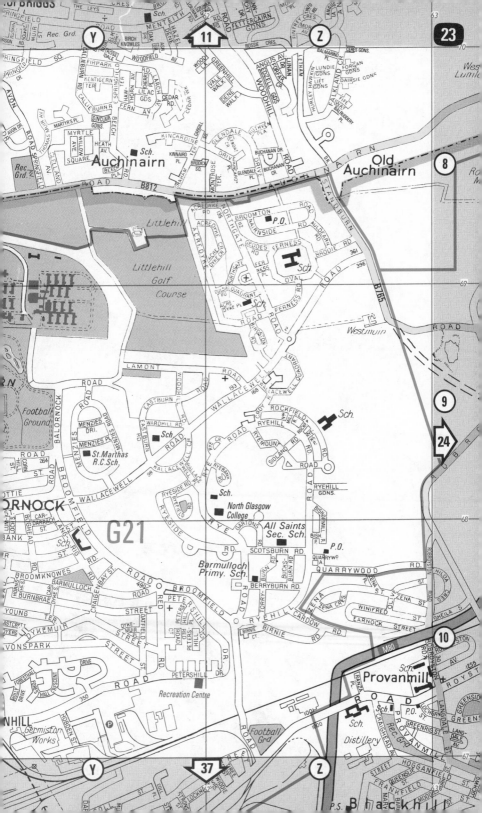

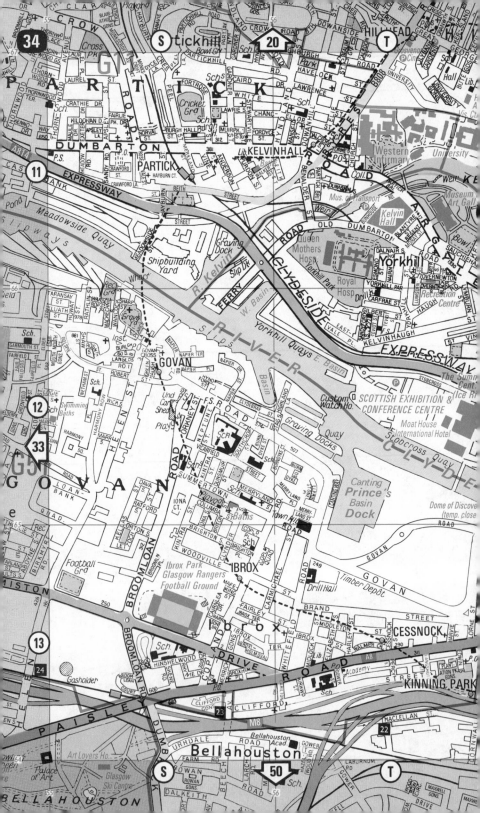

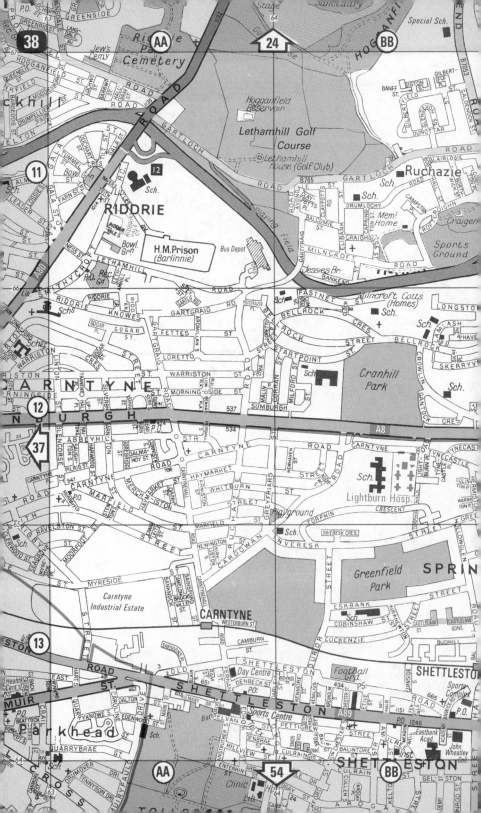

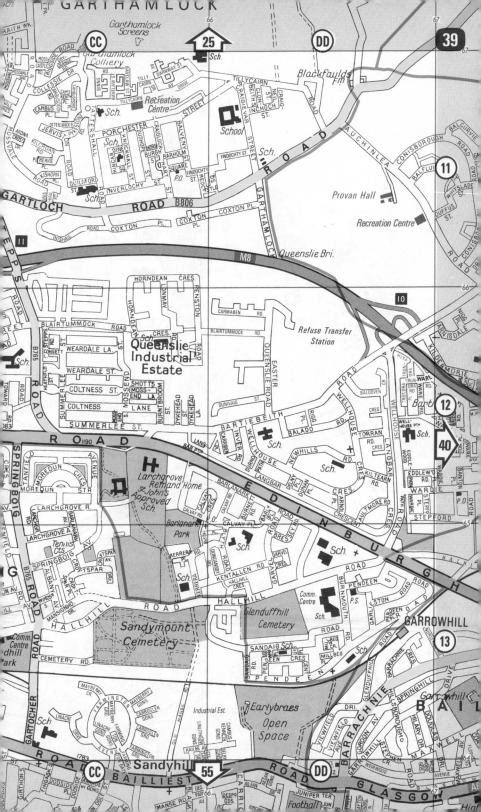

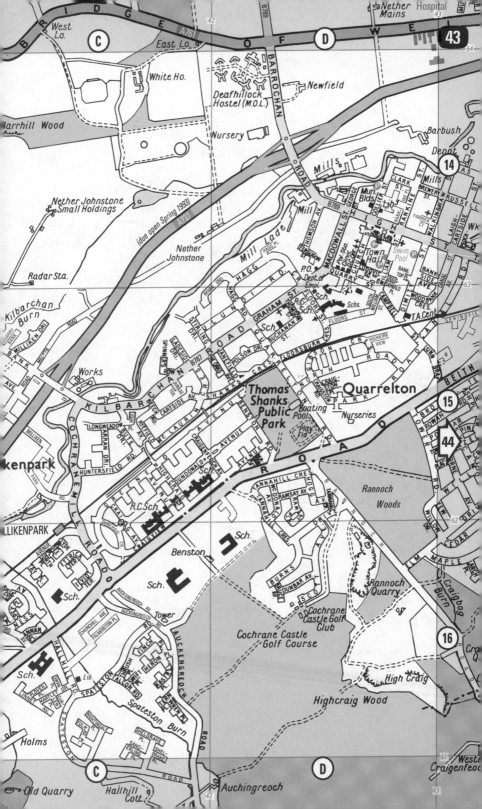

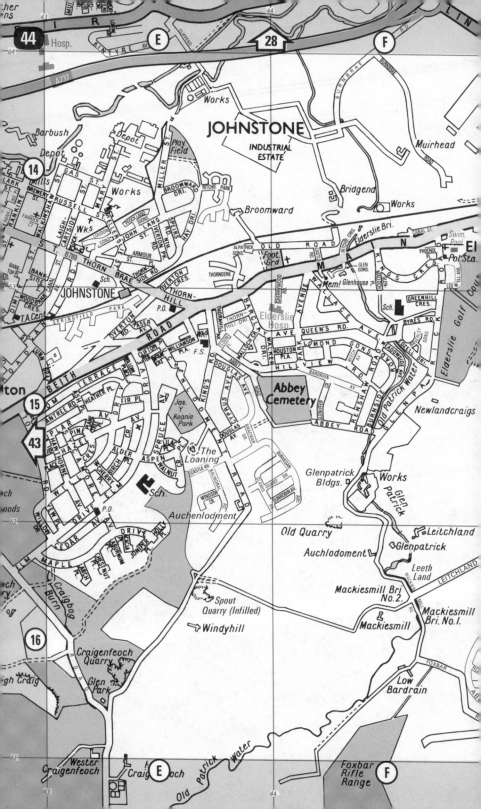

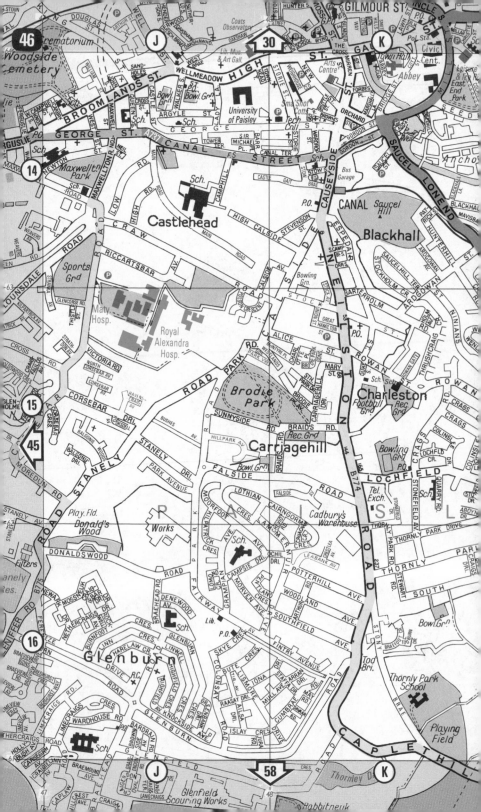

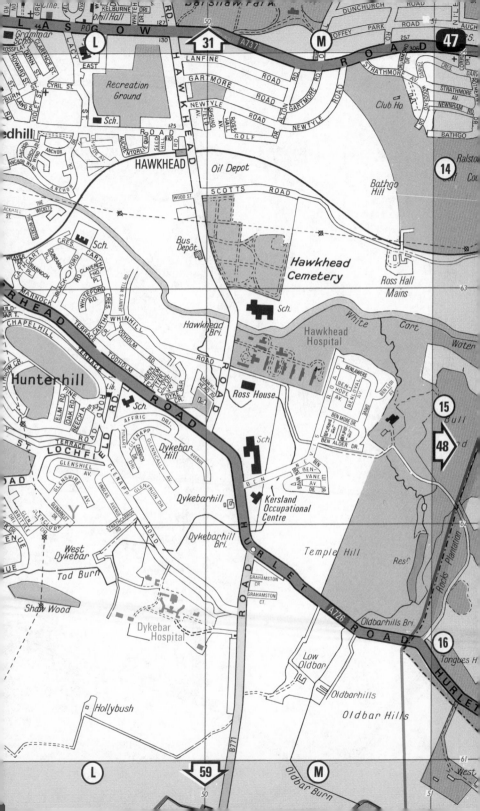

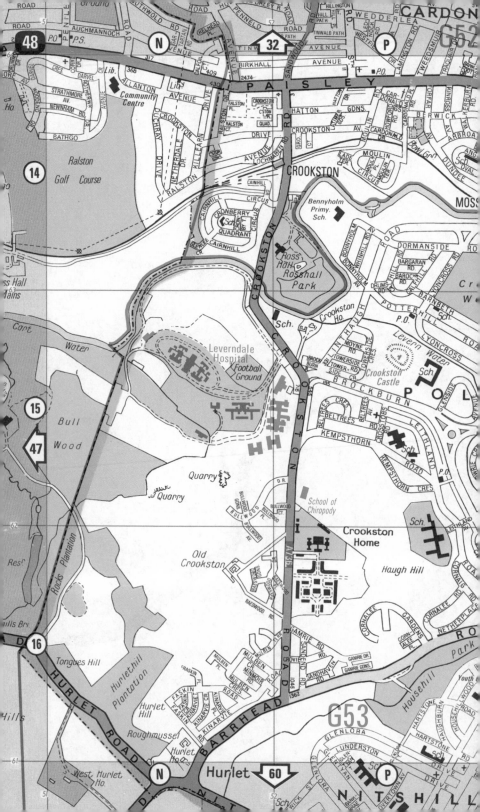

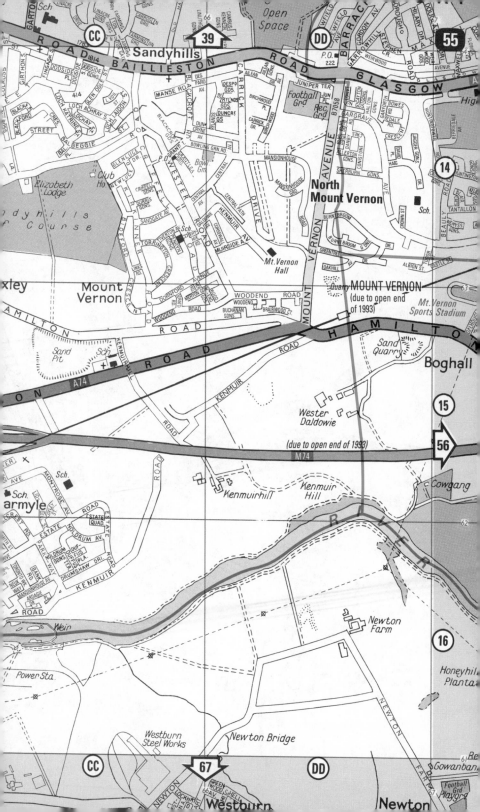

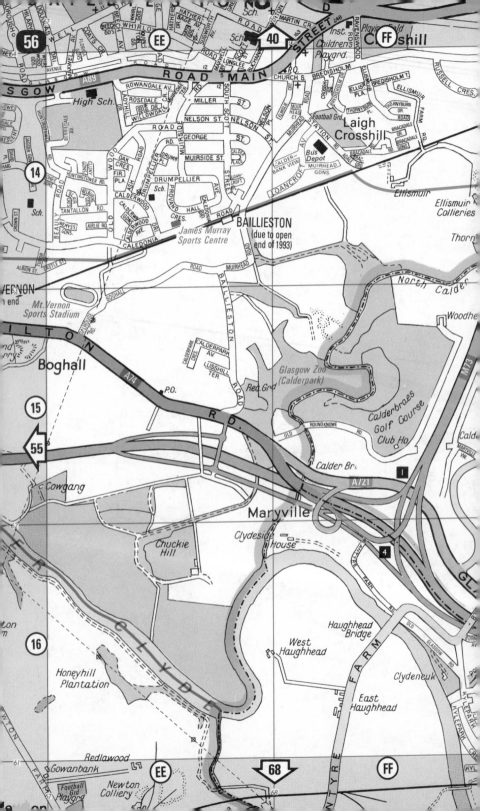

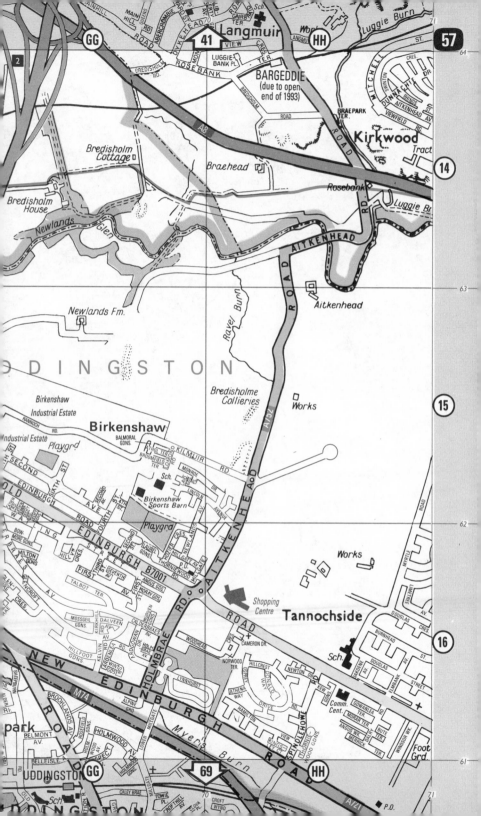

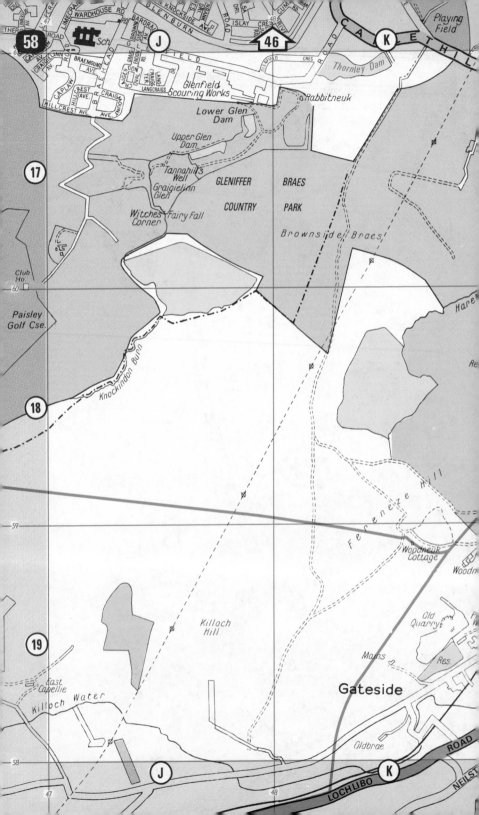

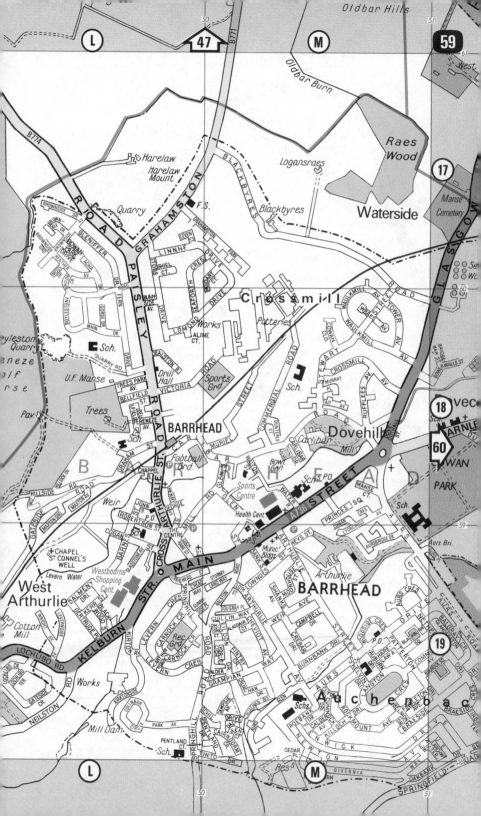

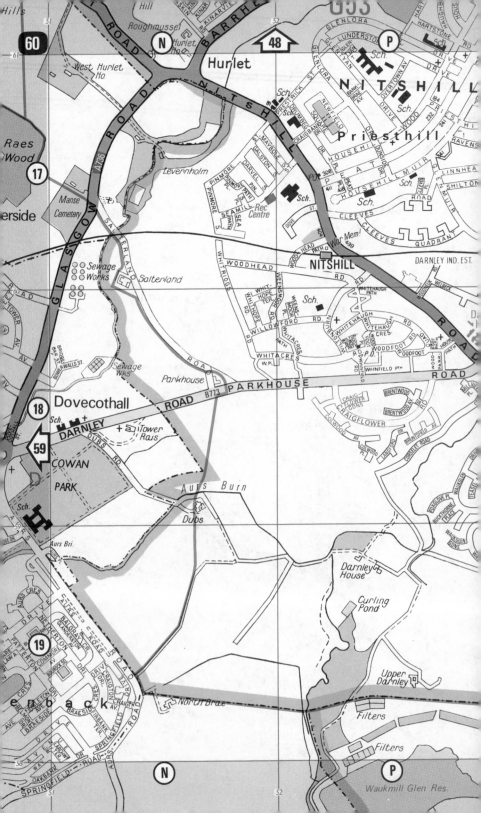

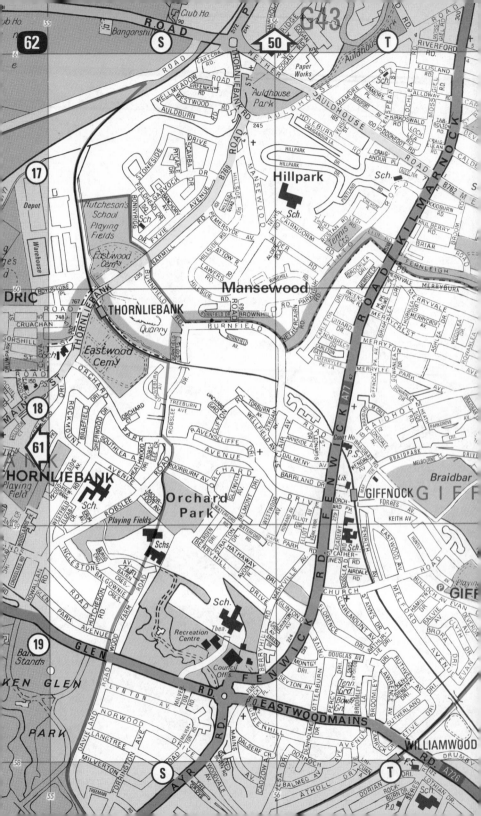

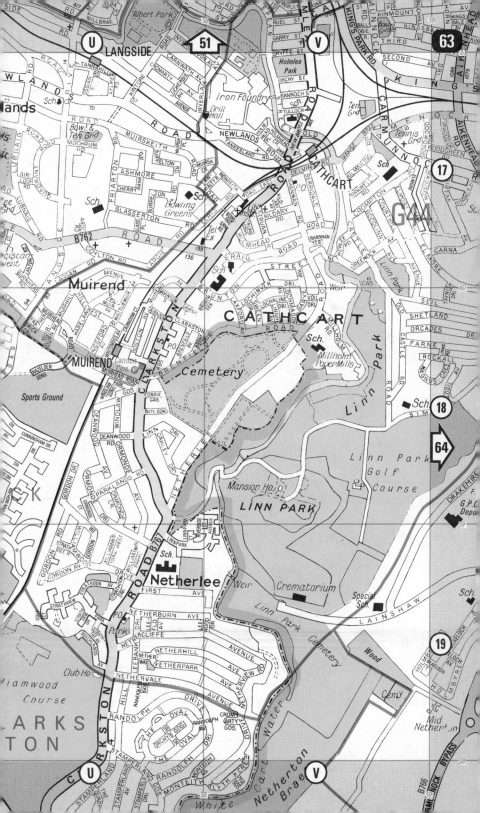

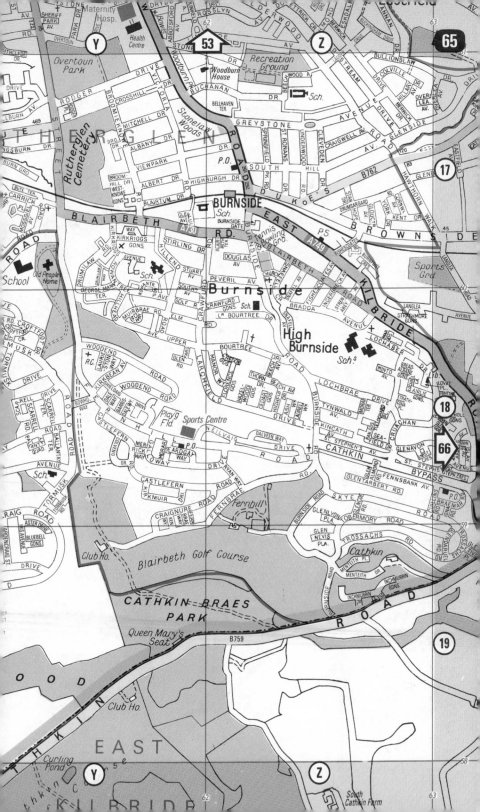

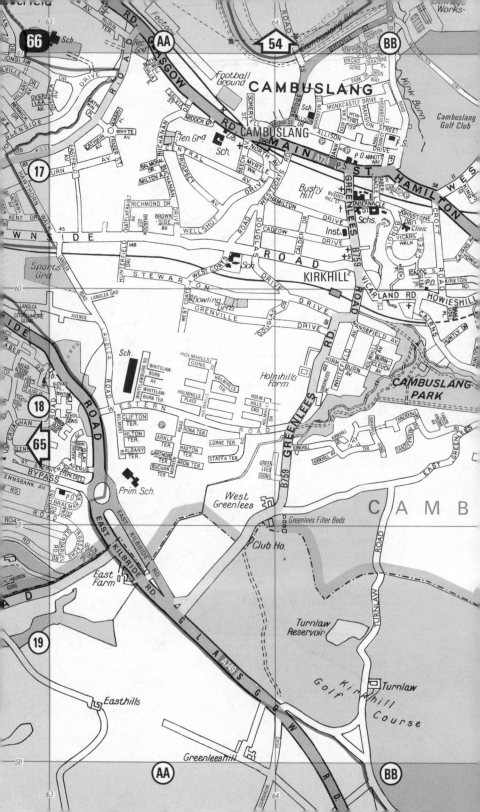

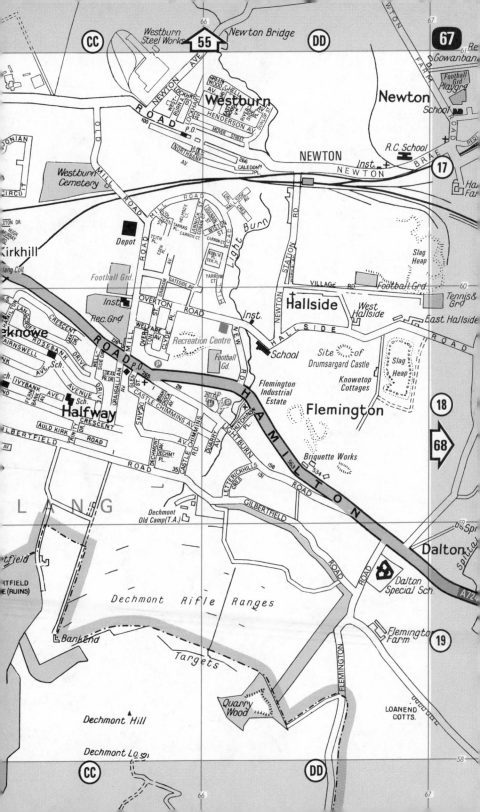

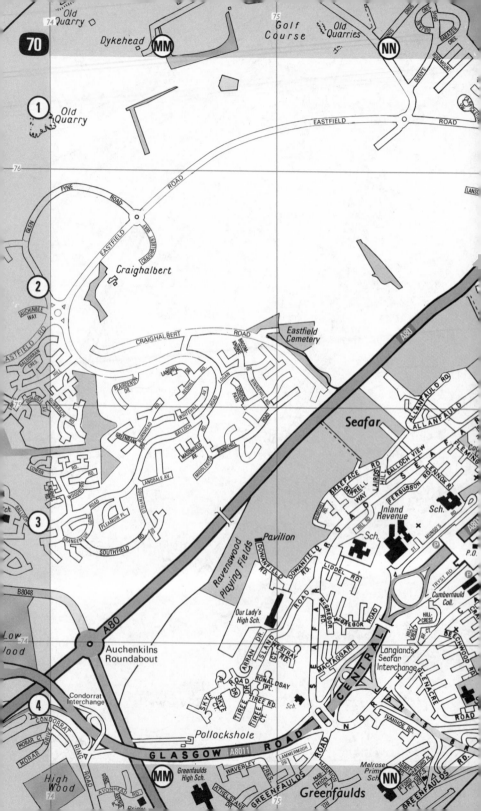

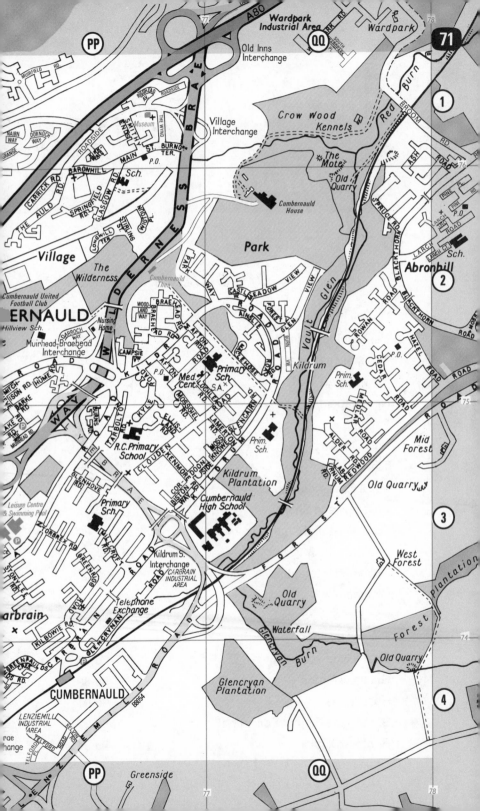

Glasgow

Information

Contents

History & Development

The City of Glasgow began life as a makeshift hamlet of huts huddled round a 6thC church, built by St. Mungo on the banks of a little salmon river - the Clyde. It was called Gleschow, meaning 'beloved green place' in Celtic. The cathedral was founded in 1136; the university, the second oldest in Scotland, was established in the 15thC; and in 1454 the flourishing medieval city wedged between the cathedral and the river was made a Royal burgh. The city's commercial prosperity dates from the 17thC when the lucrative tobacco, sugar and cotton trade with the New World flourished. The River Clyde, Glasgow's gateway to the Americas, was dredged, deepened and widened in the 18thC to make it navigable to the city's heart.

By the 19thC, Glasgow was the greatest shipbuilding centre in the world. From the 1820s onwards, it grew in leaps and bounds westwards along a steep ridge of land running parallel with the river. The hillside became encased in an undulating grid of streets and squares. Gradually the individualism, expressed in one-off set pieces characteristic of the 18thC and early 19thC, gave way to a remarkable coherent series of terraced squares and crescents of epic proportions - making Glasgow one of the finest of Victorian cities. But the price paid for such rapid industrialisation, the tremendous social problems manifest in the squalor of some of the worst of 19thC slums, was high. Today the city is still the commercial and industrial capita of the West of Scotland. The most notorious of the slums have been cleared but the new buildings lack that sparkling clenchfisted Glaswegian character of the 19thC. Ironically, this character was partially destroyed when the slums were cleared for it wasn't the architecture that had failed, only the bureaucrats, who designated such areas as working class ghettos.

Districts
Little remains of medieval Glasgow,

which stood on the wedge of land squeezed between the cathedral and the River Clyde. Its business centre was The Cross, a space formed by the junction of several streets - the tall, square Tolbooth Steeple, 1626, in the middle. Opposite is Trongate, an arch astride a footpath, complete with tower and steeple salvaged from 17thC St. Mary's Church - destroyed by fire in 1793. The centre of 20thC Glasgow is George Square, a tree-lined piazza planned in 1781 and pinned down by more than a dozen statues including an 80 foot high Doric column built in 1837 to carry a statue of Sir Walter Scott. Buildings of interest: the monumental neo-Baroque City Chambers 1883-88 which takes up the east side and the Merchants' House 1874, on the west. To the south of the square, in a huddle of narrow streets, is the old Merchant City. Of interest here is the elegant Trades House, 85 Glassford Street, built by Robert Adam in 1794. An elegant Ionic portico stands on a rusticated ground storey flanked by domed towers. Hutcheson's Hospital, 158 Ingram Street, is an handsome Italianate building designed by David Hamilton in 1805. Nearby is Stirling's Library, originally an 18thC private residence, it became the Royal Exchange in 1827 when the Corinthian portico was added. To the north west is Kelvingrove, Victorian Glasgow at its best. Built around a steep saddle of land, landscaped by Paxton in 1850 and lined along its edge with handsome terraces.

Last but not least are the banks of the River Clyde. From Clyde Walkway on the north bank you can see: the Suspension Bridge of 1871 with its pylons in the form of triumphal arches; the old clipper ship, C.V. Carrick, a contemporary of the Cutty Sark, moored by Victoria bridge; 17thC Merchants' Steeple; the Gothic Revival St. Andrew's R.C. Cathedral of 1816; the church, built 1739, in nearby St. Andrew's Square is a typical copy of London's St. Martin-in-the-Fields.

City of Glasgow Local Information Guide

Useful Information

Area of City 79 sq. miles (approx)

Population (Glasgow City)
(1989 estimate) 696,577

Early Closing Days
Tuesday with alternative of Saturday.
Most of the shops in the central area
operate six-day trading.

Electricity 240 volts A.C.

Emergency Services
Police, Fire and Ambulance. Dial 999
on any telephone.

Licensing Hours
Public Houses
Daily (except Sundays) 11 a.m. to 2.30
p.m. and 5 to 11 p.m. (many open
continuously 11 a.m. to 11 p.m.)
Sundays, 12.30 to 2.30 p.m. and 6.30
to 10.30 p.m.
Restaurants, Hotels and Public Houses
with catering facilities, same as above
but can be extended for drinks with
meals.

Information Bureau

Tourist Information Centres:
35 - 39 St. Vincent Place
Glasgow. 041 204 4400
Town Hall, Abbey Close,

Paisley. 041 889 0711

Glasgow Airport 041 848 4440

Strathclyde Transport Travel Centre
St. Enoch Square
Open Monday - Saturday 9.30 a.m. to
5.30 p.m. 041 226 4826 (Monday to
Saturday 7 a.m. to 9 p.m., Sunday 9
a.m. to 7.30 p.m.) for City services,
ferry services, local airlines, train and
express services. Free timetables are
available.

Help & Advice

British Broadcasting Corporation
Queen Margaret Drive, G12 8DQ.
041 339 8844

British Council
6 Belmont Crescent, G12 8ES.
041 339 8651

British Telecom Scotland
Glasgow Area
Westergate Chambers, 11 Hope Street,
Glasgow, G2 6AB. All Enquiries 041
220 1234 or dial 100 and ask for
FREEFONE BT GLASGOW.

Chamber of Commerce
30 George Square, G2 1EG.
041 204 2121.

Citizens Advice Bureau
87 Bath Street, Glasgow, G2 4HW
041 331 2345/6/7/8
119 Main Street, Glasgow, G40 1HA
041 554 0336
27 Dougrie Drive, Castlemilk, Glasgow,
G45 9AD 041 634 0338

139 Main Street (Town Hall),
Rutherglen, G73 2JJ   041 647 5100
216 Main Street, Barrhead, G78 1SN
041 881 2032
1145 Maryhill Road, Glasgow, G20 9AZ
041 946 6373/4
46 Township Centre, Easterhouse,
Glasgow, G34 9DS 041 771 2328

Consumer Advice Centre
St. Enoch House, 1 St. Enoch Square,
Glasgow, G1 4BH   041 204 0262

Customs and Excise
21 India Street, G2 4PZ   041 221 3828

H.M. Immigration Office
Admin Block D, Argyll Avenue, Glasgow
Airport   041 887 4115

Housing Aid and Advice
Shelter, 53 St. Vincent Crescent,
Glasgow, G3 8NQ   041 221 8895/6

Legal Aid and Advice
Castlemilk Advice and Law Centre
27 Dougrie Drive, Glasgow, G45 9AD
041 634 0338

Law Centre
30 Dougrie Drive, G45 9AG
 041 634 0313

Lost Property
Strathclyde Passenger Transport
Executive
Glasgow Central Station 041 335 4362
(Scotrail Trains)
Glasgow Queen Street Station 041 335
3276 (Scotrail Trains and Underground)
St. Enoch Underground Station
 041 248 6950 (City Buses)
Other Buses - Office of bus company.
Trains - Station of arrival.
Elsewhere in City - Strathclyde Police.
Lost Property Department, 173 Pitt
Street, G2 041 204 1468

Passport Office
Northgate 96 Milton Street, Glasgow,
G4 0BT 041 332 0271

**Registrar of Births, Deaths and
Marriages**
1 Martha Street, G1 4PF 041 225 7677
Hours - Monday to Friday 9.15 a.m. to
4.00 p.m.

Births must be registered within twenty-
one days, deaths within eight days and
marriages within three days. The
Registrar should be consulted at least
one month before intended date of
marriage.

**Royal Scottish Society for the
Prevention of Cruelty to Children**
15 Annfield Place, G31 2XE
041 556 1156

**RNID - Royal National Institute for
the Deaf**
9 Clairmont Gardens, Glasgow, G3
7LW 041 332 0343

Samaritans
218 West Regent Street, Glasgow, G2
4DQ 041 248 4488

**Scottish Society for the Mentally
Handicapped**
13 Elmbank Street, Glasgow, G2 4QA
041 226 4541

Scottish Television
Cowcaddens, G2 041 332 9999

**Society for the Prevention of Cruelty
to Animals**
15 Royal Terrace, G3 7NY (Business
Hours) 041 332 0716

Newspapers

Morning Daily
Daily Record
Anderston Quay, G3 8DA.
041 248 7000

Glasgow Herald
195 Albion Street, G1   041 552 6255

Scottish Daily Express
Park Circus Place, G3   041 332 9600

The Scotsman
181 - 195 West George Street, G2 2LB
041 221 6485

Evening Daily
Evening Times
195 Albion Street, G1   041 552 6255

Weekly
Scottish Sunday Express
Park Circus Place, G3   041 332 9600

Sunday Mail
Anderston Quay, G3 8DA
041 248 7000

Sunday Post
144 Port Dundas Road, G4 0HF
 041 332 9933

Parking

Car Parking in the central area of Glasgow is controlled. Parking meters are used extensively and signs indicating restrictions are displayed at kerbsides and on entry to the central area. Traffic Wardens are on duty.

British Rail Car Parks
(Open 24 hours)
Central Station
Queen Street Station

Multi-Storey Car Parks
(Open 24 hours)
Anderston Cross: Cambridge Street: George Street: Mitchell Street: Port Dundas Road: Waterloo Street.

(Limited Opening)
Charing Cross: Cowcaddens Road: St. Enoch Centre:Sauchiehall Street Centre

Surface Car Parks
Cathedral Street (Concert Hall):Dunlop Street: High Street: Ingram Street: King Street: McAlpine Street: Oswald Street: Shuttle Street:

Post Offices

Head Post Office
George Square, G2 041 248 2882
Open Monday to Thursday 9 a.m. to 5.30 p.m. Fridays 9.30 a.m. to 5.30 p.m. Saturdays 9 a.m. to 12.30 p.m.
Closed Sunday.

Branch Offices
85-91 Bothwell Street, G2
216 Hope Street, G2
533 Sauchiehall Street, G3

Taxis

Glasgow has over 1400 traditional London type taxis, all licensed by the Glasgow District Council and all fitted with meters sealed and approved by the Council. A fare card stating the current tariff is displayed in a prominent position within each taxi. At the time of publishing a three mile journey costs £3.10 and waiting time is charged at 13½p per minute. The total price of each journey is shown on the meter. Fares are normally reviewed annually by the council. Each taxi can carry a maximum of five passengers.

The major taxi companies in the city offer City tours at fixed prices, listing the places of interest to be visited, leaflets are available at all major hotel reception areas. Tours vary from 2 to 3 hours and in price between £20 and £28. A tour "Glasgow by Night" is also available at a cost of £10.00.

Any passenger wishing to travel to a destination outside the Glasgow District Boundary should ascertain from the driver the fare to be charged or the method of calculating the fare PRIOR to making the journey.

Complaints
Any complaints regarding the conduct of a taxi driver should be addressed to the Senior Enforcement Officer, Town Clerk's Office, City Chambers, Glasgow. 041 227 4535

Local Government

Strathclyde Regional Council
Strathclyde House, 20 India Street
Glasgow, G2 4PF
041 204 2900

District Councils:

Argyll & Bute
District Council Headquarters
Kilmory, Lochgilphead PA31 8RT
0546 2127

Bearsden & Milngavie
Municipal Building, Boclair
Bearsden G61 2TQ
041 942 2262

Clydebank
Council Offices, Rosebery Place
Clydebank G81 1TG
041 941 1331

Clydesdale
Clydesdale District Offices
Lanark ML11 7JT
0555 61331

Cumbernauld & Kilsyth
Council Offices, Bron Way
Cumbernauld G67 1DZ
0236 722131

Cummock & Doon Valley
Council Offices, Lugar
Cummock KA18 3JQ
0290 22111

Cunninghame
Cunninghame House
Irvine KA12 8EE
0294 74166

Dumbarton
Crosslet House
Dumbarton G82 3NS
0389 65100

East Kilbride
Civic Centre
East Kilbride G74 1AB
0352 71200

Eastwood
Council Offices
Eastwood Park, Rouken Glen Road
Rouken Glen, Giffnock
Glasgow G46 6UG
041 638 6511
041 638 1101

Glasgow City
City Chambers
Glasgow G2 1DU
041 221 9600

Hamilton
Town House
102 Cadzow Street
Hamilton ML3 6HH
0698 282323

Inverclyde
Municipal Buildings
Greenock PA15 1LY
0475 24400

Kilmarnock & Loudoun
Civic Centre
Kilmarnock KA1 1BY
0563 21140

Kyle & Carrick
Burns House
Burns Statue Square
Ayr KA7 1UT
0292 281511

Monklands
Municipal Buildings
Dunbeth Road
Coatbridge ML5 3LF
0236 441200

Motherwell
P.O. Box 14
Civic Centre
Motherwell ML1 1TW
0698 266166

Renfrew
Municipal Buildings
Cotton Street
Paisley PA1 1BU
041 889 5400

Strathkelvin
Tom Johnston House
Civic Way
Kirkintilloch
Glasgow G66 4TJ
041 776 7171

Buildings & Shops

Interesting Buildings

Victorian Glasgow was extremely eclectic architecturally. Good examples of the Greek Revival style are Royal College of Physicians 1845, by W.H. Playfair and the Custom House 1840, by G.L. Taylor. The Queen's Room 1857, by Charles Wilson, is a handsome temple used now as a Christian Science church. The Gothic style is seen at its most exotic in the Stock Exchange 1877, by J. Burnet. The new Victorian materials and techniques with glass, wrought and cast iron were also ably demonstrated in the buildings of the time. Typical are: Gardener's Stores 1856, by J. Baird; the Buck's Head, Argyle Street, an amalgam of glass and cast iron; and the Egyptian Halls of 1873, in Union Street, which has a masonry framework. Both are by Alexander Thomson. The Templeton Carpet Factory 1889, Glasgow Green, by William Leiper, is a Venetian Gothic building complete with battlemented parapet.

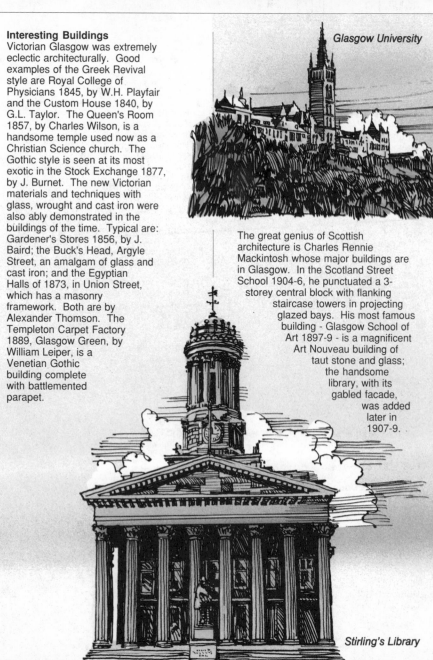

Glasgow University

The great genius of Scottish architecture is Charles Rennie Mackintosh whose major buildings are in Glasgow. In the Scotland Street School 1904-6, he punctuated a 3-storey central block with flanking staircase towers in projecting glazed bays. His most famous building - Glasgow School of Art 1897-9 - is a magnificent Art Nouveau building of taut stone and glass; the handsome library, with its gabled facade, was added later in 1907-9.

Stirling's Library

Galleries & museums

Scotland's largest tourist attraction, The Burrell Collection, is situated in Pollok Country Park, Haggs Road and has more than 8,000 objects, housed in an award winning gallery. The Museum and Art Gallery, Kelvingrove Park, Argyle Street, a palatial sandstone building with glazed central court, has one of the best municipal collections in Britain; superb Flemish, Dutch and French paintings, drawings, prints, also ceramics, silver, costumes and armour, as well as a natural history section. The recently refurbished McLellan Galleries in Sauchiehall Street provide an important venue for touring and temporary art exhibitions. Provand's Lordship c1471, in Castle Street, is Glasgow's oldest house and now a museum of 17th-18thC furniture and household articles. Pollok House, Pollok Country Park, a handsome house designed by William Adam in 1752, has paintings by William Blake and a notable collection of Spanish paintings, including works by El Greco. The Museum of Transport, housed in Kelvin Hall, Bunhouse Road, has a magnificent collection of trams, cars, ships models, bicycles, horse-drawn carriages and 7 steam locos. The People's Palace, The Green built 1898 with a huge glazed Winter Garden, has a lively illustrated history of the city. But the oldest museum in Glasgow is the Hunterian Museum, University of Glasgow, University Avenue, opened in 1807, it has a fascinating collection of manuscripts, early painted books, as well as some fine archaeological and geological exhibits. 400-year old Haggs Castle, St. Andrew's Drive, is now a children's museum with practical demonstrations and exhibits showing how everyday life has changed over the centuries.

Streets & shopping

The Oxford Street of Glasgow is Sauchiehall (meaning 'willow meadow') Street. This together with Buchanan Street, Argyle Street, Princes Square and St. Enoch Centre form the main shopping area. Here you will find the department stores, boutiques and

Old Sheriff Court

general shops. All three streets are partly pedestrianised, but the most exhilarating is undoubtedly Buchanan Street. Of particular interest is the spatially elegant Argyll Arcade 1828, the Venetian Gothic-style Stock Exchange 1877, the picturesque Dutch gabled Buchanan Street Bank building 1896 and the Glasgow Royal Concert Hall (opened 1990). In Glasgow Green is The Barrows, the city's famous street market, formed by the junction of London Road and Kent Street. The Market is open weekends. Some parts of the city have EC Tue.

Museum & Art Gallery Kelvingrove

Cathedrals & Churches

Glasgow Cathedral is a perfect example of pre-Reformation Gothic architecture. Begun in 1238, it has a magnificent choir and handsome nave with shallow projecting transepts. On a windy hill to the east is the Necropolis, a cemetery with a spiky skyline of Victoriana consisting of pillars, temples and obelisks, dominated by an 1825 Doric column carrying the statue of John Knox. Other churches of interest: Landsdowne Church built by J. Honeyman in 1863; St. George's Tron Church by William Stark 1807; Caledonian Road Church, a temple and tower atop a storey-high base, designed by Alexander Thomson in 1857; a similar design is to be found at the United Presbyterian Church, St. Vincent Street, 1858, but on a more highly articulated ground storey; Queen's Cross Church 1897 is an amalgam of Art Nouveau and Gothic Revival by the brilliant Charles Rennie Mackintosh.

Churches within the central area of Glasgow are:

Church of Scotland
Glasgow Cathedral
Castle Street
Renfield St. Stephen's Church
262 Bath Street
St. George's Tron Church
165 Buchanan Street
St. Columba Church (Gaelic)
300 St. Vincent Street

Baptist
Adelaide Place Church
209 Bath Street

Congregational
Hillhead Centre
1 University Avenue

Episcopal Church in Scotland
Cathedral Church of St. Mary
300 Great Western Road

First Church of Christ Scientist
1 La Bell Place, Clifton Street
(off Sauchiehall Street)

Free Church of Scotland
265 St. Vincent Street

German Speaking Congregation
Services held at 7 Hughenden Terrace

Greek Orthodox Cathedral
St. Luke's, 27 Dundonald Road

Jewish Orthodox Synagogue
Garnethill, 29 Garnet Street

Methodist
Woodlands Church
229 Woodlands Road

Roman Catholic
St. Andrew's Cathedral
190 Clyde Street
St. Aloysius' Church
25 Rose Street

Unitarian Church
72 Berkeley Street

United Free
Wynd Church
427 Crown Street

Entertainment

As Scotland's commercial and industrial capital, Glasgow offers a good choice of leisure activities. The city now has many theatres where productions ranging from serious drama to pantomime, pop and musicals are performed. The Theatre Royal, Hope Street is Scotland's only opera house and has been completely restored to its full Victorian splendour. The Royal Scottish National Orchestra gives concerts at the Glasgow Royal Concert Hall every Saturday night in winter and is the venue for the proms in June. Cinemas are still thriving in Glasgow, as are the many public houses, some of which provide meals and live entertainment. In the city centre and Byres Road, West End, there is a fair number of restaurants where traditional home cooking, as well as international cuisines, can be sampled. More night life can be found at the city's discos and dance halls.

Outdoors, apart from the many parks and nature trails, there is Calderpark Zoological Gardens, situated 6 miles from the centre between Mount Vernon and Uddingston. Here you may see white rhinos, black panthers and iguanas among many species. Departing from Stobcross Quay, you can also cruise down the Clyde in 'P.S. Waverley' - the last sea-going paddle-steamer in the world.

Cinemas

Cannon Cinema, 380 Clarkston Road
041 637 2641
MGM Film Centre
326 Sauchiehall Street 041 332 9513
(Admin Dept), 326 Sauchiehall Street
041 332 1592
326 Sauchiehall Street
041 332 1593
Caledonian Associated Cinemas Ltd
Regent House, 72 Renfield Street
041 332 0606
Glasgow Film Theatre
12 Rose Street (Box Off)
041 332 6535
Grosvenor Cinema
Ashton Lane 041 339 4298

Kelburne Cinema
(Manager), Glasgow Road, Paisley. 041 889 3612
Odeon Film Centre
56 Renfield Street 041 332 8701

Halls

City Halls, Candleriggs
Couper Institute
86 Clarkston Road
Dixon Halls, 650 Cathcart Road
Glasgow Royal Concert Hall
2 Sauchiehall Street
Govan Hall, Summertown Road
Kelvin Hall, Argyle Street,
Langside Hall, 5 Langside Avenue
Partick Burgh Hall, 9 Burgh Hall Street,
Pollokshaws Hall
2025 Pollokshaws Road,
Woodside Hall, Glenfarg Street
(More information about the above G.D.C. halls and others from the Director, Halls and Theatres Department, Candleriggs 041 552 1202).

Theatres

Arches Theatre
Midland Street 041 221 9736
Citizens' Theatre
Gorbals Street 041 429 0022
King's Theatre
Bath Street 041 227 5511
Mitchell Theatre and Moir Hall
Granville Street 041 227 5511
New Athenaeum Theatre
Renfrew Street 041 332 5057
Old Athenaeum Theatre
Buchanan Street 041 332 2333
Pavilion Theatre
Renfield Street 041 332 1846
Theatre Royal
Hope Street 041 332 9000
Tramway
Albert Drive 041 227 5511
Tron Theatre
38 Parnie Street. 041 552 4267
The Ticket Centre
Glasgow's Central Box Office for Arches Theatre, Centre for Contemporary Arts, Citizens' Theatre, City Hall at Candleriggs, G1, Kelvin Hall, King's Theatre, Mitchell Theatre, New Athenaeum Theatre, Old Athenaeum Theatre, Theatre Royal, Tron Theatre.
Open Monday to Saturday 10.30 a.m. to 6.30 p.m. 041 227 5511

Sport & Recreation

For both spectator and participant, football is Glasgow's favourite sport. Both Celtic and Rangers, Scotland's most famous rival teams, have their grounds within the City. Glasgow houses Scotland's national football stadium at Hampden Park.

Badminton

Scottish Badminton Union's Cockburn Centre, Bogmoor Place, G51 4TQ.
041 445 1218

Bowling Greens

There are greens in all the main Parks. Information about clubs from the Scottish Bowling Association: 50 Wellington Street, G2. 041 221 8999

Cricket Grounds

Cartha Haggs Road, G41.
Clydesdale Beaton Road, G41.
Huntershill Crowhill Road, Bishopbriggs.
Poloc 'Shawholm', 2060 Pollokshaws Road, G43.
West of Scotland Peel Street, G11.

Football Grounds

Celtic Park (Celtic F.C.)
95 Kerrydale Street, G40
Firhill Park (Partick Thistle F.C. & Clyde F.C.)
Firhill Road, G20
Hampden Park (Queen's Park F.C.)
Somerville Drive, G42
Ibrox Stadium (Rangers F.C.)
Edmiston Drive, G51
Kilbowie Park (Clydebank F.C.)
Argyll Road, Clydebank
Mertland
Kirkintilloch
St. Mirren Park (St. Mirren F.C.)
Love Street, Paisley

Golf Courses

Glasgow District Council
9 holes
Alexandra Park, Alexandra Parade, G31
King's Park, Carmunnock Road, G44
Knightswood, Lincoln Avenue, G13
Ruchill, Brassey Street, G20

18 holes
Lethamhill, Cumbernauld Road, G33
Littlehill, Auchinairn Road, G64.
Linn Park, Simshill Road, G44

(Charges displayed)
Douglaston Golf Course, Strathblane Road, Milngavie. (Five miles from Glasgow). Open to the public daily. 041 956 5750 for charges.

Putting Greens
There are putting greens in some of the main parks.

Pitch & Putt
Courses at Bellahouston Park, Queen's Park, Rouken Glen and several others.

Rugby Grounds

Auldhouse (Hutchesons'/Aloysians)
Thornliebank

Garscadden (Glasgow University)
Garscadden Road South, G15.

Hughenden (Hillhead High School)
Hughenden Road, G12.

New Anniesland (Glasgow Acad.)
Helensburgh Drive, G13.

Old Anniesland (Glasgow High School F.P. & Kelvinside Academicals)
Crow Road, G11.

Westerlands (Glasgow University)
Ascot Avenue, G12.

Sports Centres

Bellahouston Bellahouston Drive, G52. 041 427 5454

Burnhill Toryglen Road, Rutherglen, G73.
041 643 0327

Crownpoint Crownpoint Road, Bridgeton, G40.
041 554 8274

James Murray Caledonia Road, Baillieston, G69.
041 773 0881

Springburn Springburn Way, Springburn, G21.
041 558 2666

Helenvale Park Outdoor Sports Complex, Helenvale Street, G31. 041 554 4109

Swimming Baths

Glasgow District Council
Castlemilk, 137 Castlemilk Drive, G45.
Drumchapel, 199 Drumry Road East, G15.
Easterhouse, Bogbain Road, G34.
Govan, Harhill Street, G51.
Govanhill, 99 Calder Street, G42.
North Woodside, Braid Square, G4.
Pollokshaws (Dry-Land/Water Sports Complex) Ashtree Road, G43.
Rutherglen, 44 Greenhill Road, G73.
Shettleston, Elvan Street, G32.
Temple, Knightscliffe Avenue, G13.
Whitehall, Onslow Drive, G31.
Whiteinch, Medwyn Street, G14. (Open to public lunchtime and evenings).

Hours
Monday to Friday 9 a.m. to 9 p.m.
Saturday 9 a.m. to 1 p.m.
* Sunday 9 a.m. to 1 p.m.

Charges
Admission charges are minimal. OAPs free at certain times.

Turkish Baths/ Sun Beds

available at:
Govanhill   041 423 0233

Pollokshaws 041 632 2200
Shettleston 041 778 1346
Whiteinch 041 959 2465

Sauna at:
Castlemilk 041 634 8254
Drumchapel 041 944 5812
Rutherglen 041 647 4530
Whitehill 041 551 9969

Men and women on separate
days. Telephone direct to
baths for more information.

Hours
(All the year round).
Monday to Friday 9 a.m. to 9
p.m.
Saturday 9 a.m. to 1 p.m.

Tennis

There are courts in some of
the main parks. Information
about clubs from the Secretary
of the West of Scotland Lawn
Tennis Association: Mr N.
Floyd, 1 Boclair Road,
Bearsden 041 942 0162.

Weather

The City of Glasgow is on the same
latitude as the City of Moscow, but
because of its close proximity to the
warm Atlantic Shores, and the
prevailing westerly winds, it enjoys a
more moderate climate. Summers are
generally cool and winters mostly mild,
this gives Glasgow fairly consistent
summer and winter temperatures.
Despite considerable cloud the City is
sheltered by hills to the south-west and
north and the average rainfall for
Glasgow is usually less than 40 inches
per year. The following table shows the
approximate average figures for
sunshine, rainfall and temperatures to
be expected in Glasgow throughout the
year.

Weather Forecasts
For the Glasgow Area including Loch
Lomond and the Clyde Coast:
Weatherline
0898 500421 (Recording)
The Glasgow Weather Centre
(Meteorological Office), 33 Bothwell
Street, G2 041 248 3451

Month	Hours of Sunshine	Inches of Rainfall	Temperature °C		
			Ave. Max.	Ave. Min.	High/Low
Jan	36	3.8	5.5	0.8	−18
Feb	62	2.8	6.3	0.8	−15
Mar	94	2.4	8.8	2.2	21
Apr	147	2.4	11.9	3.9	22
May	185	2.7	15.1	6.2	26
June	181	2.4	17.9	9.3	30
July	159	2.9	18.6	10.8	29
Aug	143	3.5	18.5	10.6	31
Sept	106	4.1	16.3	9.1	−4
Oct	76	4.1	13.0	6.8	−8
Nov	47	3.7	8.7	3.3	−11
Dec	30	4.2	6.5	1.9	−12

Parks & Gardens

There are over 70 public parks within the city. The most famous is Glasgow Green. Abutting the north bank of the River Clyde, it was acquired in 1662. Of interest are the Winter Gardens attached to the People's Palace. Kelvingrove Park is an 85-acre park laid out by Sir Joseph Paxton in 1852. On the south side of the city is the 148-acre Queen's Park, Victoria Road, established 1857 - 94. Also of interest: Rouken Glen, Thornliebank, with a spectacular waterfall, walled garden, nature trail and boating facilities; Victoria Park, Victoria Park Drive, with its famous Fossil Grove flower gardens and yachting pond. In Great Western Road are the Botanic Gardens. Founded in 1817, the gardens' 42 acres are crammed with natural attractions, including the celebrated Kibble Palace glasshouse with its fabulous tree ferns, exotic plants and white marble Victorian statues.

The main public parks in Glasgow are:

Alexandra
671 Alexandra Parade, G31.

Bellahouston
Paisley Road West, G52.

Botanic Gardens
730 Gt. Western Road, G12.

Hogganfield Loch
Cumbernauld Road, G33.

Kelvingrove
Sauchiehall Street, G3.

King's
325 Carmunnock Road, G44.

Linn
Clarkston Road at Netherlee Road, G44.

Queen's
Victoria Road, G42.

Rouken Glen
Rouken Glen Road, G46.

Springburn
Broomfield Road, G21.

Tollcross
461 Tollcross Road, G32.

Victoria
Victoria Park Drive North, G14.

Kibble Palace

Public Transport

The City of Glasgow has one of the most advanced, fully integrated public transport systems in the whole of Europe. The Strathclyde Transport network consists of; the local British Rail network, the local bus services and the fully modernised Glasgow Underground, with links to Glasgow Airport and the Steamer and Car Ferry Services.
Note: Although the information in this section is correct at the time of printing it should be checked before use.

Bus Services and Tours

Long Distance Coach Service
Buchanan Bus Station 041 332 9191
Scottish City Link Coaches Ltd provide express services to London and most parts of Scotland including Campbeltown, Tarbert, Ardrishaig, Inveraray, Oban, Fort William, Skye, Stirling, Perth, Dundee, Arbroath, Montrose, Aberdeen, Aviemore, Inverness and Edinburgh.

Local Bus Services
A comprehensive network of local bus services is provided by a variety of operators within the City of Glasgow and also direct to the following destinations:
Airdrie, Ardrossan, Ayr, Balfron, Barrhead, Bearsden, Beith, Bellshill, Bishopbriggs, Bishopton, Blantyre, Bo'ness, Caldercruix, Cambuslang, Campsie Glen, Carluke, Clydebank, Coatbridge, Cumbernauld, Denny, Drymen, Dunfermline, Duntocher, Eaglesham, East Kilbride, Erskine, Falkirk, Glenrothes, Grangemouth, Hamilton, Irvine, Johnstone, Kilbarchan, Kilbirnie, Killearn, Kilmarnock, Kilsyth, Kirkintilloch, Kirkcaldy, Lanark, Largs, Larkhall, Lennoxtown, Lochwinnoch, Motherwell, Milngavie, Newton Mearns, Old Kilpatrick, Paisley, Prestwick, Renfrew, Saltcoats,

Shotts, Stirling, Strathblane, Strathaven, Uddingston, Wishaw.

These services depart from City Centre bus stops or from Anderston or Buchanan Bus Station. For information contact St. Enoch Travel Centre 041 226 4826; lines open 7 a.m. - 9 p.m. Monday - Saturday and 0900 - 1930 Sundays.

Coach Hire and Day, Half Day and Extended Tours
Scottish City Link Coaches
Buchanan Bus Station
041 332 8055
Private hire and seasonal tours
041 332 8055

Haldane's of Cathcart
Delvin Road, G44 041 637 2234

Strathclyde Buses Ltd.
197 Victoria Road, G42 7AD
041 636 3190
Private hire and seasonal tours

British Rail

Passenger enquiries: 041 204 2844
Sleeper reservations: 041 221 2305

Local Strathclyde Transport trains serve over 170 stations in Glasgow and Strathclyde (see map). ScotRail services operate to most destinations in Scotland. InterCity services operate to England.

Glasgow Queen Street Station
for services to Cumbernauld, Edinburgh, Falkirk, Stirling, Perth, Dundee, Arbroath, Montrose, Aberdeen, Pitlochry, Aviemore, Inverness, Dumbarton, Balloch, Helensburgh, Oban, Fort William, Mallaig, Coatbridge, Airdrie.

Glasgow Central Station
for services to Gourock (ferry connection to Dunoon), Greenock, Wemyss Bay (ferry connection to Rothesay), Paisley, Johnstone, Largs, Ardrossan (ferry connection to Brodick), Irvine, Ayr, Girvan, Stranraer, East Kilbride, Kilmarnock, Dumfries, Motherwell, Hamilton, Lanark, Carlisle, Shotts, Edinburgh, Berwick, Newcastle.
London and destinations on West and East Coast Main Lines.

OBAN
FORT WILLIAM
MALLAIG

Balloch

Milngavie

Alexandria

Ardlui
Arrochar and Tarbet
Garelochhead
Helensburgh Upper
Helensburgh Central

Renton

Dumbarton Central

Hillfoot

Bishopbriggs

Craigendoran Cardross Dalreoch
Dumbarton East
Kilpatrick
Dalmuir

Bowling

Singer Drumchapel

Bearsden

Springburn

Barnh

RIVER CLYDE

Clydebank

Drumry

Westerton

Alexar

Kilcreggan

Gourock

Fort Matilda

Yoker

Anniesland

Duke S
C

Dunoon

Greenock West

Garscadden

Kelvinhall Kelvinbridge
Cow-
caddens

Greenock Central

Scotstounhill

Jordanhill

Hillhead St. George's
Cross
Buchanan St.

High Street

Cartsdyke

Bogston

Rothesay

Branchton

Hyndland
Partick

Exhibition
Centre

Charing
Cross
Anderston

QUEEN
STREET

Bellgrove

Inverkip

IBM Whinhill

Port Glasgow

Govan

Argyle St. Bridgeton

Woodhall

Ibrox

St. Enoch

Wemyss Bay

Langbank

GLASGOW
AIRPORT

Cessnock

CENTRAL

Cumbrae Slip

Bishopton

Kinning Park

Bridge Street

Largs

Paisley St. James

Hillington
West East

Shields
Road

Rutherg

Johnstone

Paisley
Gilmour St

Cardonald

West St.

Can

Milliken Park

Crookston Corkerhill

Fairlie

Lochwinnoch

Paisley
Canal

Hawkhead Mosspark

Dumbreck
Pollokshields
West

Pollokshields
East

West Kilbride

Glengarnock

Dalry

Crossmyloof

Queen's Park

Burnsid

Brodick

Stevenson
Saltcoats

Kilwinning

Maxwell Park

Shawlands

Crosshill Croftfoot

Irvine

Pollokshaws West

Kennishead

Pollokshaws
East

King's
Park

Ardrossan
Harbour Town

Ardrossan
South Beach

Barassie

Priesthill & Darnley

Nitshill

Langside

Cathcart

Mount
Florida

Barrhead

Dunlop

Thornliebank

Muirend

Troon

Stewarton

Giffnock

Clarkston Thorntonhall

Prestwick

Kilmaurs

Kilmarnock

Busby Hairmyres

Newton-on-Ayr

Williamwood

Ayr

Auchinleck

Whitecraigs

Maybole

Girvan

New Cumnock

Patterson

Barrhill

STRANRAER

DUMFRIES
CARLISLE

Neilston

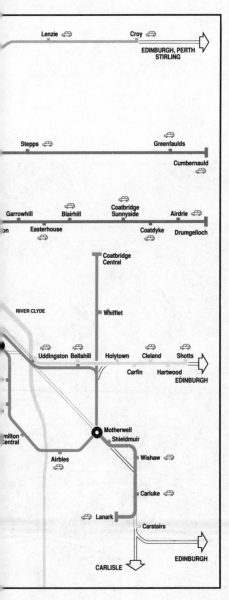

Lenzie 🚗

Croy 🚗

EDINBURGH, PERTH
STIRLING

Stepps 🚗

Greenfaulds 🚗

Cumbernauld 🚗

Garrowhill Blairhill Coatbridge Sunnyside 🚗 Airdrie 🚗

Easterhouse 🚗 Coatdyke 🚗 Drumgelloch

Coatbridge Central

RIVER CLYDE

Whifflet

Uddingston 🚗 Bellshill 🚗 Holytown 🚗 Cleland 🚗 Shotts 🚗

Carfin Hartwood
EDINBURGH

Motherwell
Shieldmuir

Hamilton Central

Airbles 🚗

Wishaw 🚗

Carluke 🚗

Lanark 🚗

Carstairs

EDINBURGH

CARLISLE

RAIL NETWORK

 Interchange with British Rail

 Ⓤ **Glasgow Underground**

Travelator Link between Buchanan St Ⓤ and Queen Street

 Prestwick Airport

 Glasgow Airport

 AIRLINK BUS
Glasgow Airport from Paisley Gilmour Street

 Inter-terminal Bus Link

 Interchange with Ferries (---- Summer Only)

 Park-and-Ride Station car parks

87

Glasgow *(Abbotsinch)* Airport

Glasgow Airport is located eight miles west of Glasgow alongside the M8 motorway at Junction 28. It is linked by a bus service to Anderston Cross Bus Station, the journey time is 25 minutes and buses leave at 30 minute intervals. There is a frequent coach service linking the Airport with all major bus and rail terminals in the City and a Coach/Air link to and from Prestwick Airport.

The Airport Terminal has a restaurant, grill, buffet, three bars, lounges, shop, post office and banking facilities.

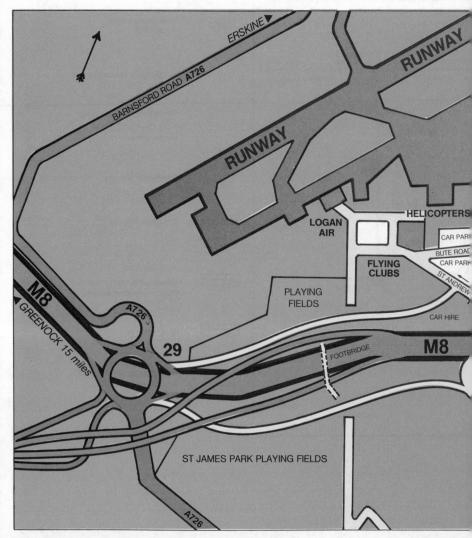

Car parking is available with a graduated scale of charges. The Airport telephone no is 041 887 1111.

Airlines

(Domestic Routes)
Air U.K.
Reservations   0345 666777

British Airways
66 Gordon Street
Glasgow, G1 3RS
Reservations   041 332 9666

British Caledonian Airways
(contact British Airways)

British Midland
Merlin House, Mossland Road,
Hillington, Glasgow. G54 4XZ
Reservations   0332 810552

Loganair Ltd.
Glasgow Airport (administration)
041 889 3181
Trident House, Renfrew Road, Paisley.

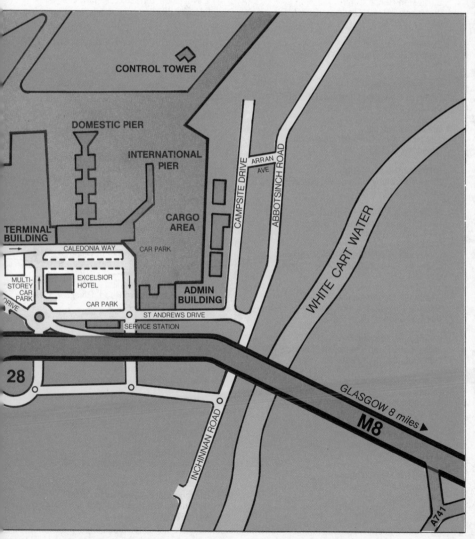

Hospitals

**Greater Glasgow Health Board
(Administration)
112 Ingram Street, Glasgow, G1 1ET.
041 552 6222**

Acorn Street Psychiatric Day Hospital
23 Acorn Street, Bridgeton, Glasgow, G40
4AA. 041 556 4789

Baillieston Health Centre
20 Muirside Road, Glasgow, G69 7AD.
041 771 0871

Belvidere Hospital
London Road, Glasgow G31 4PG.
041 554 1855

Birdston Hospital
Milton of Campsie, Glasgow, G65 8BY.
041 776 6114

Blawarthill Hospital
129 Holehouse Drive, Knightswood,
Glasgow, G13 3TG. 041 954 9547

Bridgeton Health Centre
201 Abercromby Street, Glasgow, G40
2EA. 041 554 1866

Broomhill & Lanfine Hospitals
Kilsyth Road, Kirkintilloch, Glasgow, G66
1RR. 041 776 5141

Carsewell House (Psychiatric Outpatient)
5 Oakley Terrace, Glasgow, G31 2HX.
041 554 6267

Castlemilk Health Centre
Dougrie Drive, Castlemilk, Glasgow, G45.
041 634 3434

Cannisburn Hospital
Switchback Road, Bearsden, Glasgow,
G61 1QL. 041 942 2255

Charing Cross (Alcohol and Drug) Day
Centre
8 Woodside Crescent, Glasgow, G3 7UL.
041 332 5463

Children's Home Hospital
Strathblane, Glasgow, G63 9EP.
0360 70203

Clydebank Health Centre
Kilbowie Road, Clydebank, G81 2TQ.
041 952 2080

Cowglen Hospital
Boydstone Road, Glasgow, G53 6XJ.
041 632 9106

Darnley Hospital
755 Nitshill Road, Glasgow, G53 7RR.
041 881 1005

Douglas Inch Centre
2 Woodside Terrace, Glasgow, G3 7UY.
041 332 3844

Drumchapel Hospital
129 Drumchapel Road, Glasgow, G15
6PX. 041 944 2344

Duke Street Hospital
253 Duke Street, Glasgow, G31 1HY.
041 556 5222

Duntocher Hospital
Duntocher, Clydebank, G81 5QU.
0389 74294

Easterhouse Health Centre
9 Auchinlea Road, Glasgow, G34 9QU.
041 771 0781

Gartloch Hospital,
Gartloch Road, Gartcosh, Glasgow, G69
8EJ. 041 771 0771

Gartnavel General Hospital
1053 Great Western Road, Glasgow, G12
0YN. 041 334 8122

Gartnavel Royal Hospital
1055 Great Western Road, Glasgow, G12
0XH. 041 334 6241

Glasgow Dental Hospital and School
378 Sauchiehall Street, Glasgow, G2 3JZ.
041 332 7020

Glasgow Eye Infirmary
3 Sandyford Place, Glasgow, G3 7NB.
041 204 0721

Glasgow Homeopathic Hospital
1000 Great Western Road, Glasgow, G12
0AA. 041 339 0382

Glasgow Royal Infirmary
84 Castle Street, Glasgow, G4 0SF.
041 552 3535

Glasgow Royal Maternity Hospital
Rottenrow, Glasgow, G4 0NA.
041 552 3400

Glasgow School of Chiropody
757 Crookston Road, Glasgow, G53 7UA.
041 883 0418

Glasgow School of Occupational Therapy
29 Sherbrooke Avenue, Glasgow, G41
4ER. 041 427 3032

Gorbals Health Centre
45 Pine Place, Glasgow, G5 0BQ.
041 429 6291

Govan Health Centre
5 Drumoyne Road, Glasgow G51 4BJ.
041 440 1212

Govanhill Health Centre
233 Calder Street, Glasgow, G42 7DR.
041 424 3003

Knightswood Hospital
125 Knightswood Road, Glasgow, G12
2XG. 041 954 9641

Lennox Castle Hospital
Lennoxtown, Glasgow, G65 7LB.
0360 313000

Lenzie Hospital
Auchinloch Road, Kirkintilloch, Glasgow,
G66 5DF. 041 776 1208

Leverndale Hospital
510 Crookston Road, Glasgow, G53 7TU.
041 882 6255

Lightburn Hospital
Carntyne Road, Glasgow, G32 6ND.
041 774 5102

Maryhill Health Centre
41 Shawpark Street, Glasgow, G20 9DR.
041 946 7151

Mearnskirk Hospital
Newton Mearns, Glasgow, G77 5RZ.
041 639 2251

Parkhead Health Centre
101 Salamanca Street, Glasgow, G31
5BA. 041 556 5232

Parkhead Hospital
81 Salamanca Street, Glasgow,
041 554 7951

Philipshill Hospital
East Kilbride Road, Busby, Glasgow, G76
9HW. 041 639 9777

Pollock Health Centre
21 Cowglen Road, Glasgow, G53 6EQ.
041 880 8899

Possilpark Health Centre
85 Denmark Street, Glasgow, G22 5EG.
041 336 5311

Queen Mother's Hospital
Yorkhill, Glasgow, G3 8SH. 041 339 8888

Royal Hospital for Sick Children
Yorkhill, Glasgow, G3 8SJ. 041 339 8888

Royal Samaritan Hospital for Women
69 Coplaw Street, Glasgow, G42 7JF.
041 649 4545

Ruchill Hospital
Bilsland Drive, Glasgow, G20 9NB.
041 946 7120

Rutherglen Health Centre
130 Stonelaw Road, Rutherglen, Glasgow,
G73 2PQ. 041 647 7171

Rutherglen Maternity Hospital
120 Stonelaw Road, Rutherglen, Glasgow,
G73 2PG. 041 647 0011

Shettleston Health Centre
420 Old Shettleston Road, Glasgow, G32
7JZ. 041 778 9191

Southern General Hospital
1345 Govan Road, Glasgow, G51 4TF.
041 445 2466

Springburn Health Centre
200 Springburn Way, Glasgow, G21 1TR.
041 558 0101

Stobhill General Hospital
133 Balornock Road, Glasgow, G21 3UW.
041 558 0111

Thornliebank Health Centre
20 Kennishead Road, Glasgow, G46 8NY.
041 620 2222

Townhead Health Centre
16 Alexandra Parade, Glasgow, G31 2ES.
041 552 3477

Victoria Geriatric Unit
Mansionhouse Road, Glasgow, G41 3DX.
041 649 4511

Victoria Infirmary
Langside Road, Glasgow, G42 9TY.
041 649 4545

Waverley Park Hospital
Kirkintilloch, Glasgow, G66 2HE.
041 776 2461

Western Infirmary
Dumbarton Road, Glasgow, G11 6NT.
041 339 8822

Woodilee Hospital
Kirkintilloch, Glasgow, G66 3UG.
041 777 8000

Woodside Health Centre
Barr Street, Glasgow, G20 7LR.
041 332 9977

Strathclyde Further Education

Anniesland College
Hatfield Drive, Glasgow, G12 0YE.
041 357 3969

Ayr College
Dam Park, Ayr, KA8 0EU. 0292 265184

Bell College of Technology
Almada Street, Hamilton, Lanarkshire,
ML3 0JB. 0698 283100

Cambuslang College
Hamilton Road, Cambuslang, Glasgow,
G72 7BS. 041 641 6600

**Cardonald College of Further
Education**
690 Mosspark Drive, Glasgow, G52
3AY. 041 883 6151

Central College of Commerce
300 Cathedral Street, G1 2TA.
041 552 3941

Clydebank College
Kilbowie Road, Clydebank,
Dunbartonshire, G81 2AA.
041 952 7771

Coatbridge College
Kildonan Street, Coatbridge,
Lanarkshire, ML5 3LS. 0236 422316

Cumbernauld College
Town Centre, Cumbernauld, Glasgow,
G67 1HU. 0236 731811

Glasgow Caledonian University
Cowcaddens Road, Glasgow G4 0BA
041 331 3000

**Glasgow College of Building and
Printing**
60 North Hanover Street, Glasgow, G1
2BP. 041 332 9969

**Glasgow College of Food
Technology**
230 Cathedral Street, Glasgow, G1
2TG. 041 552 3751

Glasgow College of Nautical Studies
21 Thistle Street, Glasgow, G5 9XB.
041 429 3201

Glasgow College of Technology
Cowcaddens Road, Glasgow, G4 0BA.
041 332 7090

James Watt College
Finnart Street, Greenock, Renfrewshire,
PA16 8HF. 0475 24433

John Wheatley College
1346-1364 Shettleston Road, Glasgow,
G32 9AT. 041 778 2426

Kilmarnock College
Holehouse Road, Kilmarnock, Ayrshire,
KA3 7AT. 0563 23501

Langside College
50 Prospecthill Road, Glasgow, G42
9LB. 041 649 4991

Motherwell College
Dalzell Drive, Motherwell, Lanarkshire,
ML4 2DD. 0698 59641

North Glasgow College
110 Flemington Street, Glasgow, G21
4BX. 041 558 9001

Reid Kerr College, The
Renfrew Road, Paisley, Renfrewshire,
PA13 4DR. 041 889 4225

Stow College
43 Shamrock Street, Glasgow, G4 9LD.
041 332 1786

University of Glasgow
University Avenue, Glasgow.
041 339 8855

University of Strathclyde
George Street, Glasgow, G1 1XQ.
041 552 4400

Renfrew District

A selection of leisure, recreational and cultural attractions in Renfrew District:

Barrhead Sports' Centre
The Centre contains swimming pools, sports halls, activity rooms and sauna suite. Bar and restaurant facilities add to the wide range of sporting and leisure activities available.

Barshaw Park, Glasgow Road, Paisley
The park is extensive with formal and informal areas. It adjoins the public golf course and incorporates a boating pond, playgrounds, model "ride-on" railway and a nature corner.

Castle Semple Country Park, Lochwinnoch
Castle Semple Loch is a popular feature for sailing and fishing. Canoes, rowing boats and sailing boards for hire. Fishing permits available. 0505 842882

Coats Observatory
The Observatory has traditionally recorded astronomical and meteorological information since 1882. Now installed with a satellite picture receiver, it is one of the best equipped Observatories in the country. Monday, Tuesday, Thursday 2 -8 p.m., Wednesday, Friday, Saturday 10 a.m. - 5 p.m. 041 889 3151

Erskine Bridge
The bridge is an impressive high level structure opened by HRH Princess Anne in 1971 and provides a direct link from Renfrew District to Loch Lomond and the Trossachs. The bridge replaced the Erskine Ferry and affords extensive views up and down river to pedestrian users.

Finlayston Estate
Off the A8 at Langbank. The Estate is now a garden centre with woodland walks. The house has connections with John Knox and Robert Burns and is open April to August on Sundays from 2.30 - 4.30 p.m. At other times groups by appointment. Estate open all year round. 047 554 285.

Formakin Estate, By Bishopton
A group of buildings and landscaped grounds designed in the Arts and Crafts style at the turn of the century. The estate has a visitor centre, tea room and offers walks, trails, picnic areas and play areas. Open 7 days 11 a.m. - 6 p.m. 0505 863400.

Gleniffer Braes Country Park, Glenfield Road, Paisley
1,000 breathtaking acres including Glen Park nature trail, picnic and children's play areas. Open dawn till dusk, the park affords extensive walks and spectacular views from this elevated moorland area, and contains an area reserved for model aero flying. 041 884 3794

Houston Village
Houston was developed in the 18th century as an estate village. The traditional smiddy building, village pubs and terraced houses combine to create a quiet, sleepy atmosphere which has successfully survived the development of extensive modern housing on its periphery.

Inchinnan Bridges
Early 19th century stone bridges over the White Cart and Black Cart rivers close to St. Conval's stone, and the site of the Inchinnan Church which houses the graves of the Knights Templar, whose order was introduced to Scotland in 1153 by King David I.

Johnstone Castle
The remnants of a 1700 building formerly a much larger structure but demolished in the 1950's. The castle has significant historical links with the Cochrane and Houston families, major landowners who were instrumental in the development of the Burgh of Johnstone.

Kilbarchan Village
A good example of an 18th Century weaving village with many original buildings still fronting the narrow streets. A focal point is the steeple building in the square, originally a school and meal market and now used as public meeting rooms. A cycle route/footpath system links it to Glasgow and the Clyde Coast.

Lagoon Leisure Centre, Paisley
Ultra-modern complex housing superb ice rink and extensive "fun" pool featuring artificial wave machine and water slides. Also has cafe/bar facilities. Unique within the area, the complex is easily reached by public transport and has ample parking. Monday - Friday 10 a.m. - 10 p.m., Saturday and Sunday 10 a.m. - 5.00 p.m. 041 889 4000.

Laigh Kirk, Paisley

Originally built in 1738, the Laigh Kirk has been converted to an Arts Centre, with a theatre, workshop, bistro and bar open daily 10 a.m. - 11 p.m. For further information 041 887 1010.

Linwood Sports Centre

A wide range of indoor and outdoor sporting activities include football and rugby pitches, games hall, squash courts, BMX track, fitness trail, tennis courts and conditioning suite.

Lochwinnoch Village

An attractive rural village close to the Castle Semple Water Park, Muirshiel Country Park and the R.S.P.B. nature reserve, Lochwinnoch contains a small local museum with displays reflecting agricultural, social and industrial aspects of village life. Museum open Monday, Wednesday and Friday 10 a.m. - 1 p.m., 2 - 5 p.m. and 6 - 8 p.m. Tuesday and Saturday 10 a.m. - 1 p.m. and 2 - 5 p.m. Open most days throughout the year, visitors should telephone 0505 842615.

Muirshiel Country Park

Four miles north of Lochwinnoch, the park features trails of varying length radiating from the Information Centre. Open daily 9 a.m. - 4.30 p.m. (Winter), 9 a.m. - 7.30 p.m. (Summer). 0505 842803.

Paisley Abbey

Birthplace of the Stewart Dynasty, the Abbey dates, in part, to the 12th century and features regimental flags, relics, the Barochan Cross and beautiful stained glass windows. Monday - Saturday 10 a.m. - 12.30 p.m., 1.30 - 3.30 p.m. 041 889 3630.

Paisley Arts Centre

Converted 18th century church. Performing arts, works by local artists and participatory events and includes bar and bistro. Box office open 7 days 10 a.m. - 8 p.m. Further information 041 887 1007.

Paisley Museum and Art Gallery, High Street, Paisley

In addition to the world famous collection of Paisley shawls, the Museum traces the history of the Paisley pattern, the development of weaving techniques and houses collections of local and natural history, ceramics and paintings. Monday - Saturday 10 a.m - 5 p.m. 041 889 3151.

Paisley Town Hall

A Renaissance style building by the River Cart in the heart of Paisley, it features a slim clock tower and houses a Tourist Information Centre. It accommodates many exhibitions during the year and is also available for conferences and functions. Monday - Saturday 9 a.m. - 5 p.m. 041 887 1007.

Paisley Town Trail

An easy-to-follow route taking in the town's historic and architecturally significant buildings. Visitors can spend an hour or two walking round the trail and referring to a printed guide and wall plaques on the main buildings.

Renfrew Town Hall

The Town Hall has a "fairy-tale" style to its 105 feet high spire and was the administrative centre of the Royal Burgh of Renfrew. Originally the principal town in the area, Renfrew was strategically placed on the River Clyde, and a passenger ferry continues to operate daily.

Robert Tannahill, Weaver Poet

The works of Tannahill ranks with those of Burns. Born 1774 he took his own life in 1810 and is buried in a nearby graveyard. Visitors can visit his early home, site of his death, and his grave, and read his works in Paisley Library.

Royal Society for Protection of Birds, Lochwinnoch

An interesting visitor centre with observation tower, hides, displays and gift shop. Thursday, Friday, Saturday and Sunday 10 a.m. - 5 p.m. Shop open 7 days. 0505 842663.

Sma' Shot Cottages, Paisley

Fully restored and furnished artisan's house of the Victorian era; exhibition room displaying photographs plus artefacts of local interest. 18th Century weaver's loomshop with combined living quarters. Open Wednesday & Saturday May - September 1 - 5 p.m. Group visits arranged by appointment. Tel: 041 812 2513 or 041 889 0530.

The Clyde Estuary

Visitors travelling along the rural route to the Old Greenock Road above Langbank village at the western end of the District are able to take advantage of extensive views of the upper and lower Clyde Estuary, the Gareloch and the mountains beyond.

Thomas Coats Memorial Church

Open Monday - Friday 9 a.m. - 12 noon. Visitors should check in advance. Another gift from the Coats family to Paisley, the church was built in 1894 and constructed of red sandstone, is one of the finest Baptist Churches in the country. Tel: 041 889 9980.

Wallace Monument, Elderslie

The monument was erected in 1912 and marks the birthplace of the Scottish Patriot, Sir William Wallace. It stands adjacent to the reconstructed foundation plan of the adjacent Wallace Buildings which dated from the 17th Century.

Weaver's Cottage, Kilbarchan

This cottage, built in 1723, houses the last of the village's 800 looms and demonstrations are still given. It contains displays of weaving and domestic utensils, with Cottage garden and refreshments. Open Monday, Tuesday, Thursday, Friday 2 - 5 p.m., Saturday 10 a.m. - 1 p.m. and 2 - 5 p.m.

INDEX TO STREETS

General Abbreviations

All.	Alley	Dr.	Drive	Mkt.	Market	St.	Street/Saint
App.	Approach	E.	East	Ms.	Mews	Sta.	Station
Arc.	Arcade	Esp.	Esplanade	Mt.	Mount	Ter.	Terrace
Av.	Avenue	Ex.	Exchange	N.	North	Trd.	Trading
Bk.	Bank	Fm.	Farm	Par.	Parade	Twr.	Tower
Bldgs.	Buildings	Gdns.	Gardens	Pas.	Passage	Vill.	Villa
Boul.	Boulevard	Gra.	Grange	Pk.	Park	Vills.	Villas
Bri.	Bridge	Grn.	Green	Pl.	Place	Vw.	View
Cft.	Croft	Gro.	Grove	Prom.	Promenade	W.	West
Circ.	Circus	Ho.	House	Quad.	Quadrant	Wd.	Wood
Clo.	Close	Ind.	Industrial	Rd.	Road	Wds.	Woods
Cor.	Corner	La.	Lane	Ri.	Rise	Wf.	Wharf
Cotts.	Cottages	Ln.	Loan	S.	South	Wk.	Walk
Cres.	Crescent	Lo.	Lodge	Sch.	School	Yd.	Yard
Ct.	Court	Mans.	Mansions	Sq.	Square		

District Abbreviations

Bail.	Baillieston	Clark.	Clarkston	Giff.	Giffnock	Pais.	Paisley
Barr.	Barrhead	Clyde.	Clydebank	John.	Johnstone	Renf.	Renfrew
Bear.	Bearsden	Coat.	Coatbridge	Kilb.	Kilbarchan	Ruth.	Rutherglen
Bish.	Bishopbriggs	Cumb.	Cumbernauld	Kirk.	Kirkintilloch	Step.	Stepps
Blan.	Blantyre	Dalm.	Dalmuir	Lenz.	Lenzie	Thorn.	Thornliebank
Both.	Bothwell	E.K.	East Kilbride	Linw.	Linwood	Udd.	Uddingston
Chr.	Chryston	Gart.	Gartcosh	Old K.	Old Kilpatrick		

NOTES

The figures and letters following a street name indicate the postal district for that street with the page number and square where it will be found in the atlas. Thus the postal district for Abbey Drive is G14, and it will be found on page 19 in square H12.

A street name followed by the name of another street in italics does not appear on the map, but will be found adjoining or near the latter.

Abbey Clo., Pais.	46	K14	Aberuthven Dr. G32	54	BB14	Afton Rd., Cumb.	71	PP2
Abbey Dr. G14	19	R10	Abiegail Pl., Blan.	68	FF19	Afton St. G41	51	U16
Abbey Rd., John.	44	F15	Abington St. G20	21	V10	Agamemnon St., Dalm.	4	K7
Abbeycraig Rd. G34	40	FF11	Aboukir St. G51	33	R12	Aigas Cotts. G13	19	R9
Abbeydale Way G73	65	Z18	Aboyne Dr., Pais.	46	K15	*Crow Rd.*		
Neilvaig Dr.			Aboyne St. G51	33	R13	Aikenhead Rd. G42	51	V14
Abbeyhill St. G32	38	AA12	Acacia Dr. G78	59	L17	Ailean Dr. G32	55	DD14
Abbot St. G41	51	U15	Acacia Dr., Pais.	45	H15	Ailean Gdns. G32	55	DD14
Frankfort St.			Acacia Pl., John.	44	E16	Ailort Av. G44	63	V17
Abbot St., Pais.	30	K13	Academy Rd., Giff.	62	T19	*Lochinver Dr.*		
Abbotsburn Way, Pais.	30	J12	Academy St. G32	54	BB14	Ailsa Dr. G42	51	U16
Abbotsford, Bish.	11	Z7	Acer Cres. G78	45	H15	Ailsa Dr. G73	64	X17
Abbotsford Av. G73	53	Y16	Achamore Pl. G15	6	N6	Ailsa Dr., Clyde.	5	M5
Abbotsford Ct., Cumb.	70	NN4	*Achamore Rd.*			Ailsa Dr., Pais.	46	J16
Abbotsford Cres., Pais.	44	F16	Achamore Rd. G15	6	N6	Ailsa Dr., Udd.	69	HH18
Abbotsford La. G5	51	V14	Achray Dr., Pais.	45	H15	Ailsa Rd., Bish.	11	Y7
Cumberland St.			Acorn Ct. G40	52	X14	Ailsa Rd., Renf.	31	M11
Abbotsford Pl. G5	51	V14	*Acorn St.*			Ainslie Rd. G52	32	P12
Abbotsford Pl., Cumb.	70	NN4	Acorn St. G40	52	X14	Ainslie Rd., Cumb.	71	QQ2
Abbotsford Rd., Bear.	7	Q5	Acre Dr. G20	8	T7	Airdale St., Giff.	62	T19
Abbotsford Rd., Clyde.	5	L7	Acre Rd. G20	8	S7	Aird's La. G1	36	W13
Abbotsford Rd., Cumb.	70	NN4	Acredyke Cres. G21	23	Z8	*Bridgegate*		
Abbotshall Av. G15	6	N6	Acredyke Pl. G21	23	Z9	Airgold Dr. G15	6	N6
Abbotsinch Rd., Pais.	30	K11	Acredyke Rd. G21	23	Y8	Airgold Pl. G15	6	N6
Abbott Cres., Clyde.	17	M8	Acredyke Rd. G73	52	X16	Airlie Gdns. G73	65	Z18
Aberconway St., Clyde.	17	M8	Acrehill St. G33	37	Z11	Airlie Rd., Bail.	56	EE14
Abercorn Av. G52	32	N12	Adams Ct. La. G2	35	V12	Airlie St. G12	20	S10
Abercorn Pl. G23	9	U7	*Howard St.*			Airlour Rd. G43	63	U17
Abercorn St., Pais.	30	K13	Adamswell St. G21	22	X10	Airth Dr. G52	49	R14
Abercrombie Cres.,	41	GG13	Adamswell Ter., Chr.	15	HH7	Airth La. G51	49	R14
Bail.			Addiewell St. G32	38	BB12	Airth Pl. G51	49	R14
Abercromby Dr. G40	36	X13	Addison Gro., Thorn.	61	R18	Airthrey Av. G14	19	R10
Abercromby Sq. G40	36	X13	Addison Pl., Thorn.	61	R18	Aitken St. G31	37	Z12
Abercromby St. G40	36	X13	Addison Rd. G12	20	T10	Aitkenhead Av., Coat.	57	HH14
Aberdalgie Path G34	40	EE12	Addison Rd., Thorn.	61	R18	Aitkenhead Rd., Udd.	57	HH16
Aberdalgie Rd. G34	40	EE12	Adelphi St. G5	36	W13	Alasdair Ct., Barr.	59	M19
Aberdour St. G31	37	Z12	Admiral St. G41	35	U13	Albany Av. G32	39	CC13
Aberfeldy St. G31	37	Z12	Advie Pl. G42	51	V16	Albany Cotts. G13	19	R9
Aberfoyle St. G31	37	Z12	*Prospecthill Rd.*			*Crow Rd.*		
Aberlady Rd. G51	33	R12	Affric Dr., Pais.	47	L15	Albany Dr. G73	65	Y17
Abernethy Dr., Linw.	28	E13	Afton Cres., Bear.	8	S6	Albany Pl., Both.	69	HH19
Abernethy St. G31	37	Z12	Afton Dr., Renf.	18	N10	*Marguerite Gdns.*		

95

Street	Page	Grid
Albany Quad. G32	39	CC13
Mansionhouse Dr.		
Albany St. G40	53	Y14
Albany Ter. G72	66	AA18
Albany Way, Pais.	30	K12
Abbotsburn Way		
Albert Av. G42	51	U15
Albert Ct. G41	51	U14
Albert Dr.		
Albert Cross G41	51	U14
Albert Dr. G41	50	T15
Albert Dr. G73	65	Y17
Albert Dr., Bear.	8	S7
Albert Rd. G42	51	V15
Albert Rd., Clyde.	5	L6
Albert Rd., Lenz.	13	CC6
Albert Rd., Renf.	17	M10
Alberta Ter. G12	20	T10
Saltoun St.		
Albion St. G1	36	W12
Albion St., Bail.	55	DD14
Albion St., Pais.	30	K13
Alcaig Rd. G52	49	R15
Alder Av., Lenz.	12	BB5
Alder Ct., Barr.	59	M19
Alder Pl. G43	62	T17
Alder Pl., John.	44	E15
Alder Rd. G43	62	T17
Alder Rd., Cumb.	71	QQ3
Alder Rd., Dalm.	4	K5
Alderman Pl. G13	19	Q9
Alderman Rd. G13	18	N8
Aldersdyke Pl., Blan.	68	FF19
Alderside Dr., Udd.	57	GG16
Alexandra Av. G33	25	CC9
Alexandra Av., Lenz.	13	CC6
Alexandra Ct. G31	37	Y12
Roebank St.		
Alexandra Cross G31	37	Y12
Duke St.		
Alexandra Dr., Pais.	45	H14
Alexandra Dr., Renf.	17	M10
Alexandra Gdns., Lenz.	13	CC6
Alexandra Par. G31	37	Y12
Alexandra Pk. St. G31	37	Y12
Alexandra Rd., Lenz.	13	CC6
Alford St. G21	22	W10
Alfred Ter. G52	20	T10
Cecil St.		
Algie St. G41	51	U16
Alice St. G5	52	W14
Alice St., Pais.	46	K15
Aline Ct., Barr.	59	L18
Allan Av., Renf.	32	N11
Allan Pl. G40	53	Y14
Allan St. G40	53	Y15
Allander Gdns., Bish.	10	X6
Allander Rd., Bear.	7	Q6
Allander St. G22	22	W10
Allands Av., Renf.	16	J9
Allanfauld Rd., Cumb.	70	NN2
Allanton Av., Pais.	48	N14
Allanton Dr. G52	32	P13
Allerton Gdns., Bail.	55	DD14
Alleysbank Rd. G73	53	Y15
Allison Dr. G72	66	BB17
Allison Pl. G42	51	V15
Prince Edward St.		
Allison Pl., Gart.	27	GG10
Allison St. G42	51	V15
Allnach Pl. G34	41	GG12
Alloway Cres. G73	64	X17
Alloway Dr. G73	64	X17
Alloway Dr., Clyde.	5	M6
Alloway Rd. G43	62	T17
Alma St. G40	37	Y13
Almond Av., Renf.	32	N11
Almond Cres., Pais.	45	G15
Almond Dr., Lenz.	12	BB5
Almond Rd. G33	25	CC9
Almond Rd., Bear.	7	Q7
Almond St. G33	37	Z11
Almond Vale, Udd.	57	HH16
Hamilton Vw.		
Alness Cres. G52	49	R14
Alpatrick Gdns., John.	44	E14
Alpine Gro., Udd.	57	GG16
Alsatian Av., Clyde.	5	M7
Alston La. G40	36	X13
Claythorn St.		
Altnacreag Gdns., Chr.	15	HH6
Alton Gdns. G12	20	T10
Great George St.		
Alton Rd., Pais.	47	M14
Altyre St. G32	54	AA14
Alva Gdns. G52	49	R15
Alva Gate G52	49	R15
Alva Pl., Lenz.	13	DD6
Alyth Gdns. G52	49	R14
Ambassador Way, Renf.	31	M11
Cockels Ln.		
Amisfield St. G20	21	U9
Amochrie Dr., Pais.	45	H16
Amochrie Rd., Pais.	45	G15
Amulree Pl. G32	54	BB14
Amulree St. G32	38	BB13
Ancaster Dr. G13	19	R9
Ancaster La. G13	19	Q8
Great Western Rd.		
Anchor Av., Pais.	47	L14
Anchor Cres., Pais.	47	L14
Anchor Dr., Pais.	47	L14
Anchor Wynd, Pais.	47	L14
Ancroft St. G20	21	V10
Anderson Dr., Renf.	17	M10
Anderson Gdns., Blan.	69	GG19
Station Rd.		
Anderson Quay G3	35	U13
Anderson St. G11	34	S11
Andrew Av., Lenz.	13	CC6
Andrew Av., Renf.	18	N10
Andrew Dr., Clyde.	17	M8
Andrew Sillars Av. G72	67	CC17
Andrews St., Pais.	30	K13
Anglegate G14	19	Q10
Angus Av. G52	49	Q14
Angus Av., Bish.	23	Z8
Angus Gdns., Udd.	57	GG16
Angus La. G64	11	Z7
Angus Oval G52	48	P14
Angus Pl. G52	48	P14
Angus St. G21	22	X10
Angus St., Clyde.	18	N8
Angus Wk., Udd.	57	HH16
Annan Dr. G73	53	Z16
Annan Dr., Bear.	7	Q6
Annan Dr., Pais.	45	G15
Annan Pl., John.	43	C16
Annan St. G42	51	V16
Annandale St. G42	51	V14
Annbank St. G31	36	X13
Anne Av., Renf.	17	M10
Anne Cres., Lenz.	13	CC6
Annette St. G42	51	V15
Annfield Gdns., Blan.	68	FF19
Annfield Pl. G31	36	X12
Annick Dr., Bear.	7	Q7
Annick St. G32	38	BB13
Annick St. G72	67	CC17
Anniesdale Av. G33	25	CC9
Anniesland Cres. G14	18	P9
Anniesland Mans. G13	19	R9
Ancaster Dr.		
Anniesland Rd. G13	19	Q9
Anniesland Rd. G14	18	P9
Anson St. G40	52	X14
Anson Way, Renf.	31	M11
Britannia Way		
Anstruther St. G32	38	AA13
Anthony St. G2	35	V12
Cadogan St.		
Antonine Gdns., Clyde.	5	L5
Antonine Rd., Bear.	6	P5
Anworth St. G32	54	BB14
Appin Rd. G31	37	Y12
Appin Ter. G73	65	Z18
Lochaber Dr.		
Appin Way, Udd.	69	HH18
Bracken Ter.		
Appleby St. G22	21	V10
Applecross Gdns., Chr.	15	GG6
Applecross St. G22	21	V10
Appledore Cres., Udd.	69	HH18
Apsley La. G11	34	S11
Apsley St. G11	34	S11
Aray St. G20	20	T9
Arbroath Av. G52	48	P14
Arcadia St. G40	36	X13
Arcan Cres. G15	6	P7
Archerfield Av. G32	54	BB15
Archerfield Cres. G32	54	BB15
Archerfield Dr. G32	54	BB15
Archerfield Gro. G32	54	BB15
Archerhill Av. G13	18	N8
Archerhill Cotts. G13	18	P8
Archerhill Rd.		
Archerhill Cres. G13	18	P8
Archerhill Gdns. G13	18	P8
Archerhill Rd.		
Archerhill Rd. G13	18	P8
Archerhill Sq. G13	18	P8
Kelso St.		
Archerhill St. G13	18	P8
Archerhill Rd.		
Archerhill Ter. G13	18	P8
Archerhill Rd.		
Ard Pl. G42	52	X16
Ard Rd., Renf.	17	L10
Ard St. G32	54	BB14
Ardagie Dr. G32	55	CC16
Ardagie Pl. G32	55	CC16
Ardbeg Av. G73	66	AA18
Ardbeg Av., Bish.	11	Z7
Ardbeg St. G42	51	V15
Ardconnel St. G46	61	R18
Arden Av. G46	61	R19
Arden Dr., Giff.	62	S19
Arden Pl. G46	61	R19
Stewarton Rd.		
Ardencraig Cres. G44	64	W19
Ardencraig Dr. G45	64	X19
Ardencraig La. G45	64	W19
Ardencraig Rd.		
Ardencraig Quad. G45	64	X19
Ardencraig Rd. G45	64	W19
Ardencraig St. G45	65	Y19
Ardencraig Ter. G45	64	X19
Ardenlea Rd., Udd.	57	GG16
Ardenlea St. G40	53	Y14
Ardery St. G11	34	S11
Apsley St.		
Ardessie Pl. G20	20	T9
Ardessie St. G23	8	T7
Torrin Rd.		
Ardfern St. G32	54	BB14
Ardgay Pl. G32	54	BB14
Ardgay St. G32	54	BB14
Ardgay Way G73	65	Y18
Ardgour Dr., Linw.	28	E13
Ardgowan Av., Pais.	46	K14
Ardgowan Dr., Udd.	57	GG16
Ardgowan St., Pais.	46	K15
Ardholm St. G32	38	BB13
Ardhu Pl. G15	6	N6
Ardlamont Sq., Linw.	28	F13
Ardlaw St. G51	33	R13
Ardle Rd. G43	63	U17
Ardlui St. G32	54	AA14
Ardmaleish Cres. G45	64	X19
Ardmaleish Rd. G45	64	W19
Ardmaleish St. G45	64	W19
Ardmaleish Ter. G45	64	X19
Ardmay Cres. G44	52	W16
Ardmillan St. G33	38	AA12
Ardmore Oval, Pais.	29	H13
Ardmory Av. G42	52	W16
Ardmory La. G42	52	X16
Ardnacross Dr. G33	39	CC11
Ardnahoe Av. G42	52	W16
Ardnahoe Pl. G42	52	W16
Ardneil Rd. G51	33	R13
Ardnish St. G51	33	R12
Ardo Gdns. G51	34	S13
Ardoch Gro. G72	66	AA17

Avondale Dr., Pais.	31	L13
Avondale St. G33	38	BB11
Avonhead Av. G67	70	MM4
Avonhead Gdns. G67	70	MM4
Avonhead Pl. G67	70	MM4
Avonhead Rd. G67	70	MM4
Avonspark St. G21	23	Y10
Aylmer Rd. G43	63	U17
Ayr Rd., Giff.	62	S19
Ayr St. G21	22	X10
Aytoun Rd. G41	50	T14
Back Causeway G31	37	Z13
Back Sneddon St., Pais.	30	K13
Backmuir Rd. G15	6	P6
Bagnell St. G21	22	X9
Baillie Dr., Both.	69	HH18
Baillieston Rd. G32	55	CC14
Baillieston Rd., Udd.	56	EE15
Bain Sq. G40	36	X13
Bain St.		
Bain St. G40	36	X13
Bainsford St. G32	38	AA13
Baird Av. G52	32	N12
Baird Dr., Bear.	7	Q5
Baird St. G4	36	W11
Bairdsbrae G4	21	V10
Possil Rd.		
Baker Pl. G41	51	U15
Baker St.		
Baker St. G41	51	U15
Bakewell Rd., Bail.	40	EE13
Balaclava St. G2	35	V13
McAlpine St.		
Balado Rd. G33	39	DD12
Balbeg St. G51	33	R13
Balbeggie Pl. G32	55	CC14
Balbeggie St. G32	55	CC14
Balblair Rd. G52	49	R15
Balcarres Av. G12	20	T9
Balcomie St. G33	38	BB11
Balcurvie Rd. G34	40	EE11
Baldinnie Rd. G34	40	EE12
Baldorran Cres., Cumb.	70	LL2
Baldoven Cres. G33	39	DD12
Baldovie Rd. G52	49	Q14
Baldragon Rd. G34	40	EE11
Baldric Rd. G13	19	Q9
Baldwin Av. G13	7	Q7
Balerno Dr. G52	49	R14
Balfluig St. G34	39	DD11
Balfour St. G20	20	T9
Balfron Rd. G51	33	R12
Balfron Rd., Pais.	31	M13
Balgair Dr., Pais.	31	L13
Balgair St. G22	21	V9
Balgair Ter. G32	38	BB13
Balglass St. G22	21	V10
Balgonie Av. G78	45	H15
Balgonie Av., Pais.	45	H15
Balgonie Dr., Pais.	46	J15
Balgonie Rd. G52	49	R14
Balgonie Wds., Pais.	46	J15
Balgownie Cres., Thorn.	62	S19
Balgray Cres., Barr.	60	N19
Balgraybank St. G21	23	Y10
Balgrayhill Rd. G21	22	X9
Balintore St. G32	38	BB13
Baliol La. G3	35	U11
Woodlands Rd.		
Baliol St. G3	35	U11
Ballaig Av., Bear.	7	Q5
Ballaig Cres. G33	25	CC9
Ballantay Quad. G45	65	Y18
Ballantay Rd. G45	65	Y18
Ballantay Ter. G45	65	Y18
Ballantyne Rd. G52	32	P12
Ballater Dr., Bear.	7	R7
Ballater Dr., Pais.	47	L15
Ballater St., Renf.	16	J8
Ballater Pl. G5	52	W14
Ballater St. G5	36	W13
Ballayne Dr., Chr.	15	HH7
Ballindalloch Dr. G31	37	Y12
Balloch Gdns. G52	49	R14
Balloch Rd., Cumb.	70	MM3
Balloch Vw., Cumb.	70	NN3
Ballochmill Rd. G73	53	Z16
Ballogie Rd. G44	51	V16
Balmarino Pl. G64	11	Z7
Balmartin Rd. G23	8	T7
Balmerino Pl., Bish.	23	Z8
Angus Av.		
Balmoral Cres. G42	51	V15
Queens Dr.		
Balmoral Cres., Renf.	16	K9
Balmoral Dr. G32	54	BB16
Balmoral Dr. G72	66	AA17
Balmoral Dr., Bear.	8	S7
Balmoral Gdns., Blan.	68	FF19
Balmoral Gdns., Udd.	57	GG15
Balmoral Rd., John.	44	E15
Balmoral St. G14	18	P10
Balmore Pl. G22	21	V9
Balmore Rd.		
Balmore Rd. G23	9	U5
Balmore Sq. G22	21	V9
Balmuildy Rd., Bish.	9	V6
Balornock Rd. G21	23	Y9
Balruddery Pl. G64	23	Z8
Balshagray Av. G11	19	R10
Balshagray Cres. G11	19	R10
Balshagray Dr. G11	19	R10
Balshagray La. G11	19	R10
Balshagray Pl. G11	19	R10
Balshagray Dr.		
Baltic Ct. G40	53	Y14
Baltic St.		
Baltic La. G40	53	Y14
Baltic Pl. G40	52	X14
Baltic St. G40	53	Y14
Balure St. G31	37	Z12
Balvaird Cres. G73	53	Y16
Balvaird Dr. G73	53	Y16
Balveny St. G33	39	CC11
Balvicar Dr. G42	51	U15
Balvicar St. G42	51	U15
Balvie Av. G15	6	P7
Balvie Av., Giff.	62	T19
Banavie Rd. G11	20	S10
Banchory Av. G43	62	S17
Banchory Av., Renf.	16	J8
Banchory Cres., Bear.	8	S7
Banff St. G33	38	BB11
Bangorshill St. G46	61	R18
Bank Rd. G32	55	CC16
Bank St. G12	35	U11
Bank St. G72	66	BB17
Bank St., Barr.	59	M19
Bank St., Pais.	46	K14
Bankbrae Av. G53	60	P17
Bankend St. G33	38	BB11
Bankfoot Dr. G52	48	P14
Bankfoot Rd. G52	48	P14
Bankfoot Rd., Pais.	29	H13
Bankglen Rd. G15	6	P6
Bankhall St. G42	51	V15
Bankhead Av. G13	18	P9
Bankhead Dr. G73	53	Y16
Bankhead Rd. G73	64	X17
Bankier St. G40	36	X13
Banknock St. G32	38	AA13
Bankside Av., John.	43	D14
Banktop Pl., John.	43	D14
Banling Grn. Rd. G44	63	V17
Clarkston Rd.		
Bannatyne Av. G31	37	Y12
Banner Dr. G13	7	Q7
Banner Rd. G13	7	Q7
Bannercross Av., Bail.	40	EE13
Bannercross Dr., Bail.	40	EE13
Bannercross Gdns., Bail.	40	EE13
Bannercross Dr.		
Bannerman Pl., Clyde.	5	M7
Bannerman St., Clyde.	5	L7
Bantaskin St. G20	20	T8
Banton Pl. G33	39	DD12
Barassie Ct., Both.	69	GG19
Barassie Cres., Cumb.	70	NN1
Barbae Pl., Udd.	69	HH18
Hume Dr.		
Barberry Av. G53	60	P19
Barberry Gdns. G53	60	P19
Barberry Av.		
Barberry Pl. G53	60	P19
Barberry Av.		
Barbreck Rd. G42	51	U15
Pollokshaws Rd.		
Barcaldine Av., Chr.	14	EE7
Barclay Av., John.	44	E15
Barclay Sq., Renf.	31	L11
Barclay St. G21	22	X9
Balgrayhill Rd.		
Barcraigs Dr., Pais.	46	K16
Bard Av. G13	18	P8
Bardowie St. G22	21	V10
Bardrain Av., John.	44	F15
Bardrain Rd., Pais.	46	J16
Bardrill Dr., Bish.	10	X7
Bardykes Rd., Blan.	68	FF19
Barfillan Dr. G52	33	R13
Barfillan Rd. G52	33	R13
Bargaran Rd. G53	48	P14
Bargarron Dr., Pais.	31	L12
Bargeddie St. G33	37	Z11
Barhill Cres., Kilb.	42	B15
Barholm Sq. G33	39	CC11
Barke Rd., Cumb.	71	PP2
Barlanark Av. G32	39	CC12
Barlanark Pl. G32	39	CC13
Hallhill Rd.		
Barlanark Pl. G33	39	DD12
Barlanark Rd. G33	39	CC12
Barlia Dr. G45	64	X18
Barlia St. G45	64	X18
Barlia Ter. G45	64	X18
Barloch St. G22	22	W10
Barlogan Av. G52	33	R13
Barlogan Quad. G52	33	R13
Barmill Rd. G43	62	S17
Barmulloch Rd. G21	23	Y10
Barn Grn. G78	42	B14
Barnard Gdns., Bish.	11	Y6
Barnard Ter. G40	53	Y14
Barnbeth Rd. G53	48	P15
Barnes Rd. G20	21	V9
Barnes St., Barr.	59	L19
Barnflat St. G73	53	Y15
Barnhill Dr. G21	23	Y10
Foresthall Dr.		
Barnkirk Av. G15	6	P6
Barns St., Clyde.	5	M7
Barnsford Av., Renf.	16	J9
Barnsford Rd., Pais.	29	H11
Barnton St. G32	38	AA12
Barochan Cres., Pais.	45	H14
Barochan Rd. G53	48	P14
Baron Rd., Pais.	31	L13
Baron St., Renf.	31	M11
Baronald Dr. G12	20	S9
Baronald Gate G12	20	S9
Baronald St. G73	53	Y15
Baronhill, Cumb.	71	PP1
Barons Ct. Dr., John.	45	G14
Barons Ct. Gdns., John.	45	G14
Barons Ct. Rd., John.	45	G14
Barons Gate, Both.	69	GG18
Barony Dr., Bail.	40	EE13
Barony Gdns., Bail.	40	EE13
Barony Dr.		
Barr Cres., Clyde.	5	L5
Barr Pl., Pais.	46	J14
Barr St. G20	21	V10
Barra Av., Renf.	31	M11
Barra Cres., Old K.	4	J5
Barra Gdns., Old K.	4	J5
Barra Rd.		
Barra Rd., Old K.	4	J5
Barra St. G20	20	T8
Barrachnie Ct., Bail.	39	DD13
Barrachnie Cres.		
Barrachnie Cres., Bail.	39	DD13
Barrachnie Rd., Bail.	39	DD13

98

Name		
Barrack St. G4	36	X13
Barrhead Rd. G43	48	N16
Barrhead Rd., Pais.	47	L14
Barrie Quad., Clyde.	5	L6
Barrie Rd. G52	32	P12
Barrington Dr. G4	35	U11
Barrisdale Rd. G20	20	T8
Barrisdale Way G73	65	Y18
Barrland Dr., Giff.	62	T18
Barrland St. G41	51	V14
Barrochan Rd., John.	43	D14
Barrowfield St. G40	37	Y13
Barrwood St. G33	38	AA11
Barscube Ter., Pais.	47	L14
Barshaw Dr., Pais.	31	L13
Barshaw Pl., Pais.	31	M13
Barshaw Rd. G52	32	N13
Barterholm Rd., Pais.	46	K15
Bartholomew St. G40	53	Y14
Bartiebeith Rd. G33	39	DD12
Basset Av. G13	18	P8
Basset Cres. G13	18	P8
Bath La. G2	35	V12
Blythswood St.		
Bath La. W. G3	35	U12
North St.		
Bath St. G2	35	V12
Bathgate St. G31	37	Y13
Bathgo Av., Pais.	48	N14
Batson St. G42	51	V15
Battle Pl. G41	51	U16
Battleburn St. G32	54	BB14
Battlefield Av. G42	51	V16
Battlefield Cres. G42	51	V16
Battlefield Gdns.		
Battlefield Gdns. G42	51	V16
Battlefield Rd. G42	51	V16
Bavelaw St. G33	39	CC11
Bayfield Av. G15	6	P6
Bayfield Ter. G15	6	P6
Beaconsfield Rd. G12	20	S9
Beard Cres., Gart.	27	GG9
Beardmore Cotts., Renf.	16	K9
Beardmore St., Dalm.	4	J6
Beardmore Way, Dalm.	4	J6
Bearford Dr. G52	32	P13
Bearsden Rd. G13	19	R8
Beaton Rd. G41	51	U15
Beattock St. G31	37	Z13
Beaufort Av. G43	62	T17
Beaufort Gdns., Bish.	10	X7
Beauly Dr., Pais.	45	G15
Beauly Pl. G20	20	T9
Beauly Pl., Bish.	11	Z7
Beauly Pl., Chr.	14	FF7
Beauly Rd., Bail.	56	EE14
Beaumont Gate G12	34	T11
Bedale Rd., Bail.	55	DD14
Bedford Av., Clyde.	5	M7
Onslow Rd.		
Bedford La. G5	35	V13
Bedford Row G5	35	V13
Dunmore St.		
Bedford St. G5	35	V13
Bedlay Ct., Chr.	15	HH6
Bedlay St. G21	22	X10
Mollinsburn St.		
Bedlay St. G21	22	X10
Petershill Rd.		
Bedlay Wk., Chr.	15	HH6
Beech Av. G41	50	S14
Beech Av. G72	66	AA17
Beech Av. G73	65	Z18
Beech Av., Bail.	40	EE13
Beech Av., John.	44	F15
Beech Av., Pais.	47	L15
Beech Dr., Dalm.	5	L5
Beech Gdns., Bail.	40	EE13
Beech Gro., Barr.	59	M19
Arthurlie Av.		
Beech Pl., Bish.	23	Y8
Beech Rd., Bish.	23	Y8
Beech Rd., John.	43	C15
Beech Rd., Lenz.	13	CC5
Beechcroft Pl., Blan.	69	GG19
Beeches Av., Clyde.	4	K5
Beeches Rd., Clyde.	4	K5
Beeches Ter., Clyde.	4	K5
Beechgrove St. G40	53	Y15
Beechlands Av., Giff.	63	U19
Beechmount Cotts. G14	18	N9
Dumbarton Rd.		
Beechmount Rd., Lenz.	13	CC6
Beechwood Av. G11	19	R10
Beechwood Dr.		
Beechwood Av. G73	65	Z17
Beechwood Ct., Bear.	7	R6
Beechwood Dr. G11	19	R10
Beechwood Dr., Renf.	31	L11
Beechwood Gro., Barr.	59	M19
Arthurlie Av.		
Beechwood La., Bear.	7	R6
Beechwood Ct.		
Beechwood Pl. G11	19	R10
Beechwood Dr.		
Beechwood Rd., Cumb.	70	NN3
Beil Dr. G13	18	N8
Beith Rd., John.	42	B16
Beith St. G11	34	S11
Belgrave La. G12	21	U10
Belgrave Ter.		
Belgrave Ter. G12	21	U10
Belhaven Cres. La. G12	20	T10
Lorraine Rd.		
Belhaven Ter. G12	20	T10
Belhaven Ter. W. G12	20	T10
Bell St. G1	36	W13
Bell St., Clyde.	17	M8
Bell St., Renf.	17	M10
Bellahouston Dr. G52	49	R14
Bellahouston La. G52	49	R14
Bellairs Pl., Blan.	68	FF19
Belleisle Av., Udd.	57	GG16
Belleisle St. G42	51	V15
Bellevue Pl. G21	36	X11
Bellfield Cres., Barr.	59	L18
Bellfield St. G31	37	Y13
Bellfield St., Barr.	59	L18
Bellflower Gdns. G53	61	Q18
Bellgrove St. G31	36	X13
Bellrock Cres. G33	38	BB12
Bellrock St. G33	38	BB12
Bellscroft Av. G73	52	X16
Bellshaugh Gdns. G12	20	T9
Bellshaugh La. G12	20	T9
Bellshaugh Pl. G12	20	T9
Bellshaugh Rd. G12	20	T9
Bellshill Rd., Both.	69	HH19
Bellshill Rd., Udd.	69	GG17
Belltrees Cres., Pais.	45	H14
Bellwood St. G41	51	U16
Belmar Ct., Linw.	28	F13
Belmont Av., Udd.	57	GG16
Belmont Cres. G12	21	U10
Belmont Dr. G73	53	Y16
Belmont Dr., Barr.	59	M19
Belmont Dr., Giff.	62	S18
Belmont La. G12	20	T10
Great Western Rd.		
Belmont Rd. G21	22	X9
Belmont Rd. G72	66	AA18
Belmont Rd., Pais.	31	L13
Belmont St. G12	21	U10
Belmont St., Clyde.	17	L8
Belses Dr. G52	33	Q13
Belstane Pl., Udd.	69	HH18
Appledore Cres.		
Belsyde Av. G15	6	P7
Beltane St. G3	35	U12
Beltrees Av. G53	48	P15
Beltrees Cres. G53	48	P15
Beltrees Rd. G53	48	P15
Belvidere Cres., Bish.	11	Y6
Bemersyde, Bish.	11	Z7
Bemersyde Av. G43	62	S17
Bemersyde Rd. G78	45	G16
Ben Alder Dr., Pais.	47	M15
Ben Buie Way, Pais.	47	M15
Ben Lawers Dr., Cumb.	70	MM3
Balloch Rd.		
Ben Ledi Av., Pais.	47	M15
Ben Lui Dr., Pais.	47	M15
Ben More Dr., Pais.	47	M15
Ben Nevis Rd., Pais.	47	M15
Ben Venue Way, Pais.	47	M15
Ben Wyvis Dr., Pais.	47	M15
Benalder St. G11	34	T11
Benarty Gdns., Bish.	11	Y7
Bencroft Dr. G44	64	X17
Bengairn St. G31	37	Z12
Bengal Pl. G43	50	T16
Christian St.		
Bengal St. G43	50	T16
Benhar Pl. G33	38	AA12
Benholme St. G32	54	AA14
Benhope Av., Pais.	47	M15
Benlawers Dr., Pais.	47	M15
Benloyal Av., Pais.	47	M15
Benmore St. G21	22	X9
Bennan Sq. G42	52	W15
Benston Pl., John.	43	D15
Benston Rd., John.	43	D15
Bentall St. G5	52	W14
Bentinck St. G3	35	U11
Bents Rd., Bail.	40	EE13
Benvane Av., Pais.	47	M15
Benview Gdns., Bish.	11	Y7
Benview St. G20	21	U10
Benview Ter., Pais.	47	L15
Berelands Cres. G73	52	X16
Berelands Pl. G73	52	X16
Beresford Av. G14	19	R10
Berkeley St. G3	35	U12
Berkeley Ter. La. G3	35	U11
Elderslie St.		
Berkley Dr., Blan.	68	FF19
Bernard Path G40	53	Y14
Bernard St. G40	53	Y14
Bernard Ter. G40	53	Y14
Berneray St. G22	22	W8
Berridale Av. G44	63	V17
Berriedale Av., Bail.	56	EE14
Berryburn Rd. G21	23	Z10
Berryhill Dr., Giff.	62	S19
Berryhill Rd., Cumb.	70	NN3
Berryhill Rd., Giff.	62	S19
Berryknowes Av. G52	33	Q13
Berryknowes La. G52	33	Q13
Berryknowes Rd. G52	49	Q14
Berryknowes Rd., Chr.	26	FF8
Bertram St. G41	51	U15
Bertrohill Ter. G33	39	CC12
Stepps Rd.		
Bervie St. G51	33	R13
Berwick Cres., Linw.	28	E12
Berwick Dr. G52	48	P14
Berwick Dr. G73	53	Z16
Betula Dr., Dalm.	5	L5
Bevan Gro., John.	43	C16
Beverley Rd. G43	62	T17
Bevin Av., Clyde.	5	M7
Bideford Cres. G32	55	CC14
Biggar Pl. G31	37	Y13
Biggar St. G31	37	Y13
Bigton St. G33	38	BB11
Bilbao St. G5	52	W14
Bilsland Ct. G20	21	V9
Bilsland Dr.		
Bilsland Dr. G20	21	U9
Binend Rd. G53	49	Q16
Binnie Pl. G40	36	X13
Binniehill Rd., Cumb.	70	MM2
Binns Rd. G33	39	CC11
Birch Cres., John.	44	E15
Birch Dr., Lenz.	13	CC5
Birch Gro., Udd.	57	HH16
Burnhead St.		
Birch Knowle, Bish.	23	Y8
Birch Rd., Dalm.	5	L5
Birch Vw., Bear.	8	S5
Birchfield Dr. G14	18	P10
Birchlea Dr., Giff.	62	T18
Birchwood Av. G32	55	DD14
Birchwood Dr., Pais.	45	H15
Birchwood Pl. G32	55	DD14

Birdston Rd. G21	23	Z9	Blairdardie Rd. G15	6	P7	Borgie Cres. G72	66	BB17
Birgidale Av. G45	64	W19	Blairdenan Av., Chr.	15	HH6	Borland Rd., Bear.	8	S6
Birgidale Rd. G45	64	W19	Blairdenon Dr., Cumb.	70	MM2	Borron St. G4	22	W10
Birgidale Ter. G45	64	W19	Blairgowrie Rd. G52	49	Q14	Borthwick St. G33	38	BB11
Birkdale Ct., Both.	69	GG19	Blairhall Av. G41	51	U16	Boswell Sq. G52	32	N12
Birken Rd., Lenz.	13	DD6	Blairhill Av., Chr.	14	EE5	Botanic Cres. G20	20	T10
Birkenshaw St. G31	37	Y12	Blairlogie St. G33	38	BB11	Bothlyn Cres., Gart.	27	GG8
Birkenshaw Way, Pais.	30	K12	Blairston Av., Both.	69	HH19	Bothlynn Dr. G33	25	CC9
Abbotsburn Way			Blairston Gdns., Both.	69	HH19	Bothlynn Rd., Chr.	26	FF8
Birkhall Av. G52	48	N14	Blairston Av.			Bothwell La. G2	35	V12
Birkhall Av., Renf.	16	J8	Blairtum Dr. G73	65	Y17	West Campbell St.		
Birkhall Dr., Bear.	7	R7	Blairtummock Rd. G32	39	CC12	Bothwell Pk. Rd. G71	69	HH19
Birkhill Av., Bish.	11	Y6	Blake Rd., Cumb.	71	PP3	Bothwell Rd., Udd.	69	GG17
Birkhill Gdns., Bish.	11	Z6	Blane St. G4	36	W11	Bothwell St. G2	35	V12
Birkmyre Rd. G51	33	R13	Blantyre Fm. Rd., Blan.	68	FF19	Bothwell St. G72	66	AA17
Birks Rd., Renf.	31	L11	Blantyre Mill Rd., Both.	69	GG19	Bothwell Ter. G12	35	U11
Tower Dr.			Blantyre Rd., Both.	69	HH19	Bank St.		
Birkwood St. G40	53	Y15	Blantyre St. G3	34	T11	Bothwick Way, Pais.	45	G16
Birmingham Rd., Renf.	31	L11	Blaven Ct., Bail.	56	FF14	Crosbie Dr.		
Birnam Av., Bish.	11	Y6	Bracadale Rd.			Boundary Rd. G73	52	X15
Birnam Cres., Bear.	8	S5	Blawarthill St. G14	18	N9	Bourne Ct., Renf.	16	J8
Birnam Gdns., Bish.	11	Y7	Blenheim Av. G33	25	CC9	Bourne Cres., Renf.	16	J8
Birnam Rd. G31	53	Z14	Blenheim Ct. G33	25	DD9	Bourock Sq., Barr.	60	N19
Birness Dr. G43	50	T16	Blenheim Av.			Bourtree Dr. G73	65	Z18
Birness St. G43	50	T16	Blenheim La. G33	25	DD9	Bouverie St. G14	18	N9
Birnie Ct. G21	23	Z10	Blesdale Ct., Clyde.	5	L7	Bouverie St. G73	52	X16
Birnie Rd. G21	23	Z10	Blochairn Rd. G21	37	Y11	Bowden Dr. G52	32	P13
Birnock Av., Renf.	32	N11	Bluebell Gdns. G45	65	Y19	Bower St. G12	21	U10
Birsay Rd. G22	21	V8	Bluevale St. G31	37	Y13	Bowerwalls St., Barr.	60	N18
Bishop Gdns., Bish.	10	X7	Blyth Pl. G32	39	CC13	Bowes Cres., Bail.	55	DD14
Bishop St. G2	35	V12	Blyth Rd. G33	39	DD13	Bowfield Av. G52	32	N13
Bishopmill Pl. G21	23	Z10	Blythswood Av., Renf.	17	M10	Bowfield Cres. G52	32	N13
Bishopmill Rd. G21	23	Z10	Blythswood Ct. G2	35	V12	Bowfield Dr. G52	32	N13
Bisset Cres., Clyde.	4	K5	Cadogan St.			Bowfield Pl. G52	32	N13
Black St. G4	36	W11	Blythswood Dr., Pais.	30	K13	Bowfield Ter. G52	32	N13
Blackburn Sq., Barr.	59	M19	Blythswood Rd., Renf.	17	M9	Bowfield Cres.		
Blackburn St. G51	34	T13	Blythswood Sq. G2	35	V12	Bowhouse Way G73	65	Y18
Blackbyres Rd., Barr.	59	M17	Blythswood St. G2	35	V12	Bowling Grn. La. G14	19	Q10
Blackcraig Av. G15	6	P6	Boclair Av., Bear.	7	R6	Westland Dr.		
Blackcroft Gdns. G32	55	CC14	Boclair Cres., Bear.	8	S6	Bowling Grn. Rd. G14	19	Q10
Blackcroft Rd. G32	55	CC14	Boclair Cres., Bish.	11	Y7	Bowling Grn. Rd. G32	55	CC14
Blackfaulds Rd. G73	52	X16	Boclair Rd., Bear.	8	S6	Bowling Grn. Rd. G44	63	V17
Blackford Cres. G32	55	CC14	Boclair Rd., Bish.	11	Y7	Bowling Grn. Rd., Chr.	26	FF8
Blackford Pl. G32	55	CC14	Boclair St. G13	19	R8	Bowman St. G42	51	V15
Blackford Rd., Pais.	47	L14	Boden St. G40	53	Y14	Bowmont Gdns. G12	20	T10
Blackfriars St. G1	36	W12	Bodmin Gdns., Chr.	15	GG6	Bowmont Hill, Bish.	11	Y6
Blackhall La., Pais.	46	K14	Gartferry Rd.			Bowmont Ter. G12	20	T10
Blackhall St., Pais.	46	K14	Bogany Ter. G45	64	X19	Bowmore Gdns. G73	66	AA18
Blackhill Cotts. G23	9	V7	Bogbain Rd. G34	40	EE12	Bowmore Gdns., Udd.	57	GG16
Blackhill Pl. G33	37	Z11	Boggknowe, Udd.	56	FF16	Bowmore Rd. G52	33	R13
Blackhill Rd. G23	8	T7	Old Edinburgh Rd.			Boyd St. G42	51	V15
Blackie St. G3	34	T11	Boghall Rd., Udd.	56	EE15	Boydstone Pl. G46	61	R17
Blacklands Pl., Lenz.	13	DD6	Boghall St. G33	38	BB11	Boydstone Rd. G43	61	R17
Blacklaw La., Pais.	30	K13	Boghead Rd. G21	23	Y10	Boyle St., Clyde.	17	M8
Blackstone Av. G53	49	Q16	Boghead Rd., Lenz.	12	BB6	Boyleston Rd., Barr.	59	L18
Blackstone Cres. G53	49	Q15	Bogleshole Rd. G72	54	AA16	Boyndie Path G34	40	EE12
Blackstone Rd.,	29	G12	Bogmoor Rd. G51	33	Q12	Boyndie St. G34	40	EE12
Candren			Bogside Pl., Bail.	40	FF12	Brabloch Cres., Pais.	30	K13
Blackstoun Av., Linw.	28	E13	Whamflet Av.			Bracadale Dr., Bail.	56	FF14
Blackstoun Oval, Pais.	29	H13	Bogside Rd. G33	24	BB9	Bracadale Gdns., Bail.	56	FF14
Blackstoun Rd., Pais.	29	H13	Bogside St. G40	53	Y14	Bracadale Gro., Bail.	56	FF14
Blackthorn Av., Lenz.	12	BB5	Bogton Av. G44	63	U18	Bracadale Rd., Bail.	56	FF14
Blackthorn Gro., Lenz.	12	BB5	Bogton Av. La. G44	63	U18	Bracken Rd., Barr.	59	L17
Blackthorn Rd., Cumb.	71	QQ2	Bogton Av.			Bracken St. G22	21	V9
Blackthorn St. G22	22	X9	Boleyn Rd. G41	51	U15	Bracken Ter., Udd.	69	HH18
Blackwood Av., Linw.	28	E13	Bolivar Ter. G42	52	W16	Brackenbrae Av., Bish.	10	X7
Blackwood St. G13	19	R8	Bolton Dr. G42	51	V16	Brackenbrae Rd., Bish.	10	X7
Blackwood St., Barr.	59	L19	Bon Accord St., Clyde.	17	L8	Brackenrig Rd. G46	61	R19
Blackwoods Cres., Chr.	15	GG7	Bonawe St. G20	21	U10	Brackla Av. G13	18	N8
Blacurvie Rd. G34	40	EE11	Boness St. G40	53	Y14	Bracora Pl. G20	20	T9
Bladda La., Pais.	46	K14	Bonhill St. G22	21	V10	Glenfinnan Dr.		
Blades Ct., Gart.	27	HH9	Bonnar St. G40	53	Y14	Bradan Av. G13	18	N8
Bladnoch Dr. G15	7	Q7	Bonnaughton Rd.,	6	P5	Bradda Av. G73	65	Z18
Moraine Av.			Bear.			Bradfield Av. G12	20	T9
Blaeloch Av. G45	64	W19	Bonnyholm Av. G53	48	P14	Braeface Rd., Cumb.	70	NN3
Blaeloch Dr. G45	64	W19	Bonnyrigg Dr. G43	62	S17	Braefield Dr., Thorn.	62	S18
Blaeloch Ter. G45	64	W19	Bonyton Av. G13	18	N9	Braefoot Cres., Pais.	46	K16
Blair Cres., Bail.	56	EE14	Boon Dr. G15	6	P7	Braehead Rd., Cumb.	71	PP2
Blair Rd., Pais.	32	N13	Boquhanran Pl., Clyde.	5	L6	Braehead Rd., Pais.	58	J17
Blair St. G32	38	AA13	Albert Rd.			Braehead St. G5	52	W14
Blairatholl Av. G11	20	S10	Boquhanran Rd., Clyde.	4	K7	Braemar Av., Dalm.	4	K6
Blairatholl Gdns. G11	20	S10	Borden La. G13	19	R9	Braemar Cres., Bear.	7	R7
Blairbeth Dr. G44	51	V16	Borden Rd. G13	19	R9	Braemar Dr., John.	44	E15
Blairbeth Rd. G73	65	Y17	Boreland Dr. G13	18	P8	Braemar Rd. G73	66	AA18
Blairbeth Ter. G73	65	Y18	Boreland Pl. G13	18	P9	Braemar Rd., Renf.	16	J9

Name	Map	Grid
Braemar St. G42	51	U16
Braemar Vw., Dalm.	4	K5
Braemount Av., Pais.	58	J17
Braes Av., Clyde.	17	M8
Braeside Av. G73	53	Z16
Braeside Av., Chr.	15	GG7
Braeside Cres., Bail.	41	GG13
Braeside Cres., Barr.	60	N19
Braeside Dr., Barr.	59	M19
Braeside Pl. G72	66	BB18
Braeside St. G20	21	U10
Braeview Av., Pais.	45	H16
Braeview Dr., Pais.	45	H16
Braeview Gdns., Pais.	45	H16
Braeview Rd., Pais.	45	H16
Braid Sq. G4	35	V11
Braid St. G4	35	V11
Braidbar Fm. Rd., Giff.	62	T18
Braidbar Rd., Giff.	62	T18
Braidcraft Rd. G53	49	Q15
Braidfauld Gdns. G32	54	AA14
Braidfauld Pl. G32	54	AA15
Braidfauld St. G32	54	AA15
Braidfield Rd., Clyde.	5	L5
Braidholm Cres., Giff.	62	T18
Braidholm Rd., Giff.	62	T18
Braidpark Cres., Giff.	62	T18
Braidpark Dr., Giff.	62	T18
Braids Rd., Pais.	46	K15
Bramley Pl., Lenz.	13	DD6
Branchock Av. G72	67	CC18
Brand St. G51	34	T13
Brandon Gdns. G72	66	AA17
Brandon St. G31	36	X13
Branscroft G78	42	B14
Brassey St. G20	21	U9
Breadalbane Gdns. G73	65	Z18
Breadalbane St. G3	35	U12
Brech Av., Bail.	41	GG13
Brechin Rd., Bish.	11	Z7
Brechin St. G3	35	U12
Breck Av. G78	44	F16
Brediland Rd., Linw.	28	E13
Brediland Rd., Pais.	45	G15
Bredisholm Dr., Bail.	56	FF14
Bredisholm Rd., Bail.	57	GG14
Bredisholm Ter., Bail.	56	FF14
Brenfield Av. G44	63	U18
Brenfield Dr. G44	63	U18
Brentwood Av. G53	60	P18
Brentwood Dr. G53	60	P18
Brentwood Sq. G53	60	P18
Brentwood Dr.		
Brereton St. G42	52	W15
Bressey Rd. G33	39	DD13
Brewery St., John.	43	D14
Brewster Av., Pais.	31	L12
Briar Dr., Clyde.	5	L6
Briar Neuk, Bish.	23	Y8
Briar Rd. G43	62	T17
Briarlea Dr., Giff.	62	T18
Briarwood Ct. G32	55	DD15
Briarwood Gdns. G32	55	DD15
Woodend Rd.		
Brick La., Pais.	30	K13
Bridge of Weir Rd., Linw.	28	E13
Bridge St. G72	66	BB17
Bridge St., Dalm.	4	K6
Bridge St., Linw.	28	F13
Bridge St., Pais.	46	K14
Bridgebar St., Barr.	60	N18
Bridgeburn Dr., Chr.	15	GG7
Bridgegate G1	36	W13
Bridgend Rd. G53	49	Q16
Bridgeton Cross G40	36	X13
Brigham Pl. G23	21	U8
Broughton Rd.		
Brighton Pl. G51	34	S13
Brighton St. G51	34	S13
Brightside Av., Udd.	69	HH17
Brisbane Ct., Giff.	62	T18
Braidbar Dr.		
Brisbane St. G42	51	V16
Brisbane St., Dalm.	4	J6
Britannia Way, Clyde.	5	L7
Britannia Way, Renf.	31	M11
Briton St. G51	34	S13
Broad Pl. G40	36	X13
Broad St.		
Broad St. G40	36	X13
Broadford St. G4	36	W11
Harvey St.		
Broadholm St. G22	21	V9
Broadleys Av., Bish.	10	X6
Broadlie Dr. G13	18	P9
Broadloan, Renf.	31	M11
Broadwood Dr. G44	63	V17
Brock Oval G53	61	Q17
Brock Pl. G53	49	Q16
Brock Rd. G53	49	Q16
Brock Ter. G53	61	Q17
Brock Way G67	71	PP3
North Carbrain Rd.		
Brockburn Rd. G53	48	P15
Brockburn Ter. G53	49	Q16
Brockville St. G32	38	AA13
Brodick Sq. G64	23	Y8
Brodick St. G21	37	Y11
Brodie Pk. Av., Pais.	46	K15
Brodie Pk. Gdns., Pais.	46	K15
Brodie Pl., Renf.	31	L11
Brodie Rd. G21	23	Z8
Brognowe, Udd.	56	FF16
Glasgow Rd.		
Brook St. G40	36	X13
Brooklands Av., Udd.	57	GG16
Brooklea Dr., Giff.	62	T17
Brookside St. G40	37	Y13
Broom Cres., Barr.	59	L17
Broom Dr., Clyde.	5	L6
Broom Gdns., Lenz.	12	BB5
Broom Path, Bail.	55	DD14
Tudor St.		
Broom Rd. G43	62	T17
Broom Rd. G67	71	QQ1
Broom Ter., John.	44	E15
Broomdyke Way, Pais.	30	J12
Broomfield Av. G21	23	Y10
Broomfield Rd.		
Broomfield Av. G72	53	Z16
Broomfield Pl. G21	22	X9
Broomfield Rd.		
Broomfield Rd. G21	22	X9
Broomfield Ter., Udd.	57	GG15
Broomhill Av. G11	33	R11
Broomhill Av. G32	54	BB16
Broomhill Cres. G11	19	R10
Broomhill Dr. G11	19	R10
Broomhill Dr. G73	65	Y17
Broomhill Gdns. G11	19	R10
Broomhill La. G11	19	R10
Broomhill Path G11	33	R11
Broomhill Pl. G11	19	R10
Broomhill Rd. G11	33	R11
Broomhill Ter. G11	33	R11
Broomieknowe Dr. G73	65	Y17
Broomieknowe Rd. G73	65	Y17
Broomielaw G1	35	V13
Broomknowe, Cumb.	70	MM2
Broomknowe, Pl. G66	13	DD6
Broomknowes Rd. G21	23	Y10
Broomlands Av., Renf.	16	J8
Broomlands Cres., Renf.	16	J8
Broomlands Gdns., Renf.	16	J8
Broomlands Rd., Cumb.	71	PP4
Broomlands St., Pais.	46	J14
Broomlands Way, Renf.	16	K8
Broomlea Cres., Renf.	16	J8
Broomley Dr. G46	62	T19
Broomley La., Giff.	62	T19
Broomloan Ct. G51	34	S13
Broomloan Pl. G51	34	S13
Broomloan Rd. G51	34	S13
Broompark Circ. G31	36	X12
Broompark Dr. G31	36	X12
Broompark Dr., Renf.	16	J8
Broompark St. G31	36	X12
Broomton Rd. G21	23	Z8
Broomward Dr., John.	44	E14
Brora Dr., Bear.	8	S6
Brora Dr., Giff.	62	T19
Brora Dr., Renf.	18	N10
Brora Gdns., Bish.	11	Y7
Brora La. G31	37	Z11
Brora St.		
Brora Rd., Bish.	11	Y7
Brora St. G33	37	Z11
Broughton Dr. G23	21	U8
Broughton Gdns. G23	9	U7
Broughton Rd. G23	21	U8
Brown Av., Clyde.	17	M8
Brown Pl. G72	66	BB17
Allison Dr.		
Brown Rd., Cumb.	70	NN3
Brown St. G2	35	V12
Brown St., Pais.	30	J13
Brown St., Renf.	31	L11
Brownhill Rd. G43	62	S18
Brownlie St. G42	51	V16
Browns La., Pais.	46	K14
Brownsdale Rd. G73	52	X16
Brownside Av. G72	66	AA17
Brownside Av., Barr.	59	L17
Brownside Av., Pais.	46	J16
Brownside Cres., Barr.	59	L17
Brownside Dr. G13	18	N9
Brownside Dr., Barr.	59	L17
Brownside Gro., Barr.	59	L17
Brownside Rd. G72	65	Z17
Brownside Rd. G73	65	Z17
Bruce Av., John.	43	D16
Bruce Av., Pais.	31	L12
Bruce Rd. G41	51	U14
Bruce Rd., Pais.	31	L13
Bruce Rd., Renf.	31	L11
Bruce St., Clyde.	5	L7
Bruce Ter., Blan.	69	GG19
Brucefield Pl. G34	40	FF12
Brunstance Rd. G34	40	EE11
Brunswick Ho., Dalm.	4	J5
Perth Cres.		
Brunswick St. G1	36	W12
Brunton St. G44	63	V17
Brunton Ter. G44	63	U18
Bruntsfield Av. G53	60	P18
Bruntsfield Gdns. G53	60	P18
Bruntsfield Av.		
Brydson Pl., Linw.	28	E13
Fulwood Av.		
Buccleuch Av. G52	32	N12
Buccleuch La. G3	35	V11
Scott St.		
Buccleuch St. G3	35	V11
Buchan St. G5	35	V13
Norfolk St.		
Buchan Ter. G72	66	AA18
Buchanan Cres. G64	23	Z8
Buchanan Dr. G64	23	Z8
Buchanan Dr. G72	66	AA17
Buchanan Dr. G73	65	Y17
Buchanan Dr., Bear.	8	S6
Buchanan Dr., Bish.	23	Z8
Buchanan Dr., Lenz.	13	CC6
Buchanan Gdns. G32	55	DD15
Buchanan St. G1	35	V12
Buchanan St., Bail.	56	EE14
Buchanan St., John.	43	D15
Buchlyvie Gdns., Bish.	22	X8
Hillcroft Ter.		
Buchlyvie Path G34	40	EE12
Buchlyvie Rd., Pais.	32	N13
Buchlyvie St. G34	40	EE12
Buckingham Bldgs. G12	20	T10
Great Western Rd.		
Buckingham Dr. G32	54	BB16
Buckingham Dr. G73	53	Z16
Buckingham St. G12	20	T10
Buckingham Ter. G12	20	T10
Great Western Rd.		
Bucklaw Gdns. G52	49	Q14
Bucklaw Pl. G52	49	Q14
Bucklaw Ter. G52	49	Q14
Buckley St. G22	22	W9
Bucksburn Rd. G21	23	Z10

Street	No.	Grid
Buckthorne Pl. G53	60	P18
Buddon St. G40	53	Z14
Budhill Av. G32	38	BB13
Bulldale St. G14	18	N9
Bullionslaw Dr. G73	65	Z17
Bulloch Av., Giff.	62	T19
Bullwood Av. G53	48	N15
Bullwood Ct. G53	48	N15
Bullwood Dr. G53	48	N15
Bullwood Gdns. G53	48	N15
Bullwood Pl. G53	48	N15
Bunessan St. G52	33	R13
Bunhouse Rd. G3	34	T11
Burgh Hall La. G11	34	S11
Fortrose St.		
Burgh Hall St. G11	34	S11
Burgh La. G12	20	T10
Vinicombe St.		
Burghead Dr. G51	33	R12
Burghead Pl. G51	33	R12
Burgher St. G31	37	Z13
Burleigh Rd., Udd.	69	HH18
Burleigh St. G51	34	S12
Burlington Av. G12	20	S9
Burmola St. G22	21	V10
Burmouth Rd. G33	39	DD13
Burn Gdns., Blan.	68	FF19
Burn Ter. G72	54	AA16
Burn Vw., Cumb.	71	QQ2
Burnacre Gdns., Udd.	57	GG16
Burnbank Dr., Barr.	59	M19
Burnbank Gdns. G20	35	U11
Burnbank Pl. G4	36	X12
Drygate		
Burnbank Ter. G20	35	U11
Burnbrae, Clyde.	5	L5
Burnbrae Av., Chr.	15	HH7
Burnbrae Av., Linw.	28	F13
Bridge St.		
Burnbrae Ct., Lenz.	13	CC6
Auchinloch Rd.		
Burnbrae Dr. G73	65	Z17
East Kilbride Rd.		
Burnbrae Rd., John.	44	F14
Burnbrae Rd., Lenz.	13	DD7
Burnbrae St. G21	23	Y10
Burncleuch Av. G72	66	BB18
Burncrooks Ct., Clyde.	4	K5
Burndyke Ct. G51	34	T12
Burndyke Sq. G51	34	T12
Burndyke St. G51	34	S12
Burnett Rd. G33	39	DD12
Burnfield Av., Giff.	62	S18
Burnfield Cotts., Giff.	62	S18
Burnfield Dr. G43	62	S18
Burnfield Gdns., Giff.	62	T18
Burnfield Rd.		
Burnfield Rd., Giff.	62	S17
Burnfoot Cres. G73	65	Z17
Burnfoot Cres., Pais.	46	J16
Burnfoot Dr. G52	32	P13
Burngreen Ter., Cumb.	71	PP1
Burnham Rd. G14	18	P10
Burnham Ter. G14	18	P10
Burnham Rd.		
Burnhead Rd. G43	63	U17
Burnhead Rd.,	70	MM3
Cumb.		
Burnhead St., Udd.	57	HH16
Burnhill Quad. G73	52	X16
Burnhill St. G73	52	X16
Burnhouse St. G20	20	T9
Burnmouth Ct. G33	39	DD13
Pendeen Rd.		
Burnpark Av., Udd.	56	FF16
Burns Dr., John.	43	D16
Burns Gro., Thorn.	62	S19
Burns Rd., Cumb.	71	PP3
Burns St. G4	35	V11
Burns St., Dalm.	4	K6
Burnside Av., Barr.	59	L18
Burnside Ct., Dalm.	4	K6
Scott St.		
Burnside Gdns., Kilb.	42	B15
Burnside Gate G73	65	Z17
Burnside Rd. G73	65	Z17
Burnside Rd., John.	44	F15
Burnside Ter. G72	67	DD18
Burntbroom Dr., Bail.	55	DD14
Burntbroom Gdns., Bail.	55	DD14
Burntbroom Rd., Udd.	55	DD14
Burntbroom St. G33	39	CC12
Burntshields Rd., Kilb.	42	A15
Burr Gdns., Bish.	11	Z7
Solway Rd.		
Burrells La. G4	36	X12
High St.		
Burrelton Rd. G43	63	U17
Burton La. G43	51	V15
Langside Rd.		
Bushes Av., Pais.	46	J15
Busheyhill St. G72	66	BB17
Bute Av., Renf.	31	M11
Bute Cres., Bear.	7	R7
Bute Cres., Pais.	46	J16
Bute Dr., John.	43	C15
Bute Gdns. G12	34	T11
Bute Gdns. G44	63	U18
Bute Rd., Pais.	30	J11
Bute Ter. G73	65	Y17
Bute Ter., Udd.	57	HH16
Butterbiggins Rd. G42	51	V14
Butterfield Pl. G41	51	U15
Pollokshaws Rd.		
Byrebush Rd. G53	49	Q15
Byres Av., Pais.	31	L13
Byres Cres.		
Byres Cres., Pais.	31	L13
Byres Rd. G11	34	T11
Byres Rd., John.	44	F15
Byron Ct., Udd.	69	HH19
Shelley Dr.		
Byron La. G11	33	R11
Sandeman St.		
Byron St. G11	33	R11
Byron St., Clyde.	4	K6
Byshot St. G22	22	W10
Cable Depot Rd., Dalm.	4	K7
Cadder Ct., Bish.	11	Y5
Cadder Gro. G20	21	U8
Cadder Rd.		
Cadder Pl. G20	21	U8
Cadder Rd. G20	21	U8
Cadder Rd., Bish.	11	Y5
Cadder Way, Bish.	11	Y5
Cadoc St. G72	66	BB17
Cadogan St. G2	35	V12
Cadzow Dr. G72	66	AA17
Cadzow St. G2	35	V12
Cadogan St.		
Caird Dr. G11	34	S11
Cairn Av., Renf.	32	N11
Cairn Dr., Linw.	28	E13
Cairn La., Pais.	30	J12
Mosslands Rd.		
Cairn St. G21	22	X9
Cairnban St. G51	33	Q13
Cairnbrook Rd. G34	40	FF12
Cairncraig St. G31	53	Z14
Cairndow Av. G44	63	U18
Cairndow Ct. G44	63	U18
Cairngorm Cres., Barr.	59	M19
Cairngorm Cres., Bear.	6	P5
Cairngorm Cres., Pais.	46	K15
Cairngorm Rd. G43	62	T17
Cairnhill Circ. G52	48	N14
Cairnhill Dr. G52	48	N14
Cairnhill Pl. G52	48	N14
Cairnhill Circ.		
Cairnhill Rd. G61	7	R7
Cairnlea Dr. G51	34	S13
Cairnmuir Rd. G52	66	AA19
Cairns Av. G72	66	BB17
Cairns Rd. G72	66	BB18
Cairnsmore Pl. G15	6	N7
Cairnsmore Rd. G15	6	N7
Cairnswell Av. G72	67	CC18
Cairnswell Pl. G72	67	CC18
Cairntoul Dr. G14	18	P9
Cairntoul Pl. G14	18	P9
Caithness St. G20	21	U10
Calcots Path G34	40	FF11
Auchengill Rd.		
Calcots Pl. G34	40	FF11
Caldarvan St. G22	21	V10
Calder Av., Barr.	59	M19
Calder Dr. G72	66	BB17
Calder Gate, Bish.	10	X6
Calder Pl., Bail.	56	EE14
Calder Rd., Pais.	29	H13
Calder Rd., Udd.	68	FF17
Calder St. G42	51	V15
Calderbank Vw., Bail.	56	FF14
Calderbraes Av., Udd.	57	GG16
Caldercuilt Rd. G20	20	T8
Caldercuilt St. G20	20	T8
Calderpark Av., Udd.	56	EE15
Calderpark Cres., Udd.	56	EE15
Caldervale, Udd.	68	FF17
Calderwood Av., Bail.	56	EE14
Calderwood Dr., Bail.	56	EE14
Calderwood Gdns., Bail.	56	EE14
Calderwood Rd. G43	62	T17
Calderwood Rd. G73	53	Z16
Caldwell Av. G13	18	P9
Caldwell Av., Linw.	28	E13
Caledon La. G12	34	T11
Highburgh Rd.		
Caledon St. G12	34	T11
Caledonia Av. G5	52	W14
Caledonia Av. G73	53	Y16
Caledonia Dr., Bail.	56	EE14
Caledonia Rd. G5	52	W14
Caledonia Rd., Bail.	56	EE14
Caledonia St. G5	52	W14
Caledonia St., Dalm.	4	K7
Caledonia St., Pais.	30	J13
Caledonia Way W., Pais.	30	J11
Caledonian Circuit G72	67	CC17
Caledonian Cres. G12	20	T10
Great Western Rd.		
Caledonian Cres. G12	35	U11
Caledonian Mans. G12	20	T10
Great Western Rd.		
Caledonian Pl. G72	67	DD17
Caley Brae, Udd.	69	GG17
Calfhill Rd. G53	48	P14
Calfmuir Rd., Chr.	14	EE5
Calgary St. G4	36	W11
Callander St. G20	21	V10
Callieburn Rd., Bish.	23	Y8
Cally Av. G15	6	P6
Calside, Pais.	46	K15
Calside Av., Pais.	46	J14
Calton Entry G40	36	X13
Gallowgate		
Calvay Cres. G33	39	CC12
Calvay Pl. G33	39	DD13
Calvay Rd. G33	39	CC12
Cambourne Rd., Chr.	15	GG6
Cambridge Av., Clyde.	5	L6
Cambridge Dr. G20	20	T9
Glenfinnan Dr.		
Cambridge La. G3	35	V11
Cambridge St.		
Cambridge Rd., Renf.	31	M11
Cambridge St. G3	35	V12
Camburn St. G32	38	AA13
Cambus Pl. G32	39	CC11
Cambusdoon Rd. G32	39	CC11
Cambuskenneth Gdns.	39	DD13
G32		
Cambuskenneth Pl. G32	39	CC11
Cambuslang Rd. G32	54	AA16
Cambuslang Rd. G72	53	Z16
Cambuslang Rd. G73	53	Y15
Cambusmore Pl. G32	39	CC11
Camden St. G5	52	W14
Camelon St. G32	38	AA13
Cameron Dr., Bear.	8	S6
Cameron Dr., Udd.	57	HH16
Cameron Sq., Clyde.	5	M5
Glasgow Rd.		

Cameron St. G20 — 21 — V10
Cameron St. G52 — 32 — N12
Cameron St., Clyde. — 17 — M8
Camlachie St. G31 — 37 — Y13
Camp Rd. G73 — 52 — X15
Camp Rd., Bail. — 40 — EE13
Campbell Dr., Barr. — 59 — M19
Campbell Dr., Bear. — 7 — Q5
Campbell St. G20 — 20 — T8
Campbell St., John. — 43 — D15
Campbell St., Renf. — 17 — M10
Camperdown St. G20 — 21 — V10
Garscube Rd.
Camphill, Pais. — 46 — J14
Camphill Av. G41 — 51 — U16
Camps Cres., Renf. — 32 — N11
Campsie Av., Barr. — 59 — M19
Campsie Dr., Pais. — 31 — L12
Campsie Dr., Pais. — 46 — J16
Campsie Dr., Pais. — 30 — K11
Campsie Pl., Chr. — 26 — FF8
Campsie St. G21 — 22 — X9
Campsie Vw., Bail. — 41 — GG13
Campsie Vw., Chr. — 26 — FF8
Campsie Vw., Cumb. — 71 — PP2
Campsie Vw G33 — 25 — CC10
Campston Pl. G33 — 38 — BB11
Camstradden Dr. E., Bear. — 7 — Q6
Camstradden Dr. W., Bear. — 7 — Q6
Camus Pl. G15 — 6 — N6
Canal Av., John. — 44 — E14
Canal Rd., John. — 43 — D15
Canal St. G4 — 36 — W11
Canal St., Clyde. — 17 — L8
Canal St., John. — 44 — F14
Canal St., Pais. — 46 — J14
Canal St., Renf. — 17 — M10
Canal Ter., Pais. — 46 — K14
Canberra Av., Dalm. — 4 — J6
Canberra Ct., Giff. — 62 — T18
Braidpark Dr.
Cander Rigg, Bish. — 11 — Y6
Candleriggs G1 — 36 — W13
Candren Rd., Linw. — 28 — F13
Candren Rd., Pais. — 45 — H14
Canmore Pl. G31 — 53 — Z14
Canmore St. G31 — 53 — Z14
Cannich Dr., Pais. — 47 — L15
Canniesburn Rd., Bear. — 7 — Q6
Canniesburn Sq., Bear. — 7 — R7
Macfarlane Rd.
Canniesburn Toll, Bear. — 7 — R6
Canonbie St. G34 — 40 — FF11
Canting Way G51 — 34 — T12
Capelrig St. G46 — 61 — R18
Caplaw Rd., Pais. — 58 — J17
Caplethill Rd., Pais. — 46 — K16
Caprington St. G33 — 38 — BB11
Cara Dr. G51 — 33 — R12
Caravelle Way, Renf. — 31 — M11
Friendship Way
Carberry Rd. G41 — 50 — T15
Carbeth St. G22 — 21 — V10
Carbisdale St. G22 — 22 — X9
Carbost St. G23 — 8 — T7
Torgyle St.
Carbrook St. G21 — 37 — Y11
Carbrook St., Pais. — 46 — J14
Cardarrach St. G21 — 23 — Y10
Cardell Dr., Pais. — 45 — H14
Cardell Rd., Pais. — 45 — H14
Carding La. G3 — 35 — U12
Argyle St.
Cardonald Dr. G52 — 48 — P14
Cardonald Gdns. G52 — 48 — P14
Cardonald Pl. Rd. G52 — 48 — P14
Cardow Rd. G21 — 23 — Z10
Cardowan Dr. G33 — 25 — CC9
Cardowan Rd. G33 — 25 — DD9
Cardowan Rd. G32 — 38 — AA13
Cardrona St. G33 — 24 — BB10
Cardross Ct. G31 — 36 — X12
Cardross St. G31 — 36 — X12

Cardwell St. G41 — 51 — V14
Cardyke St. G21 — 23 — Y10
Careston Pl., Bish. — 11 — Z7
Carfin St. G42 — 51 — V15
Carfrae St. G3 — 34 — T12
Cargill St. G31 — 54 — AA14
Cargill St. G64 — 23 — Y8
Carham Cres. G52 — 33 — Q13
Carham Dr. G52 — 33 — Q13
Carillon Rd. G51 — 34 — T13
Carisbrooke Cres., Bish. — 11 — Y6
Carlaverock Rd. G43 — 62 — T17
Carleith Av., Clyde. — 4 — K5
Carleith Quad. G51 — 33 — Q12
Carleith Ter., Clyde. — 4 — K5
Carleith Av.
Carleston St. G21 — 22 — X10
Atlas Rd.
Carleton Dr., Giff. — 62 — T18
Carleton Gdns. Giff. — 62 — T18
Carlibar Av. G13 — 18 — N9
Carlibar Dr., Barr. — 59 — M18
Carlibar Gdns., Barr. — 59 — M18
Commercial Rd.
Carlibar Rd., Barr. — 59 — L18
Carlile La., Pais. — 30 — K13
New Sneddon St.
Carlile Pl., Pais. — 30 — K13
Carlisle St. G21 — 22 — W10
Carlowrie Av., Blan. — 68 — FF19
Carlton Ct. G5 — 35 — V13
Carlton Pl. G5 — 35 — V13
Carlton Ter. G20 — 21 — U10
Wilton St.
Carlyle Av. G52 — 32 — N12
Carlyle Rd., Pais. — 30 — K13
Carlyle Ter. G73 — 53 — Y15
Carmaben Rd. G33 — 39 — DD12
Carment Dr. G41 — 50 — T16
Carment La. G41 — 50 — T16
Carmichael Pl. G42 — 51 — U16
Carmichael St. G51 — 34 — S13
Carmunnock Bypass G44 — 64 — W19
Carmunnock La. G44 — 63 — V17
Madison Av.
Carmunnock Rd. G44 — 51 — V16
Carmyle Av. G32 — 54 — BB15
Carna Dr. G44 — 64 — W17
Carnarvon St. G3 — 35 — U11
Carnbooth Ct. G45 — 64 — X19
Carnbroe St. G20 — 35 — V11
Carnegie Rd. G52 — 32 — P13
Carnock Cres., Barr. — 59 — L19
Carnock Rd. G53 — 49 — Q16
Carnoustie Ct., Both. — 69 — GG19
Carnoustie Cres., Bish. — 11 — Z7
Carnoustie St. G5 — 35 — U13
Carntyne Gdns. G32 — 38 — AA12
Abbeyhill St.
Carntyne Pl. G32 — 37 — Z12
Carntyne Rd. G31 — 37 — Z13
Carntynehall Rd. G32 — 38 — AA12
Carnwadric Rd. G46 — 61 — R18
Carnwath Av. G43 — 63 — U17
Caroline St. G31 — 38 — AA13
Carolside Dr. G15 — 6 — P6
Carradale Gdns., Bish. — 11 — Z7
Thrums Av.
Carradale Pl., Linw. — 28 — E13
Carrbridge Dr. G20 — 20 — T9
Glenfinnan Dr.
Carriagehill Dr., Pais. — 46 — K15
Carrick Cres., Giff. — 62 — T19
Carrick Dr. G32 — 55 — DD14
Carrick Dr. G73 — 65 — Y17
Carrick Rd. G73 — 64 — X17
Carrick Rd., Bish. — 11 — Z7
Carrick Rd., Cumb. — 71 — PP2
Carrick St. G2 — 35 — V12
Carrickarden Rd., Bear. — 7 — R6
Carrickstone Vw., Cumb. — 70 — NN1
Carriden Pl. G33 — 39 — DD12

Carrington St. G4 — 35 — U11
Carroglen Gdns. G32 — 39 — CC13
Carroglen Gro. G32 — 39 — CC13
Carron Ct. G72 — 67 — CC17
Carron Cres. G22 — 22 — W9
Carron Cres. G66 — 13 — DD6
Carron Cres., Bear. — 7 — Q6
Carron Cres., Bish. — 11 — Y7
Carron La., Pais. — 31 — L12
Kilearn Rd.
Carron Pl. G22 — 22 — X9
Carron St. G22 — 22 — X9
Carrour Gdns., Bish. — 10 — X7
Carsaig Dr. G52 — 33 — R13
Carse Vw. Dr., Bear. — 8 — S5
Carsebrook Av., Chr. — 14 — EE5
Chryston Rd.
Carsegreen Av., Pais. — 45 — H16
Carstairs St. G40 — 53 — Y15
Carswell Gdns. G41 — 51 — U15
Cart St., Clyde. — 17 — L8
Cartcraigs Rd. G43 — 62 — S17
Cartha Cres., Pais. — 47 — L14
Cartha St. G41 — 51 — U16
Cartside Av., John. — 43 — C15
Cartside Quad. G42 — 51 — V16
Cartside St. G42 — 51 — U16
Cartside Ter., Kilb. — 43 — C15
Kilbarchan Rd.
Cartvale La., Pais. — 30 — K13
Cartvale Rd. G42 — 51 — U16
Caskie Dr., Blan. — 69 — GG19
Cassley Av., Renf. — 32 — N11
Castle Av., Both. — 69 — GG19
Castle Av., John. — 44 — E15
Castle Av., Udd. — 69 — GG17
Castle Chimmins Av. G72 — 67 — CC18
Castle Chimmins Rd. G72 — 67 — CC18
Castle Cres. N. Ct. G1 — 36 — W12
Royal Ex. Sq.
Castle Gait, Pais. — 46 — K14
Castle Gdns., Chr. — 15 — GG7
Castle Gate, Both. — 69 — GG17
Castle Pl., Udd. — 69 — GG17
Ferry Rd.
Castle Rd. G78 — 44 — F14
Main Rd.
Castle Rd., John. — 44 — F14
Castle Sq., Dalm. — 4 — K6
Castle St. G4 — 36 — X12
Castle St. G73 — 53 — Y16
Castle St., Bail. — 56 — EE14
Castle St., Dalm. — 4 — K6
Castle St., Pais. — 46 — J14
Castle Vw., Clyde. — 5 — L6
Granville St.
Castle Way, Cumb. — 71 — QQ2
Castlebank Ct. G13 — 19 — R9
Castlebank Cres. G11 — 34 — S11
Meadowside St.
Castlebank Gdns. G13 — 19 — R9
Castlebank St. G11 — 33 — R11
Castlebank Vill. G13 — 19 — R9
Castlebay Dr. G22 — 10 — W7
Castlebay Pl. G22 — 22 — W8
Castlebay St. G22 — 22 — W8
Castlecroft Gdns., Udd. — 69 — GG17
Castlefern Rd. G73 — 65 — Y18
Castlehill Cres., Renf. — 17 — M10
Ferry Rd.
Castlehill Rd., Bear. — 6 — P5
Castlelaw Gdns. G32 — 38 — BB13
Castlelaw Pl. G32 — 38 — BB13
Castlelaw St. G32 — 38 — BB13
Castlemilk Cres. G44 — 64 — X17
Castlemilk Dr. G45 — 64 — X18
Castlemilk Ms. G44 — 64 — X17
Castlemilk Rd.
Castlemilk Rd. G44 — 52 — X16
Castleton Av. G21 — 22 — X8
Colston Rd.
Castleton Ct. G45 — 64 — X19
Cathay St. G22 — 22 — W8

Street	Pg	Grid
Cathcart Cres., Pais.	47	L14
Cathcart Pl. G73	52	X16
Cathcart Rd. G42	51	V16
Cathcart Rd. G73	52	X16
Cathedral Ct. G4	36	W12
Rottenrow E.		
Cathedral La. G4	36	W12
Cathedral St.		
Cathedral Sq. G4	36	X12
Cathedral St. G1	36	W12
Cathedral St. G4	36	X12
Catherine Pl. G3	35	U12
Hydepark St.		
Cathkin Av. G72	66	AA17
Cathkin Av. G73	53	Z16
Cathkin Bypass G73	65	Z18
Cathkin Ct. G45	64	X19
Cathkin Gdns., Udd.	57	GG15
Cathkin Pl. G72	66	AA17
Cathkin Rd. G42	51	U16
Cathkin Rd., E.K.	65	Y19
Cathkin Rd., Udd.	57	GG15
Cathkin Vw. G32	54	BB16
Cathkinview Rd. G42	51	V16
Catrine Av., Clyde.	5	M6
Causewayside St. G32	54	BB15
Causeyside St., Pais.	46	K14
Cavendish Pl. G5	51	V14
Cavendish St. G5	51	V14
Cavin Dr. G45	64	X18
Cavin Rd. G45	64	X18
Caxton St. G13	19	R9
Cayton Gdns., Bail.	55	DD14
Cecil Pl. G51	35	U13
Paisley Rd. W.		
Cecil St. G12	20	T10
Cedar Av. G78	44	E16
Cedar Av., Dalm.	4	J6
Cedar Ct. G20	35	V11
Cedar Ct. G78	42	B14
Cedar Dr., Lenz.	13	CC5
Cedar Gdns. G73	65	Z18
Cedar Pl., Barr.	59	M19
Cedar Pl., Blan.	68	FF19
Cedar Rd., Bish.	23	Y8
Cedar Rd., Cumb.	71	QQ2
Cedar St. G20	35	V11
Cedar Wk., Bish.	23	Y8
Cedric Pl. G13	19	Q8
Cedric Rd. G13	19	Q8
Celtic Pl. G20	20	T8
Maryhill Rd.		
Cemetery Rd. G32	39	CC13
Cemetery Rd. G52	49	Q14
Paisley Rd. W.		
Central Av. G11	33	R11
Broomhill Ter.		
Central Av. G32	55	CC14
Central Av. G72	66	AA17
Central Av., Clyde.	5	L7
Central Chambers G2	35	V12
Hope St.		
Central Path G32	55	DD14
Central Way, Cumb.	70	NN4
Central Way, Pais.	30	K13
Centre, The, Barr.	59	L19
Centre St. G5	35	V13
Ceres Gdns. G64	11	Z7
Cessnock Rd. G33	24	BB9
Cessnock St. G51	34	T13
Cessnock St., Clyde.	5	M6
Chachan Dr. G51	33	R12
Skipness Dr.		
Chalmers Ct. G40	36	X13
Chalmers Gate G40	36	X13
Claythorn St.		
Chalmers Pl. G40	36	X13
Claythorn St.		
Chalmers St. G40	36	X13
Chalmers St., Clyde.	5	L7
Chamberlain La. G13	19	R9
Chamberlain Rd. G13	19	R9
Chancellor St. G11	34	S11
Chapel Rd., Clyde.	5	L5
Chapel St. G20	21	U9
Chapel St. G73	52	X16
Chapelhill Rd., Pais.	47	L15
Chapelton Av., Bear.	7	R6
Chapelton Gdns., Bear.	7	R6
Chapelton St. G22	21	V9
Chaplet Av. G13	19	Q8
Chapman St. G42	51	V15
Allison St.		
Chappel St., Barr.	59	L18
Charing Cross G2	35	U11
Charing Cross La. G3	35	U12
Granville St.		
Charles Av., Renf.	17	M10
Charles Cres., Lenz.	13	CC6
Charles St. G21	36	X11
Charlotte La. G1	36	W13
London Rd.		
Charlotte La. S. G1	36	W13
Charlotte St.		
Charlotte Pl., Pais.	46	K15
Charlotte St. G1	36	W13
Chatelherault Av. G72	66	AA17
Chatton St. G23	8	T7
Cheapside St. G3	35	U12
Chelmsford Dr. G12	20	S9
Cherry Bk., Lenz.	12	BB5
Cherry Cres., Clyde.	5	L6
Cherry Pl., Bish.	23	Y8
Cherry Pl., John.	44	E15
Cherrybank Rd. G43	63	U17
Cherrywood Rd., John.	44	F15
Chester St. G32	38	BB13
Chesterfield Av. G12	20	S9
Chesters Pl. G73	53	Y16
Chesters Rd., Bear.	7	Q6
Chestnut Dr., Dalm.	5	L5
Chestnut Dr., Lenz.	12	BB5
Chestnut Pl., John.	44	E16
Chestnut St. G22	22	W9
Cheviot Av., Barr.	59	M19
Cheviot Rd. G43	62	T17
Cheviot Rd., Pais.	46	K16
Chirnside Pl. G52	32	P13
Chirnside Rd. G52	32	P13
Chisholm St. G1	36	W13
Christian St. G43	50	T16
Christie La., Pais.	30	K13
New Sneddon St.		
Christie Pl. G72	66	BB17
Christie St., Pais.	30	K13
Christopher St. G21	37	Y11
Chryston Rd., Chr.	26	FF8
Chryston Rd., Chr.	14	FF5
Chryston Rd., Waterside	14	EE5
Church Av. G33	25	CC9
Church Av. G73	65	Z17
Church Dr., Lenz.	13	CC5
Church Hill, Pais.	30	K13
Church La. G42	51	V15
Victoria Rd.		
Church Rd., Chr.	26	FF8
Church Rd., Giff.	62	T19
Church St. G11	34	T11
Church St., Bail.	56	FF14
Church St., Clyde.	5	L6
Church St., John.	43	D14
Church St., Kilb.	42	B14
Church St., Udd.	69	GG17
Church Vw. G72	54	BB16
Churchill Av., John.	43	C16
Churchill Cres., Udd.	69	HH18
Churchill Dr. G11	19	R10
Churchill Pl., Kilb.	42	B14
Churchill Way, Bish.	10	X7
Kirkintilloch Rd.		
Circus Dr. G31	36	X12
Circus Pl. G31	36	X12
Circus Pl. La. G31	36	X12
Circus Pl.		
Cityford Cres. G73	52	X16
Cityford Dr. G73	52	X16
Clachan Dr. G51	33	R12
Skipness Dr.		
Claddens Pl., Lenz.	13	DD6
Claddens Quad. G22	22	W9
Claddens St. G22	21	V9
Claddens Wynd G66	13	DD6
Claddon Vw., Clyde.	5	M6
Kirkoswald Dr.		
Clair Rd., Bish.	11	Z7
Clairmont Gdns. G3	35	U11
Clare St. G21	37	Y11
Claremont Av., Giff.	62	T19
Claremont Pl. G3	35	U11
Claremont Ter.		
Claremont St. G3	35	U12
Claremont Ter. G3	35	U11
Claremont Ter. La. G3	35	U11
Clifton St.		
Clarence Dr. G11	20	S10
Clarence Gdns. G11	20	S10
Clarence St., Clyde.	5	M6
Clarence St., Pais.	31	L13
Clarendon La. G20	35	V11
Clarendon St.		
Clarendon Pl. G20	35	V11
Clarendon St. G20	35	V11
Clarion Cres. G13	18	P8
Clarion Rd. G13	18	P8
Clark St. G41	35	U13
Tower St.		
Clark St., Dalm.	4	K6
Clark St., John.	43	D14
Clark St., Pais.	30	J13
Clark St., Renf.	17	L10
Clarkston Av. G44	63	U18
Clarkston Rd. G44	63	U19
Clathic Av., Bear.	8	S6
Claude Av. G72	67	DD18
Claude Rd., Pais.	31	L13
Claudhall Av., Gart.	27	GG8
Clavens Rd. G52	32	N13
Claverhouse Pl., Pais.	47	L14
Claverhouse Rd. G52	32	N12
Clavering St. E., Pais.	30	J13
Well St.		
Clavering St. W., Pais.	30	J13
King St.		
Clayhouse Rd. G33	25	DD9
Claypotts Pl. G33	38	BB11
Claypotts Rd. G33	38	BB11
Clayslaps Rd. G3	34	T11
Argyle St.		
Claythorn Av. G40	36	X13
Claythorn Circ. G40	36	X13
Claythorn Av.		
Claythorn Ct. G40	36	X13
Claythorn Pk.		
Claythorn Pk. G40	36	X13
Claythorn St. G40	36	X13
Claythorn Ter. G40	36	X13
Claythorn Pk.		
Clayton Ter. G31	36	X12
Cleddans Cres., Clyde.	5	M5
Cleddans Rd., Clyde.	5	M5
Cleddens Ct., Bish.	11	Y7
Cleeves Pl. G53	60	P17
Cleeves Quad. G53	60	P17
Cleeves Rd. G53	60	P17
Cleghorn St. G22	21	V10
Cleland La. G5	36	W13
Cleland St.		
Cleland St. G5	36	W13
Clelland Av., Bish.	23	Y8
Clerwood St. G32	37	Z13
Cleveden Cres. G12	20	S9
Cleveden Cres. La. G12	20	S9
Cleveden Dr.		
Cleveden Dr. G12	20	S9
Cleveden Dr. G73	65	Z17
Cleveden Gdns. G12	20	T9
Cleveden Pl. G12	20	S9
Cleveden Rd. G12	20	S9
Cleveland La. G3	35	U12
Cleveland St. G3	35	U11
Cliff Rd. G3	35	U11
Clifford Gdns. G51	34	S13
Clifford La. G51	34	T13
Gower St.		

Clifford Pl. G51	34	T13	Coatbridge Rd., Bail.	41	GG13	Coltness St. G33	39	CC12
Clifford St.			Coatbridge Rd., Gart.	27	GG10	Coltpark Av., Bish.	22	X8
Clifford St. G51	34	S13	Coates Cres. G53	49	Q16	Coltpark La., Bish.	22	X8
Clifton Pl. G3	35	U11	Coats Cres., Bail.	40	EE13	Coltsfoot Dr. G53	60	P18
Clifton St.			Coats Dr., Pais.	45	H14	Columba Path, Clyde.	5	M7
Clifton Rd., Giff.	62	S18	Coatshill Av., Blan.	68	FF19	*Onslow Rd.*		
Clifton St. G3	35	U11	Cobbleriggs Way, Udd.	69	GG17	Columba St. G51	34	S12
Clifton Ter. G72	66	AA18	Cobinshaw St. G32	38	BB13	Colvend Dr. G73	65	Y18
Clifton Ter., John.	44	E15	Cobinton Pl. G33	38	BB11	Colvend St. G40	52	X14
Clincart Rd. G42	51	V16	Coburg St. G5	35	V13	Colville Dr. G73	65	Z17
Clincarthill Rd. G73	53	Y16	Cochno St., Clyde.	17	M8	Colwood Av. G53	60	P18
Clinton Av., Udd.	69	GG17	Cochran St., Pais.	46	K14	Colwood Gdns. G53	60	P18
Clippens Rd., Linw.	28	E13	Cochrane St. G1	36	W12	*Colwood Av.*		
Cloan Av. G15	6	P7	Cochrane St., Barr.	59	L19	Colwood Path G53	60	P18
Cloan Cres., Bish.	11	Y6	Cochranemill Rd., John.	43	C15	*Parkhouse Rd.*		
Cloberhill Rd. G13	7	Q7	Cockels Ln., Renf.	31	L11	Colwood Pl. G53	60	P18
Cloch St. G33	38	BB12	Cockenzie St. G32	38	BB13	Colwood Sq. G53	60	P18
Clochoderick Av., Kilb.	42	B15	Cockmuir St. G21	23	Y10	*Colwood Av.*		
Mackenzie Dr.			Cogan Rd. G43	62	T17	Comedie Rd. G33	25	DD10
Clonbeith St. G33	39	DD11	Cogan St. G43	50	T16	Comely Pk. St. G31	37	Y13
Closeburn St. G22	22	W9	Cogan St., Barr.	59	L19	Comley Pl. G31	37	Y13
Cloth St., Barr.	59	M19	Colbert St. G40	52	X14	*Gallowgate*		
Clouden Rd., Cumb.	71	PP3	Colbreggan Ct., Clyde.	5	M5	Commerce St. G5	35	V13
Cloudhowe Ter., Blan.	68	FF19	*St. Helena Cres.*			Commercial Ct. G5	36	W13
Clouston Ct. G20	21	U10	Colbreggan Gdns.,	5	M5	Commercial Rd. G5	52	W14
Clouston La. G20	20	T10	Clyde.			Commercial Rd., Barr.	59	M18
Clouston St.			Colchester Dr. G12	20	S9	Commonhead Rd. G34	40	FF12
Clouston St. G20	20	T10	Coldingham Av. G14	18	N9	Commonhead Rd., Bail.	41	GG12
Clova Pl., Udd.	69	GG17	Coldstream Dr. G73	65	Z17	Commore Av., Barr.	59	M19
Clova St. G46	61	R18	Coldstream Pl., Pais.	45	H15	Commore Dr. G13	18	P8
Clover Av., Bish.	10	X7	Coldstream Pl. G21	22	W10	Comrie Rd. G33	25	CC9
Cloverbank St. G21	37	Y11	*Keppochhill Rd.*			Comrie St. G32	54	BB14
Clovergate, Bish.	10	X7	Coldstream Rd., Clyde.	5	L7	Cona St. G46	61	R18
Clunie Rd. G52	49	R14	Colebrook St. G72	66	BB17	Conan Ct. G72	67	CC17
Cluny Av., Bear.	8	S7	Colebrook Ter. G12	21	U10	Condorrat Ring Rd.,	70	MM4
Cluny Dr., Bear.	8	S7	*Colebrooke La.*			Cumb.		
Cluny Dr., Pais.	31	L13	Colebrooke La. G12	21	U10	Congleton St. G53	60	N17
Cluny Gdns. G14	19	R10	*Colebrooke St.*			*Nitshill Rd.*		
Cluny Gdns., Bail.	56	EE14	Colebrooke Pl. G12	21	U10	Congress Rd. G3	35	U12
Cluny Vill. G14	19	Q10	*Belmont St.*			Conifer Pl., Lenz.	12	BB5
Westland Dr.			Colebrooke St. G12	21	U10	Conisborough Path G34	39	DD11
Clutha St. G51	35	U13	Colegrove Cres. G32	54	AA14	*Balfluig St.*		
Paisley Rd. W.			Coleridge, Udd.	69	HH18	Conisborough Rd. G34	39	DD11
Clyde Av., Barr.	59	M19	Colfin St. G34	40	FF11	Connal St. G40	53	Y14
Clyde Av., Both.	69	GG19	Colgrain St. G20	21	V9	Conniston St. G32	38	AA12
Clyde Ct., Dalm.	4	K6	Colinbar Circle, Barr.	59	L19	Conon Av., Bear.	7	Q6
Little Holm			Colinslee Av., Pais.	46	K15	Consett La. G33	39	CC12
Clyde Pl. G5	35	V13	Colinslee Cres., Pais.	46	K15	Consett St. G33	39	CC12
Clyde Pl. G72	67	CC18	Colinslee Dr., Pais.	46	K15	*Consett La.*		
Clyde Pl., John.	43	C16	Colinslie Rd. G53	49	Q16	Contin Pl. G12	20	T9
Clyde Rd., Pais.	31	L12	Colinton Pl. G32	38	BB12	Convair Way, Renf.	31	M11
Clyde St. G1	35	V13	Colintraive Av. G33	24	AA10	*Lismore Av.*		
Clyde St., Clyde.	17	M8	Coll Av., Renf.	31	M11	Conval Way, Pais.	30	J12
Clyde St., Renf.	17	M9	Coll Pl. G21	37	Y11	*Abbotsburn Way*		
Clyde Ter., Both.	69	HH19	Coll St. G21	37	Y11	Cook St. G5	35	V13
Clyde Vale G71	69	HH19	Colla Gdns., Bish.	11	Z7	Coopers Well La. G11	34	T11
Clyde Vw., Pais.	47	L15	College La. G1	36	W13	*Dumbarton Rd.*		
Clydebrae Dr. G71	69	HH19	*High St.*			Coopers Well St. G11	34	T11
Clydebrae St. G51	34	S12	College St. G1	36	W12	*Dumbarton Rd.*		
Clydeford Dr. G32	54	AA14	Collessie Dr. G33	39	CC11	Copland Pl. G51	34	S13
Clydeford Dr., Udd.	56	FF16	Collier St., John.	43	D14	Copland Quad. G51	34	S13
Clydeford Rd. G72	54	BB16	Collina St. G20	20	T9	Copland Rd. G51	34	S13
Clydeholm Rd. G14	33	Q11	Collins St. G4	36	X12	Coplaw St. G42	51	V14
Clydeholm Ter., Clyde.	17	M8	Collylin Rd., Bear.	7	R6	Copperfield La., Udd.	57	HH16
Clydeneuk Dr., Udd.	56	FF16	Colmonell Av. G13	18	N8	*Hamilton Vw.*		
Clydesdale Av., Pais.	31	L11	Colonsay Av., Renf.	31	M11	Corbett St. G32	54	BB14
Clydeside Expressway	34	T11	Colonsay Rd. G52	33	R13	Corbiston Way, Cumb.	71	PP3
G3			Colonsay Rd., Pais.	46	J16	Cordiner St. G44	51	V16
Clydeside Expressway	19	Q10	Colquhoun Av. G52	32	P12	Corkerhill Gdns. G52	49	R14
G14			Colquhoun Dr., Bear.	7	Q5	Corkerhill Pl. G52	49	Q15
Clydeside Rd. G73	52	X15	Colston Av., Bish.	22	X8	Corkerhill Rd. G52	49	Q15
Clydesmill Dr. G32	54	BB16	Colston Dr., Bish.	22	X8	Corlaich Av. G42	52	X16
Clydesmill Gro. G32	54	BB16	Colston Gdns., Bish.	22	X8	Corlaich Dr. G42	52	X16
Clydesmill Pl. G32	54	BB16	Colston Path, Bish.	22	X8	Corn St. G4	35	V11
Clydesmill Rd. G32	54	BB16	*Colston Gdns.*			Cornaig Rd. G53	48	P16
Clydeview G11	34	S11	Colston Pl., Bish.	22	X8	Cornalee Gdns. G53	48	P16
Dumbarton Rd.			Colston Rd., Bish.	22	X8	Cornalee Pl. G53	48	P16
Clydeview La. G11	33	R11	Coltmuir Av., Bish.	22	X8	Cornalee Rd. G53	48	P16
Broomhill Ter.			*Coltmuir Dr.*			Cornhill St. G21	23	Y9
Clydeview Ter. G32	55	CC16	Coltmuir Cres., Bish.	22	X8	Cornoch St. G23	8	T7
Clydeview Ter. G40	52	X14	Coltmuir Dr., Bish.	22	X8	*Torrin Rd.*		
Newhall St.			Coltmuir Gdns., Bish.	22	X8	Cornock Cres., Clyde.	5	L6
Clynder St. G51	34	S13	*Coltmuir Dr.*			Cornock St., Clyde.	5	L6
Clyth Dr., Giff.	62	T19	Coltmuir St. G22	21	V9	Cornwall Av. G73	65	Z17
Coalhill St. G31	37	Y13	Coltness La. G33	39	CC12	Cornwall St. G41	34	T13

105

Coronation Pl., Gart.	27	GG8	Craigbank St. G22	22	W10	Craigwell Av. G73	65	Z17
Coronation Way, Bear.	8	S7	Craigbarnet Cres. G33	24	BB10	Crail St. G31	37	Z13
Corpach Pl. G34	40	FF11	Craigbo Av. G23	8	T7	Cramond Av., Renf.	32	N11
Corran St. G33	38	AA12	Craigbo Ct. G23	20	T8	Cramond St. G5	52	W15
Corrie Dr., Pais.	48	N14	Craigbo Dr. G23	20	T8	Cramond Ter. G32	38	BB13
Corrie Gro. G44	63	U18	Craigbo Pl. G23	20	T8	Cranborne Rd. G12	20	S9
Corrie Pl., Lenz.	13	DD6	Craigbo Rd. G23	20	T8	Cranbrooke Dr. G20	20	T8
Corrour Rd. G43	50	T16	Craigbo St. G23	8	T7	Cranston St. G3	35	U12
Corse Rd. G52	32	N13	Craigbog Av., John.	43	C15	Cranworth La. G12	20	T10
Corsebar Av., Pais.	46	J15	Craigdonald Pl., John.	43	D14	*Great George St.*		
Corsebar Cres, Pais.	46	J15	Craigellan Rd. G43	62	T17	Cranworth St. G12	20	T10
Corsebar Dr., Pais.	46	J15	Craigenbay Cres., Lenz.	13	CC5	Crarae Av., Bear.	7	R7
Corsebar La. G78	45	H15	Craigenbay Rd., Lenz.	13	CC6	Crathie Dr. G11	34	S11
Balgonie Av.			Craigenbay St. G21	23	Y10	Crathie La. G11	34	S11
Corsebar Rd., Pais.	46	J15	Craigencart Ct., Clyde.	4	K5	*Exeter Dr.*		
Corseford Av., John.	43	C16	*Gentle Row*			Craw Rd., Pais.	46	J14
Corsehill Pl. G34	40	FF12	Craigend Pl. G13	19	R9	Crawford Av., Lenz.	13	CC6
Corsehill St. G34	40	FF12	Craigend St. G13	19	R9	Crawford Ct., Giff.	62	S19
Corselet Rd. G53	60	P18	Craigendmuir Rd. G33	25	DD10	*Milverton Rd.*		
Corsewall Av. G32	55	DD14	Craigendmuir St. G33	37	Z11	Crawford Cres., Blan.	68	FF19
Corsford Dr. G53	61	Q17	Craigendon Oval, Pais.	58	J17	Crawford Cres., Udd.	57	GG16
Corsock St. G31	37	Z12	Craigendon Rd., Pais.	58	J17	Crawford Dr. G15	6	N7
Corston St. G33	37	Z12	Craigends Dr., Kilb.	42	B14	Crawford La. G11	34	S11
Cortachy Pl., Bish.	11	Z7	*High Barholm*			Crawford Path G11	34	S11
Coruisk Way, Pais.	45	G16	Craigenfeoch Av., John.	43	C15	*Crawford St.*		
Spencer Dr.			Craigfaulds Av., Pais.	45	H15	Crawford St. G11	34	S11
Corunna St. G3	35	U12	Craigflower Gdns. G53	60	P18	Crawford Dr., Pais.	29	H13
Coshneuk Rd. G33	24	BB9	Craigflower Rd. G53	60	P18	Crawford Gdns. G73	65	Y18
Cottar St. G20	21	U8	Craighalbert Rd. G68	70	MM2	Crawfurd Rd. G73	65	Y18
Cotton Av., Linw.	28	E13	Craighalbert Way, Cumb.	70	MM2	Crawriggs Av., Lenz.	13	CC5
Cotton St. G40	53	Y15	Craighall Rd. G4	35	V11	Crebar Dr., Barr.	59	M19
Cotton St., Pais.	46	K14	Craighead Av. G33	23	Z10	Crebar St. G46	61	R18
Coulters La. G40	36	X13	Craighead St., Barr.	59	L19	Credon Gdns. G73	65	Z18
Countess Wk., Bail.	41	HH13	Craighead Way, Barr.	59	L19	Cree Av., Bish.	11	Z7
County Av. G72	53	Z16	Craighouse St. G33	38	BB11	Cree Gdns. G32	38	AA13
County Pl., Pais.	30	K13	Craigie Pk. G66	13	DD5	*Kilmany Dr.*		
Moss St.			Craigie St. G42	51	V15	Creran St. G40	36	X13
County Sq., Pais.	30	K13	Craigiebar Dr., Pais.	46	J16	*Tobago St.*		
Couper St. G4	36	W11	Craigieburn Gdns. G20	20	S8	Crescent Ct., Dalm.	4	K6
Courthill Av. G44	63	V17	Craigieburn Rd., Cumb.	70	NN3	*Swindon St.*		
Coustonhill St. G43	50	T16	Craigiehall Pl. G51	34	T13	Crescent Rd. G13	18	P9
Pleasance St.			Craigiehall St. G51	35	U13	Cresswell La. G12	20	T10
Coustonholm Rd. G43	50	T16	*Craigiehall Pl.*			*Great George St.*		
Coventry Dr. G31	37	Y12	Craigielea Dr., Pais.	30	J13	Cresswell St. G12	20	T10
Cowal Dr., Linw.	28	E13	Craigielea Pk., Renf.	17	L10	Cressy St. G51	33	R12
Cowal Rd. G20	20	T8	Craigielea Rd., Renf.	17	M10	Crest Av. G13	18	P8
Cowal St. G20	20	T8	Craigielinn Av., Pais.	58	J17	Crestlea Av., Pais.	46	K16
Cowan Clo., Barr.	59	M18	Craigievar St. G33	39	DD11	Creswell Ter., Udd.	57	GG16
Cowan Cres., Barr.	59	M19	Craigleith St. G32	38	AA13	*Kylepark Dr.*		
Cowan La. G12	35	U11	Craiglockhart St. G33	39	CC11	Crichton Ct. G45	64	X19
Cowan St.			Craigmaddie Ter. La. G3	35	U12	Crichton St. G21	22	X10
Cowan Rd., Cumb.	70	MM3	*Derby St.*			Crieff Ct. G3	35	U12
Cowan St. G33	35	U11	Craigmillar Rd. G42	51	V16	*North St.*		
Cowan Wilson Av., Blan.	68	FF19	Craigmont Dr. G20	21	U9	Criffell Gdns. G32	55	CC14
Cowcaddens Rd. G2	35	V11	Craigmont St. G20	21	U9	Criffell Rd. G32	55	CC14
Cowden Dr., Bish.	11	Y6	Craigmore St. G31	37	Z13	Crimea St. G2	35	V12
Cowden St. G51	33	Q12	Craigmount Av., Pais.	58	J17	Crinan Gdns., Bish.	11	Y7
Cowdenhill Circ. G13	19	Q8	Craigmuir Cres. G52	32	N13	Crinan Rd., Bish.	11	Y7
Cowdenhill Pl. G13	19	Q8	Craigmuir Pl. G52	32	N13	Crinan St. G31	37	Y12
Cowdenhill Rd. G13	19	Q8	*Craigmuir Rd.*			Cripps Av., Clyde.	5	M7
Cowdie St., Pais.	30	J12	Craigmuir Rd. G52	32	N13	Croft Rd. G73	66	BB17
Cowdray Cres., Renf.	17	M10	Craigneil St. G33	39	DD11	Croft Wynd, Udd.	69	HH17
Cowell Vw., Clyde.	5	L6	Craignestock St. G40	36	X13	Croftbank Av. G71	69	HH19
Granville St.			Craignethan Gdns. G11	34	S11	Croftbank Cres., Both.	69	HH19
Cowglen Pl. G53	49	Q16	*Lawrie St.*			Croftbank Cres., Udd.	69	GG17
Cowglen Rd.			Craignure Rd. G73	65	Y18	Croftbank St. G21	22	X10
Cowglen Rd. G53	49	Q16	Craigpark G31	37	Y12	Croftbank St., Udd.	69	GG17
Cowglen Ter. G53	49	Q16	Craigpark Dr. G31	37	Y12	Croftburn Dr. G44	64	W18
Cowie St. G41	35	U13	Craigpark Ter. G31	37	Y12	Croftcroighn Rd. G33	38	BB11
Cowlairs Rd. G21	22	X10	*Craigpark*			Croftend Av. G44	64	X17
Coxhill St. G21	22	W10	Craigpark Way, Udd.	57	HH16	Croftfoor Rd. G44	64	W18
Coxton Pl. G33	39	CC11	*Newton Dr.*			Croftfoot Cotts., Gart.	27	HH9
Coylton Rd. G43	63	U17	Craigs Av., Clyde.	5	M5	Croftfoot Cres. G45	65	Y18
Craggan Dr. G14	18	N9	Craigston Pl., John.	43	D15	Croftfoot Dr. G45	64	X18
Cragielea St. G31	37	Y12	Craigston Rd., John.	43	D15	Croftfoot Quad. G45	64	X18
Crags Av., Pais.	46	K15	Craigton Av., Barr.	60	N19	Croftfoot Rd. G45	64	W18
Crags Cres., Pais.	46	K15	Craigton Dr. G51	33	R13	Croftfoot St. G45	65	Y18
Crags Rd., Pais.	46	K15	Craigton Dr., Barr.	60	N19	Croftfoot Ter. G45	64	X18
Craig Rd. G44	63	V17	Craigton Pl. G51	33	R13	Crofthead St., Udd.	69	GG17
Craigallian Av. G72	67	CC18	*Craigton Dr.*			Crofthill Av., Udd.	69	GG17
Craiganour La. G43	62	T17	Craigton Pl., Blan.	68	FF19	Crofthill Rd. G44	64	W17
Craiganour Pl. G43	62	T17	Craigton Rd. G51	33	R13	Crofthouse Dr. G44	64	X18
Craigard Pl. G73	66	AA18	Craigvicar Gdns. G32	39	CC13	Croftmont Av. G44	64	X18
Inverclyde Gdns.			*Hailes Av.*			Croftmoraig Av., Chr.	15	HH6
Craigbank Dr. G53	60	P17	Craigview Av., John.	43	C16	Crofton Av. G44	64	W18

Name	Page	Grid
Croftpark Av. G44	64	W18
Croftside Av. G44	64	X18
Croftspar Av. G32	39	CC13
Croftspar Dr. G32	39	CC13
Croftspar Pl. G32	39	CC13
Croftwood, Bish.	11	Y6
Croftwood Av. G44	64	W18
Cromart Pl., Chr.	14	FF7
Cromarty Av. G43	63	U17
Cromarty Av., Bish.	11	Z7
Cromarty Gdns., Clark.	63	V19
Crombie Gdns., Bail.	56	EE14
Cromdale St. G51	33	R13
Cromer La., Pais.	30	J12
Abbotsburn Way		
Cromer St. G20	21	U9
Cromer Way, Pais.	30	J12
Mosslands Rd.		
Crompton Av. G44	63	V17
Cromwell La. G20	35	V11
Cromwell St.		
Cromwell St. G20	35	V11
Cronberry Quad. G52	48	N14
Cronberry Ter. G52	48	N14
Crookedshields Rd. G72	66	BB19
Crookston Av. G52	48	P14
Crookston Ct. G52	48	P14
Crookston Dr. G52	48	N14
Crookston Gdns. G52	48	N14
Crookston Gro. G52	48	P14
Crookston Pl. G52	48	N14
Crookston Quad. G52	48	N14
Crookston Rd. G52	48	P15
Crookston Ter. G52	48	P14
Crookston Rd.		
Crosbie Dr. G78	45	G16
Crosbie St. G20	20	T8
Crosbie Wds., Pais.	45	H15
Cross, The G1	36	W13
Cross, The, Pais.	30	K13
Cross Arthurlie St., Barr.	59	L19
Cross Rd., Pais.	45	H15
Cross St. G32	55	CC15
Cross St., Pais.	46	J14
Crossbank Av. G42	52	X15
Crossbank Dr. G42	52	X15
Crossbank Rd. G42	52	W15
Crossbank Ter. G42	52	W15
Crossflat Cres., Pais.	31	L13
Crossford Dr. G23	9	U7
Crosshill Av. G42	51	V15
Crosshill Av., Lenz.	13	CC5
Crosshill Dr. G73	65	Y17
Crosshill Rd., Bish.	11	Z5
Crosshill Sq., Bail.	56	FF14
Crosslee St. G52	33	R13
Crosslees Ct., Thorn.	61	R18
Main St.		
Crosslees Dr., Thorn.	61	R18
Crosslees Pk., Thorn.	61	R18
Crosslees Rd., Thorn.	61	R19
Crossloan Pl. G51	33	R12
Crossloan Rd. G51	33	R12
Crossloan Ter. G51	33	R12
Crossmill Av., Barr.	59	M18
Crossmyloof Gdns. G41	50	T15
Crosspoint Dr. G23	9	U7
Invershiel Rd.		
Crosstobs Rd. G53	48	P15
Crossview Av., Bail.	40	FF13
Swinton Av.		
Crossview Pl., Bail.	40	FF13
Crovie Rd. G53	48	P16
Crow Ct., The, Bish.	10	X7
Kenmure Av.		
Crow La. G13	19	R9
Crow Rd. G11	19	R10
Crow Wd. Rd., Chr.	26	EE8
Crow Wd. Ter., Chr.	26	EE8
Crowflats Rd., Udd.	69	GG17
Lady Isle Cres.		
Crowhill Rd. G64	22	X8
Crowhill St. G22	22	W9
Crowlin Cres. G33	38	BB12
Crown Av., Clyde.	5	L6
Crown Circ. G12	20	S10
Crown Rd. S.		
Crown Ct. G1	36	W12
Virginia St.		
Crown Gdns. G12	20	S10
Crown Rd. N.		
Crown Mans. G11	20	S10
North Gardner St.		
Crown Rd. N. G12	20	S10
Crown Rd. S. G12	20	S10
Crown St. G5	52	W14
Crown St., Bail.	55	DD14
Crown Ter. G12	20	S10
Crown Rd. S.		
Crownpoint Rd. G40	36	X13
Crowpoint Rd. G40	37	Y13
Alma St.		
Croy Pl. G21	23	Z9
Rye Rd.		
Croy Pl. G21	23	Z9
Croy Rd.		
Croy Rd. G21	23	Z9
Cruachan Av., Renf.	31	M11
Cruachan Cres., Pais.	46	K16
Cruachan Dr., Barr.	59	M19
Cruachan Rd. G73	65	Z18
Cruachan St. G46	61	R18
Cruachan Way, Barr.	59	M19
Cruden St. G51	33	R13
Crum Av., Thorn.	62	S18
Crusader Av. G13	7	Q7
Cubie St. G40	36	X13
Cuilhill Rd., Bail.	41	GG12
Cuillin Way, Barr.	59	M19
Cuillins, The, Udd.	56	FF15
Cuillins Rd. G73	65	Z18
Culbin Dr. G13	18	N8
Cullen St. G32	54	BB14
Cullins, The, Chr.	15	HH6
Culloden St. G31	37	Y12
Coventry Dr.		
Culrain Gdns. G32	38	BB13
Culrain St. G32	38	BB13
Culross La. G32	55	CC14
Culross St. G32	55	CC14
Cult Rd., Lenz.	13	DD6
Cults St. G51	33	R13
Culzean Cres., Bail.	56	EE14
Huntingtower Rd.		
Culzean Dr. G32	39	CC13
Cumberland Ct. G1	36	W13
Gallowgate		
Cumberland La. G5	51	V14
Cumberland St.		
Cumberland Pl. G5	52	W14
Cumberland Pl., Pais.	46	K14
Laigh Kirk La.		
Cumberland St. G5	35	V13
Cumbernauld Rd. G31	37	Z12
Cumbrae Ct., Clyde.	5	L7
Montrose St.		
Cumbrae Rd., Pais.	46	K16
Cumbrae Rd., Renf.	31	M11
Cumbrae St. G33	38	BB12
Cumlodden Dr. G20	20	T8
Cumming Dr. G42	51	V16
Cumnock Dr., Renf.	59	M19
Cumnock Rd. G33	24	AA9
Cunard St., Clyde.	17	M8
Cunningham Dr., Clyde.	4	K5
Cunningham Dr., Giff.	63	U18
Cunningham Rd. G52	32	N12
Cunningham Rd. G73	53	Z16
Cunninghame Rd., Kilb.	42	B14
Curfew Rd. G13	7	Q7
Curle St. G14	33	Q11
Curlew Pl., John.	43	C16
Curling Cres. G44	52	W16
Currie St. G20	21	U9
Curtis Av. G44	52	W16
Curzon St. G20	21	U9
Cut, The, Udd.	69	GG17
Cuthbert St., Udd.	57	HH16
Oakdene Av.		
Cuthbertson St. G42	51	V15
Cuthelton Dr. G31	54	AA14
Cuthelton St.		
Cuthelton St. G31	53	Z14
Cuthelton Ter. G31	53	Z14
Cypress Av., Blan.	68	FF19
Cypress Av., Udd.	57	HH16
Myrtle Rd.		
Cypress Ct., Lenz.	12	BB5
Cypress St. G22	22	W9
Cyprus Av., John.	44	E15
Cyprus St., Clyde.	17	M8
Cyril St., Pais.	47	L14
Daer Av., Renf.	32	N11
Dairsie Gdns., Bish.	23	Z8
Dairsie St. G44	63	U18
Daisy St. G42	51	V15
Dakota Way, Renf.	31	M11
Friendship Way		
Dalbeth Rd. G32	54	AA15
Dalchurn Path G34	40	EE12
Dalchurn Pl.		
Dalchurn Pl. G34	40	EE12
Dalcraig Cres., Blan.	68	FF19
Dalcross La. G11	34	T11
Byres Rd.		
Dalcross St. G11	34	T11
Dalcruin Gdns. G69	15	HH6
Daldowie Av. G32	55	CC14
Dale Path G40	52	X14
Dale St. G40	52	X14
Dale Way G73	65	Y18
Daleview Av. G12	20	S9
Dalfoil Ct. G52	48	N14
Dalgarroch Av. G13	18	N8
Dalgleish Av., Clyde.	4	K5
Dalhouse Rd., Udd.	56	EE15
Dalhousie Gdns., Bish.	10	X7
Dalhousie La. G3	35	V11
Scott St.		
Dalhousie La. W. G3	35	V11
Buccleuch St.		
Dalhousie Rd., Kilb.	42	B15
Dalhousie St. G3	35	V11
Dalilea Dr. G34	40	FF11
Dalilea Path G34	40	FF11
Dalilea Dr.		
Dalilea Pl. G34	40	FF11
Dalintober St. G5	35	V13
Dalkeith Av. G41	50	S14
Dalkeith Av., Bish.	11	Y6
Dalkeith Rd., Bish.	11	Y6
Dalmahoy St. G32	38	AA12
Dalmally St. G20	21	U10
Dalmarnock Bri. G40	53	Y15
Dalmarnock Ct. G40	53	Y14
Baltic St.		
Dalmarnock Rd. G40	52	X14
Dalmary Dr., Pais.	31	L13
Dalmeny Av., Giff.	62	T18
Dalmeny Dr., Barr.	59	L19
Dalmeny St. G5	52	X15
Dalmuir St., Dalm.	4	K6
Stewart St.		
Dalnair St. G3	34	T11
Dalness Pas. G32	54	BB14
Ochil St.		
Dalness St. G32	54	BB14
Dalreoch Av., Bail.	40	FF13
Dalriada St. G40	53	Z14
Dalry Rd., Udd.	57	HH16
Myrtle Rd.		
Dalry St. G32	54	BB14
Dalserf Cres., Giff.	62	S19
Dalserf St. G31	37	Y13
Dalsetter Av. G15	6	N7
Dalsetter Pl. G15	6	P7
Dalsholm Rd. G20	20	S8
Dalskeith Av., Pais.	29	H13
Dalskeith Cres., Pais.	29	H13
Dalskeith Rd., Pais.	45	H14
Dalswinton Pl. G34	40	FF12
Dalswinton St.		

Street	Page	Ref.
Dalswinton St. G34	40	FF12
Dalton Av., Clyde.	6	N7
Dalton St. G31	38	AA13
Dalveen Av., Udd.	57	GG16
Dalveen Ct., Barr.	59	M19
Dalveen St. G32	38	AA13
Dalveen Way G73	65	Z18
Dalwhinnie Av., Blan.	68	FF19
Daly Gdns., Blan.	69	GG19
Dalziel Dr. G41	50	T14
Dalziel Quad. G41	50	T14
Dalziel Dr.		
Dalziel Rd. G52	32	N12
Damshot Cres. G53	49	Q15
Damshot Rd. G53	49	Q16
Danby Rd., Bail.	55	DD14
Danes Cres. G14	18	P9
Danes Dr. G14	18	P9
Danes La. S. G14	19	Q10
Dunglass Av.		
Dargarvel Av. G41	50	S14
Darkwood Cres., Pais.	29	H13
Darleith St. G32	38	AA13
Darluith Rd., Linw.	28	E13
Darnaway Av. G33	39	CC11
Darnaway St. G33	39	CC11
Darnick St. G21	23	Y10
Hobden St.		
Darnley Cres., Bish.	10	X6
Darnley Gdns. G41	51	U15
Darnley Path G41	61	R17
Kennisholm Av.		
Darnley Pl. G41	51	U15
Darnley Rd.		
Darnley Rd. G41	51	U15
Darnley Rd., Barr.	60	N18
Darnley St. G41	51	U15
Darroch Way, Cumb.	71	PP2
Dartford St. G22	21	V10
Darvaar Rd., Renf.	31	M11
Darvel Cres., Pais.	47	M14
Darvel St. G53	60	N17
Darwin Pl., Dalm.	4	J6
Dava St. G51	34	S12
Davaar Rd., Pais.	46	K16
Davaar St. G40	53	Y14
Daventry Dr. G12	20	S9
David Pl., Bail.	55	DD14
David Pl., Pais.	31	L12
Killarn Way		
David St. G40	37	Y13
David Way, Pais.	31	L12
Killarn Way		
Davidson Gdns. G14	19	Q10
Westland Dr.		
Davidson St. G40	53	Y15
Davidson St., Clyde.	18	N8
Davidston Pl., Lenz.	13	DD6
Davieland Rd., Giff.	62	S19
Daviot St. G51	33	Q13
Dawes La. N. G14	19	Q10
Upland Rd.		
Dawson Pl. G4	21	V10
Dawson Rd.		
Dawson Rd. G4	21	V10
Dealston Rd., Barr.	59	L18
Dean Pk. Dr. G72	67	CC18
Dean Pk. Rd., Renf.	32	N11
Dean St., Clyde.	5	M7
Deanbrae St., Udd.	69	GG17
Deanfield Quad. G52	32	N13
Deanpark Av., Udd.	69	HH18
Deans Av. G72	67	CC18
Deanside La. G4	36	W12
Rottenrow		
Deanside Rd., Renf.	32	P12
Deanston Dr. G41	51	U16
Deanwood Av. G44	63	U18
Deanwood Rd. G44	63	U18
Debdale Cotts. G13	19	R9
Whittingehame Dr.		
Dechmont Av. G72	67	CC18
Dechmont Gdns., Blan.	68	FF19
Dechmont Gdns., Udd.	57	GG15
Dechmont Pl. G72	67	CC18
Dechmont Rd., Udd.	57	GG15
Dechmont St. G31	53	Z14
Dechmont Vw., Udd.	57	HH16
Hamilton Vw.		
Dee Av. G78	45	G15
Dee Av., Renf.	18	N10
Dee Dr., Pais.	45	G15
Dee Pl., John.	43	C16
Dee St. G33	37	Z11
Deepdene Rd., Bear.	7	Q7
Deepdene Rd., Chr.	15	HH7
Delburn St. G31	53	Z14
Delhi Av., Dalm.	4	J6
Delhmont Vw., Udd.	57	HH16
Hamilton Vw.		
Delny Pl. G33	39	DD12
Delvin Rd. G44	63	V17
Denbeck St. G32	38	AA13
Denbrae St. G32	38	AA13
Dene Wk., Bish.	23	Z8
Denewood Av., Pais.	46	J16
Denham St. G22	21	V10
Denholme Dr., Giff.	62	T19
Denkenny Sq. G15	6	N6
Denmark St. G22	22	W10
Denmilne Path G34	40	FF12
Denmilne Pl. G34	40	FF12
Denmilne St. G34	40	FF12
Derby St. G3	35	U12
Derby Ter. La. G3	35	U12
Derby St.		
Derwent St. G22	21	V10
Despard Av. G32	55	DD14
Despard Gdns. G32	55	DD14
Deveron Av., Giff.	62	T19
Deveron Rd., Bear.	7	Q7
Deveron St. G33	37	Z11
Devol Cres. G53	48	P16
Devon Gdns. G12	20	S10
Hyndland Rd.		
Devon Gdns., Bish.	10	X6
Devon Pl. G42	51	V14
Devon St. G5	51	V14
Devondale Av., Blan.	68	FF19
Devonshire Gdns. G12	20	S10
Devonshire Gdns. La.	20	S10
G12		
Hyndland Rd.		
Devonshire Ter. G12	20	S10
Devonshire Ter. La. G12	20	S10
Hughenden Rd.		
Diana Av. G13	18	P8
Dick St. G20	21	U10
Henderson St.		
Dickens Av., Clyde.	4	K6
Dilwara Av. G14	33	R11
Dimity St., John.	43	D15
Dinard Dr., Giff.	62	T18
Dinart St. G33	37	Z11
Dinduff St. G34	40	FF11
Dingwall St. G3	34	T12
Kelvinhaugh St.		
Dinmont Pl. G41	51	U15
Norham St.		
Dinmont Rd. G41	50	T15
Dinwiddie St. G21	37	Z11
Dipple Pl. G15	6	P7
Dirleton Av. G41	51	U16
Dirleton Dr., Pais.	45	H15
Dirleton Gate, Bear.	7	Q7
Dixon Av. G42	51	V15
Dixon Rd. G42	52	W15
Dixon St. G1	35	V13
Dixon St., Pais.	46	K14
Dobbies Ln. G4	35	V11
Dobbies Ln. Pl. G4	36	W12
Dochart Av., Renf.	32	N11
Dochart St. G33	38	AA11
Dock St., Clyde.	17	M8
Dodhill Pl. G13	18	P9
Dodside Gdns. G32	55	CC14
Dodside Pl. G32	55	CC14
Dodside St. G32	55	CC14
Dolan St., Bail.	40	EE13
Dollar Ter. G20	20	T8
Crosbie St.		
Dolphin Rd. G41	50	T15
Don Av., Renf.	32	N11
Don Dr., Pais.	45	G15
Don Pl., John.	43	C16
Don St. G33	37	Z12
Donald Way, Udd.	57	HH16
Donaldson Dr., Renf.	17	M10
Ferguson St.		
Donaldswood Rd.,	46	J16
Pais.		
Doncaster St. G20	21	V10
Doon Cres., Bear.	7	Q6
Doon Side, Cumb.	71	PP3
Doon St., Clyde.	5	M6
Doonfoot Rd. G43	62	T17
Dora St. G40	53	Y14
Dorchester Av. G12	20	S9
Dorchester Ct. G12	20	S9
Dorchester Av.		
Dorchester Pl. G12	20	S9
Dorlin Rd. G33	25	DD9
Dormanside Rd. G53	48	P14
Dornal Av. G13	18	N8
Dornford Av. G32	55	CC15
Dornford Rd. G32	55	CC15
Dornie Dr. G32	55	CC16
Dornie Dr. G46	61	R18
Dornoch Av., Giff.	62	T19
Dornoch Pl., Bish.	11	Z7
Dornoch Pl., Chr.	14	FF7
Dornoch Rd., Bear.	7	Q7
Dornoch St. G40	36	X13
Dornoch Way, Cumb.	71	PP1
Dorset Sq. G3	35	U12
Dorset St.		
Dorset St. G3	35	U12
Dosk Av. G13	18	N8
Dosk Pl. G13	18	N8
Douglas Av. G32	54	BB15
Douglas Av. G73	65	Z17
Douglas Av., Giff.	62	T19
Douglas Av., John.	44	E15
Douglas Av., Lenz.	13	CC5
Douglas Ct., Lenz.	13	CC5
Douglas Cres., Udd.	57	HH16
Douglas Dr. G15	6	N7
Douglas Dr. G72	66	AA17
Douglas Dr., Bail.	39	DD13
Douglas Dr., Both.	69	HH19
Douglas Gdns., Bear.	7	R6
Douglas Gdns., Giff.	62	T19
Douglas Gdns., Lenz.	13	CC5
Douglas Gdns., Udd.	69	GG17
Douglas La. G2	35	V12
West George St.		
Douglas Pk. Cres., Bear.	8	S5
Douglas Pl., Bear.	7	R5
Douglas Pl., Lenz.	13	CC5
Douglas Rd., Pais.	31	L12
Douglas St. G2	35	V12
Douglas St., Pais.	30	J13
Douglas St., Udd.	57	HH16
Douglas Ter. G41	51	U14
Shields Rd.		
Douglas Ter., Pais.	30	K11
Douglaston Rd. G23	9	U7
Dougray Pl., Barr.	59	M19
Dougrie Dr. G45	64	W18
Dougrie Pl. G45	64	X18
Dougrie Rd. G45	64	W19
Dougrie St. G45	64	X18
Dougrie Ter. G45	64	W18
Doune Cres., Bish.	11	Y6
Doune Gdns. G20	21	U10
Doune Quad. G20	21	U10
Dove St. G53	60	P17
Dovecot G43	50	T16
Shawhill Rd.		
Dovecothall St., Barr.	59	M18
Dover St. G3	35	U12
Downanfield Rd., Cumb.	70	NN3
Downanhill Pl. G11	34	T11
Old Dumbarton Rd.		

Name	Page	Grid
Dowanhill St. G11	34	T11
Dowanside La. G12	20	T10
Byres Rd.		
Dowanside Rd. G12	20	T10
Dowanvale Ter. G11	34	S11
White St.		
Downcraig Dr. G45	64	W19
Downcraig Rd. G45	64	W19
Downcraig Ter. G45	64	W19
Downfield Gdns., Both.	69	GG19
Downfield St. G32	54	AA14
Downiebrae Rd. G73	53	Y15
Downs St. G21	22	X10
Dowrie Cres. G53	48	P15
Dows Pl. G4	21	V10
Possil Rd.		
Drainie St. G34	40	EE12
Westerhouse Rd.		
Drake St. G40	36	X13
Drakemire Av. G45	64	W18
Drakemire Dr. G45	64	W18
Dreghorn St. G31	37	Z12
Drem Pl. G11	34	S11
Merkland St.		
Drimnin Rd. G33	25	DD9
Drive Gdns., John.	45	G14
Drive Rd. G51	33	R12
Drochil St. G34	40	EE11
Drumbeg Dr. G53	60	P17
Drumbeg Pl. G53	60	P17
Drumbottie Rd. G21	23	Y9
Drumby Cres., Clark.	62	T19
Drumcavel Rd., Chr.	26	FF8
Drumcavel Rd., Gart.	26	FF8
Drumchapel Gdns. G15	6	P7
Drumchapel Pl. G15	6	P7
Drumchapel Rd. G15	6	P7
Drumclog Gdns. G33	24	AA9
Drumclutha Dr., Both.	69	HH19
Drumcross Rd. G53	49	Q15
Drumhead Pl. G32	54	AA15
Drumhead Rd. G32	54	AA15
Drumilaw Rd. G73	65	Y17
Drumilaw Way G73	65	Y17
Drumlaken Av. G23	8	T7
Drumlaken Ct. G23	8	T7
Drumlaken St. G23	8	T7
Drumlanrig Av. G34	40	FF11
Drumlanrig Pl. G34	40	FF11
Drumlanrig Quad. G34	40	FF11
Drumlochy Rd. G33	38	BB11
Drummond Av. G73	52	X16
Drummond Dr., Pais.	47	M14
Drummond Gdns. G13	19	R9
Crow Rd.		
Drummore Rd. G15	6	P6
Drumover Dr. G31	54	AA14
Drumoyne Av. G51	33	R12
Drumoyne Circ. G51	33	R13
Drumoyne Dr. G51	33	R12
Drumoyne Pl. G51	33	R13
Drumoyne Circ.		
Drumoyne Quad. G51	33	R13
Drumoyne Rd. G51	33	R13
Drumoyne Sq. G51	33	R12
Drumpark St. G46	61	R18
Drumpark St., Coat.	57	HH14
Dunnachie Dr.		
Drumpeller Rd., Bail.	56	EE14
Drumpellier Av., Bail.	56	EE14
Drumpellier Pl., Bail.	56	EE14
Drumpellier St. G33	37	Z11
Drumreoch Dr. G42	52	X16
Drumreoch Pl. G42	52	X16
Drumry Pl. G15	6	N7
Drumry Rd., Clyde.	5	L6
Drumry Rd. E. G15	6	N7
Drums Av., Pais.	30	J13
Drums Cres., Pais.	30	J13
Drums Rd. G53	48	P14
Drumsack Av., Chr.	26	FF8
Drumsargard Rd. G73	65	Z17
Drumshaw Dr. G32	55	CC16
Drumvale Dr., Chr.	15	GG7
Drury St. G2	35	V12
Dryad St. G46	61	R17
Dryborough Av., John.	45	H15
Dryburgh Av. G73	53	Y16
Dryburgh Gdns. G20	21	U10
Dryburgh Rd., Bear.	7	Q5
Dryburn Av. G52	32	P13
Drygate G4	36	X12
Drygrange Rd. G33	39	CC11
Drymen Pl., Lenz.	13	CC6
Drymen Rd., Bear.	7	Q5
Drymen St. G52	33	R13
Morven St.		
Drymen Wynd, Bear.	7	R6
Drynoch Pl. G22	21	V8
Drysdale St. G14	18	N9
Duart Dr., John.	44	E15
Duart St. G20	20	T8
Dubs Rd., Barr.	60	N18
Dubton Path G34	40	EE11
Dubton St. G34	40	EE11
Duchall Pl. G14	18	P10
Duchess Pl. G73	53	Z16
Duchess Rd. G73	53	Z15
Duchray Dr., Pais.	48	N14
Duchray La. G31	37	Z11
Duchray St.		
Duchray St. G33	37	Z11
Ducraig St. G32	38	BB13
Dudhope St. G33	39	CC11
Dudley Dr. G12	20	S10
Duffus Pl. G32	55	CC16
Duffus St. G34	40	EE11
Duffus Ter. G32	55	CC16
Duich Gdns. G23	9	U7
Duisdale Rd. G32	55	CC16
Duke St. G4	36	X12
Duke St. G31	36	X12
Duke St., Linw.	28	F13
Duke St., Pais.	46	K15
Dukes Gate, Both.	69	GG18
Dukes Rd. G72	65	Z17
Dukes Rd. G73	65	Z17
Dukes Rd., Bail.	41	HH13
Dulnain St. G72	67	DD17
Dulsie Rd. G21	23	Z9
Dumbarton Rd. G11	34	S11
Dumbarton Rd. G14	18	N9
Dumbarton Rd., Clyde.	4	K5
Dumbarton Rd., Clyde.	4	J6
Dumbarton Rd., Dalm.	4	J6
Dumbarton Rd., Old K.	4	J6
Dumbreck Av. G41	50	S14
Dumbreck Ct. G41	50	S14
Dumbreck Pl., Lenz.	13	DD6
Dumbreck Rd. G41	50	S14
Dumbreck Sq. G41	50	S14
Dumbreck Av.		
Dunagoil Rd. G45	64	W19
Dunagoil St. G45	64	X19
Dunagoil Ter. G45	64	X19
Dunalastair Dr. G33	24	BB9
Dunan Pl. G33	39	DD12
Dunard Rd. G73	53	Y16
Dunard St. G20	21	U10
Dunard Way, Pais.	30	J12
Mosslands Rd.		
Dunaskin St. G11	34	T11
Dunbar Av. G73	53	Z16
Dunbar Av., John.	43	D16
Dunbar Rd., Pais.	45	H15
Dunbeith Pl. G20	20	T9
Dunblane St. G4	35	V11
Dunbrach Rd., Cumb.	70	MM2
Duncan Av. G14	19	Q10
Duncan La. G14	19	Q10
Duncan Av.		
Duncan La. N. G14	19	Q10
Ormiston Av.		
Duncan St., Clyde.	5	L6
Duncansby Rd. G33	39	CC13
Dunchatt St. G31	36	X12
Dunchattan Pl. G31	36	X12
Duke St.		
Dunchurch Rd., Pais.	31	M13
Dunclutha Dr., Both.	69	HH19
Dunclutha St. G40	53	Y15
Duncombe St. G20	20	T8
Duncombe Vw., Clyde.	5	M6
Kirkoswald Dr.		
Duncraig Cres., John.	43	C16
Duncruin St. G20	20	T8
Duncruin St., Bish.	10	X7
Duncryne Av. G32	55	CC14
Duncryne Gdns. G32	55	DD14
Duncryne Pl., Bish.	22	X8
Dundas La. G1	36	W12
Dundas St. G1	36	W12
Dundasvale Ct. G4	35	V11
Maitland St.		
Dundasvale Rd. G4	35	V11
Maitland St.		
Dundee Dr. G52	48	P14
Dundee Path G52	49	Q14
Dundee Dr.		
Dundonald Av., John.	43	C15
Dundonald Rd. G12	20	T10
Dundonald Rd., Pais.	31	L12
Dundrennan Rd. G42	51	U16
Dunearn Pl., Pais.	47	L14
Dunearn St. G4	35	U11
Dunegoin St. G51	34	S12
Sharp St.		
Dunellan St. G52	33	R13
Dungeonhill Rd. G34	40	FF12
Dunglass Av. G14	19	Q10
Dunglass La. N. G14	19	Q10
Verona Av.		
Dungoil Av., Cumb.	70	LL2
Dungoil Rd., Lenz.	13	DD6
Dungoyne St. G20	20	T8
Dunira St. G32	54	AA14
Dunivaig St. G33	39	DD12
Dunkeld Av. G73	53	Y16
Dunkeld Dr., Bear.	8	S6
Dunkeld Gdns., Bish.	11	Y7
Dunkeld La., Chr.	15	HH7
Burnbrae Av.		
Dunkeld St. G31	53	Z14
Dunkenny Pl. G15	6	N6
Dunkenny Rd. G15	6	N6
Dunlop Cres., Both.	69	HH19
Dunlop Cres., Renf.	17	M10
Hairst St.		
Dunlop St. G1	36	W13
Dunlop St. G72	67	DD17
Dunlop St., Linw.	28	F13
Dunlop St., Renf.	17	M10
Hairst St.		
Dunmore La. G5	35	V13
Norfolk St.		
Dunmore St. G5	35	V13
Dunmore St., Clyde.	17	M8
Dunn St. G40	53	Y14
Dunn St., Clyde.	4	K5
Dunn St., Dalm.	4	K6
Dunn St., Pais.	47	L14
Dunnachie Dr., Coat.	57	HH14
Dunnichen Pl., Bish.	11	Z7
Dunning St. G31	53	Z14
Dunolly St. G21	37	Y11
Dunottar St. G33	38	BB11
Dunottar St., Bish.	11	Z7
Dunphail Dr. G34	40	FF12
Dunphail Rd. G34	40	FF12
Dunragit St. G31	37	Z12
Dunrobin Av., John.	44	E15
Dunrobin Rd. G31	37	Y13
Dunrod St. G32	54	BB14
Dunside Dr. G53	60	P17
Dunskaith Pl. G34	40	FF12
Dunskaith St. G34	40	FF12
Dunsmuir St. G51	34	S12
Dunster Gdns., Bish.	11	Y6
Dunswin Av., Dalm.	4	K6
Dunswin Ct., Dalm.	4	K6
Dunswin Av.		
Dunsyre Pl. G23	9	U7
Dunsyre St. G33	38	AA12
Duntarvie Cres. G34	40	FF12
Duntarvie Pl. G34	40	EE12

Name	Page	Grid	Name	Page	Grid	Name	Page	Grid
Duntarvie Quad. G34	40	FF12	East Campbell St. G1	36	X13	Edmiston Dr. G51	33	R13
Duntarvie Rd. G34	40	EE12	East Fulton Holdings, Linw.	28	E12	Edmiston Dr., Linw.	28	E13
Dunterle Ct., Barr.	59	M18	East Greenlees Av. G72	67	CC18	Edmiston St. G31	53	Z14
Dunterlie Av. G13	18	P9	East Greenlees Cres. G72	66	BB18	Edmondstone Ct., Clyde. Yokerburn Ter.	17	M8
Duntiglennan Rd., Clyde.	5	L5	East Greenlees Dr. G72	66	BB18	Edrom Path G32 Edrom St.	38	AA13
Duntocher Rd., Bear.	6	P5	East Greenlees Rd. G72	66	BB18	Edrom St. G32	38	AA13
Duntocher Rd., Clyde.	5	L5	East Hallhill Rd., Bail.	40	EE13	Edward Av., Renf.	18	N10
Duntocher Rd., Dalm.	4	K6	East Kilbride Expressway G72	66	BB19	Edward St. G3 Lumsden St.	34	T12
Duntocher St. G21 Northcroft Rd.	22	X10	East Kilbride Rd. G73	65	Z17	Edward St., Bail.	41	GG13
Duntreath Av. G13	18	N8	East La., Pais.	47	L14	Edward St., Clyde.	17	M8
Duntroon St. G31	37	Y12	East Reid St. G73	53	Z16	Edwin St. G51	34	T13
Dunure Dr. G73	64	X17	East Springfield Ter., Bish.	23	Y8	Edzell Ct. G14	33	Q11
Dunure St. G20	20	T8	East St., Kilb.	42	B14	Edzell Dr., John.	44	F15
Dunvegan Av., John.	44	F15	East Thomson St., Clyde.	5	L6	Edzell Gdns., Bish.	23	Z8
Dunvegan Ct. G13 Kintillo Dr.	18	P9	East Whitby St. G31	53	Z14	Edzell Pl. G14	33	Q11
Dunvegan Dr., Bish.	11	Y6	Eastburn Rd. G21	23	Y9	Edzell St. G14	33	Q11
Dunvegan Quad., Renf. Kirklandneuk Rd.	17	L10	Eastcote Av. G14	19	R10	Egidia Av., Giff.	62	S19
Dunvegan St. G51 Sharp St.	34	S12	Eastcroft G73	53	Y16	Egilsay Cres. G22	22	W8
Dunwan Av. G13	18	N8	Eastcroft Ter. G21	23	Y10	Egilsay Pl. G22	22	W8
Dunwan Pl. G13	18	N8	Easter Av., Udd.	69	GG17	Egilsay St. G22	22	W8
Durban Av., Dalm.	4	J6	Easter Garngaber Rd. G66	13	DD5	Egilsay Ter. G22	22	W8
Durness Av., Bear.	8	S5	Easter Ms., Udd. Church St.	69	GG17	Eglinton Ct. G5	35	V13
Durno Path G33	39	DD12	Easter Queenslie Rd. G33	39	DD12	Eglinton Dr., Giff.	62	T19
Duror St. G32	38	BB13	Eastercraigs G31	37	Y12	Eglinton La. G5 Eglinton St.	51	V14
Durris Gdns. G32	55	CC14	Easterhill Pl. G32	54	AA14	Eglinton St. G5	51	V14
Durrockstock Cres., Pais.	45	G16	Easterhill St. G32	54	AA14	Egunton Ct. G5 Cumberland St.	51	V14
Durward Av. G41	50	T15	Easterhouse Path G34	40	FF12	Eighth St., Udd.	57	GG15
Durward Cres., Pais.	45	G15	Easterhouse Pl. G34	40	FF12	Eildon Dr., Barr.	59	M19
Durwood Ct. G41	50	T15	Easterhouse Quad. G34	40	FF12	Eileen Gdns., Bish.	11	Y7
Duthil St. G51	33	Q13	Easterhouse Rd. G34	40	FF12	Elba La. G31	37	Z13
Dyce La. G11	34	S11	Eastfield Av. G72	66	AA17	Elcho St. G40	36	X13
Dyers La. G1 Turnbull St.	36	W13	Eastfield Rd. G21	22	X10	Elder Gro., Udd. Burnhead St.	57	HH16
Dyers Wynd, Pais. Gilmour St.	30	K13	Eastgate, Gart.	27	HH9	Elder St. G51	33	R12
Dyke Pl. G13	18	P8	Eastmuir St. G32	38	BB13	Elderpark Gdns. G51	33	R12
Dyke Rd. G13	18	N9	Eastvale Pl. G3	34	T12	Elderpark Gro. G51	33	R12
Dyke St., Bail.	40	FF13	Eastwood Av. G41	50	T16	Elderpark St. G51	33	R12
Dykebar Av. G13	18	P9	Eastwood Av., Giff.	62	T19	Elderslie St. G3	35	U11
Dykebar Cres., Pais.	47	L15	Eastwood Ct., Thorn. Main St.	61	R18	Eldon Gdns., Bish.	10	X7
Dykefoot Dr. G53	49	Q16	Eastwood Cres., Thorn.	61	R18	Eldon Pl., John.	44	E15
Dykehead La. G33	39	CC12	Eastwood Rd., Chr.	15	GG7	Eldon St. G3	35	U11
Dykehead Rd., Bail.	41	GG13	Eastwood Vw. G72	67	DD17	Eldon Ter. G11 Caird Dr.	34	S11
Dykehead St. G33	39	CC12	Eastwoodmains Rd., Giff.	62	T19	Elgin Dr., Linw.	28	E13
Dykemuir Pl. G21	23	Y10	Easwald Bk., Kilb.	42	B15	Elgin St. G40	37	Y13
Dykemuir Quad. G21 Dykemuir St.	23	Y10	Eccles St. G22	22	X9	Elibank St. G33	38	BB11
Dykemuir St. G21	23	Y10	Eckford St. G32	54	BB14	Elie St. G11	34	T11
			Eday St. G22	22	W9	Elizabeth Cres., Thorn.	62	S18
Eagle Cres., Bear.	6	P5	Edderton Pl. G33	40	EE12	Elizabeth St. G51	34	T13
Eagle St. G4	36	W11	Eddleston Pl. G72	67	DD17	Elizabethan Way, Renf. Cockels Ln.	31	M11
Eaglesham Ct. G51 Blackburn St.	35	U13	Eddlewood Path G33	39	DD12	Ellangowan Rd. G41	50	T16
Eaglesham Pl. G51	35	U13	Eddlewood Rd. G33	39	DD12	Ellergreen Rd., Bear.	7	R6
Earl Haig Rd. G52	32	N12	Edelweiss Ter. G11 Gardner St.	34	S11	Ellerslie St., John.	44	E14
Earl Pl. G14	19	Q10	Eden La. G33	37	Z11	Ellesmere St. G22	21	V10
Earl St. G14	18	P10	Eden Pk., Both.	69	GG19	Ellinger Ct., Dalm. Scott St.	4	K6
Earlbank Av. G14	19	Q10	Eden Pl. G72	67	CC17	Elliot Av. G78	45	G16
Earlbank La. N. G14 Dunglass Av.	19	Q10	Eden Pl., Renf.	32	N11	Elliot Av., Giff.	62	T19
Earlbank La. S. G14 Verona Av.	19	Q10	Eden St. G33	37	Z11	Elliot Dr., Giff.	62	T18
Earls Ct., Chr. Longdale Rd.	15	GG7	Edenwood St. G33	38	AA13	Elliot La. G3 Elliot St.	35	U12
Earls Gate, Both.	69	GG18	Edgam Dr. G52	33	Q13	Elliot Pl. G3	35	U12
Earls Hill G68	70	LL2	Edgefauld Av. G21	22	X10	Elliot St. G3	35	U12
Earlsburn Rd., Lenz.	13	DD6	Edgefauld Dr. G21	22	X10	Ellisland Av., Clyde.	5	M6
Earlspark Av. G43	51	U16	Edgefauld Pl. G21 Balgrayhill Rd.	22	X9	Ellisland Cres. G73	64	X17
Earn Av., Bear.	8	S6	Edgefauld Rd. G21	22	X10	Ellisland Rd. G43	62	T17
Earn Av., Renf. Almond Av.	32	N11	Edgehill La. G11 Marlborough Av.	20	S10	Ellisland Rd., Cumb.	71	PP3
Earn St. G33	38	AA11	Edgehill Rd. G11	20	S10	Ellismuir Fm. Rd., Bail.	56	FF14
Earnock St. G33	23	Z10	Edgehill Rd., Bear.	7	R5	Ellismuir Pl., Bail.	56	FF14
Earnside St. G32	38	BB13	Edgemont St. G41	51	U16	Ellismuir Rd., Bail.	56	FF14
Easdale Dr. G32	54	BB14	Edinbeg Av. G42	52	X16	Elliston Av. G53	61	Q17
East Av., Renf.	17	M10	Edinbeg Pl. G42	52	X16	Elliston Dr. G53	61	Q17
East Barns St., Clyde.	17	M8	Edinburgh Rd. G33	37	Z12	Elliston Pl. G53 Ravenscraig Dr.	61	Q17
East Bath La. G2 Sauchiehall St.	35	V12	Edington Gdns., Chr.	15	GG6	Elm Av., Lenz.	13	CC5
East Buchanan St., Pais.	30	K13	Edington St. G4	35	V11	Elm Av., Renf.	17	M10
			Edison St. G52	32	N12	Elm Bk., Bish.	11	Y7
						Elm Dr., John.	43	D16
						Elm Gdns., Bear.	7	R5

Elm Rd. G73 65 Y18
Elm Rd., Dalm. 5 L5
Elm Rd., Pais. 47 L15
Elm St. G14 19 Q10
Elm Wk., Bear. 7 R5
Elmbank Av., Udd. 57 HH16
Elmbank Cres. G2 35 V12
Elmbank St.
Elmbank La. G3 35 U12
North St.
Elmbank St. G2 35 V12
Elmbank St. La. G3 35 U12
North St.
Elmfoot St. G5 52 W15
Elmore Av. G44 63 V17
Elmore La. G44 63 V17
Elmslie Ct., Bail. 56 EE14
Elmvale Row G21 22 X10
Elmvale Row E. G21 22 X10
Elmvale Row
Elmvale Row W. G21 22 X10
Elmvale Row
Elmvale St. G21 22 X9
Elmwood Av. G11 19 R10
Elmwood Ct., Both. 69 HH19
Blantyre Mill Rd.
Elmwood Gdns. G11 19 R10
Randolph Rd.
Elmwood Gdns., Kirk. 12 BB5
Elmwood La. G11 19 Q10
Elmwood Av.
Elmwood Ter. G11 19 R10
Crow Rd.
Elphin St. G23 8 T7
Invershiel Rd.
Elphinstone Pl. G51 34 T12
Elrig Rd. G44 63 V17
Elspeth Gdns., Bish. 11 Y7
Eltham St. G22 21 V10
Elvan Ct. G32 38 AA13
Edrom St.
Elvan St. G32 38 AA13
Embo Dr. G13 18 P9
Emerson Rd., Bish. 11 Y7
Emerson St. G20 21 V9
Emily Pl. G31 36 X13
Endfield Av. G12 20 S9
Endrick Bk., Bish. 11 Y6
Endrick Dr., Bear. 7 R6
Endrick Dr., Pais. 31 L13
Endrick St. G21 22 W10
Endsleigh Gdns. G11 20 S10
Partickhill Rd.
Ensay St. G22 22 W8
Enterkin St. G32 54 AA14
Ericht Rd. G43 62 T17
Eriska Av. G14 18 P9
Erradale St. G22 21 V8
Erriboll Pl. G22 21 V8
Erriboll St. G22 21 V8
Errogie St. G34 40 EE12
Erskine Av. G41 50 S14
Erskine Sq. G52 32 N12
Erskine Vw., Clyde. 5 L6
Singer St.
Erskinefauld Rd., Linw. 28 E13
Ervie St. G34 40 FF12
Esk Av., Renf. 32 N11
Esk Dr., Pais. 45 G15
Esk St. G14 18 N9
Esk Way, Pais. 45 G15
Eskbank St. G32 38 BB13
Eskdale Dr. G73 53 Z16
Eskdale Rd., Bear. 7 Q7
Eskdale St. G42 51 V15
Esmond St. G3 34 T11
Espedair St., Pais. 46 K14
Essenside Av. G15 7 Q7
Essex Dr. G14 19 R10
Essex La. G14 19 R10
Esslemont Av. G14 18 P9
Estate Quad. G32 55 CC16
Estate Rd. G32 55 CC16
Etive Av., Bear. 8 S6
Etive Ct., Clyde. 5 M5

Etive Cres., Bish. 11 Y7
Etive Dr., Giff. 62 T19
Etive St. G32 38 BB13
Eton Gdns. G12 35 U11
Oakfield Av.
Eton La. G12 35 U11
Great George St.
Eton Pl. G12 35 U11
Oakfield Av.
Eton Ter. G12 35 U11
Oakfield Av.
Ettrick Av., Renf. 32 N11
Ettrick Ct. G72 67 DD18
Gateside Av.
Ettrick Cres. G73 53 Z16
Ettrick Oval, Pais. 45 G16
Ettrick Pl. G43 50 T16
Ettrick Ter., John. 43 C16
Ettrick Way, Renf. 32 N11
Evan Cres., Giff. 62 T19
Evan Dr., Giff. 62 T19
Evanton Dr. G46 61 R19
Evanton Pl. G46 61 R18
Evanton Dr.
Everard Ct. G21 22 X8
Everard Dr. G21 22 X8
Everard Pl. G21 22 X8
Everard Quad. G21 22 X8
Everglades, The, Chr. 26 EE8
Eversley St. G32 54 BB14
Everton Rd. G53 49 Q15
Ewart Pl. G3 34 T12
Kelvinhaugh St.
Ewing Pl. G31 37 Z13
Ewing St. G73 53 Y16
Ewing St., Kilb. 42 B14
Exchange Pl. G1 36 W12
Buchanan St.
Exeter Dr. G11 34 S11
Exeter La. G11 34 S11
Exeter Dr.
Eynort St. G22 21 V8

Fagan Ct., Blan. 69 GG19
Faifley Rd., Clyde. 5 L5
Fairbairn Cres., Thorn. 62 S19
Fairbairn Path G40 53 Y14
Ruby St.
Fairbairn St. G40 53 Y14
Dalmarnock Rd.
Fairburn St. G32 54 AA14
Fairfax Av. G44 64 W17
Fairfield Gdns. G51 33 R12
Fairfield Pl. G51 33 R12
Fairfield Pl. G71 69 HH19
Fairfield St. G51 33 R12
Fairhaven Dr. G23 20 T8
Fairhill Av. G53 49 Q16
Fairholm St. G32 54 AA14
Fairley St. G51 34 S13
Fairlie Pk. Dr. G11 34 S11
Fairway Av., Pais. 46 J16
Fairways, Bear. 6 P5
Fairyknowe Gdns. G71 69 HH19
Falcon Cres., Pais. 29 H13
Falcon Rd., John. 43 C16
Falcon Ter. G20 20 T8
Falfield St. G5 51 V14
Falkland Cres., Bish. 23 Z8
Falkland Mans. G12 20 S10
Clarence Dr.
Falkland St. G12 20 S10
Falloch Rd. G42 51 V16
Falloch Rd., Bear. 7 Q7
Fallside Rd., Both. 69 HH19
Falside Av., Pais. 46 K15
Falside Rd. G32 54 BB14
Falside Rd., Pais. 46 J15
Fara St. G23 21 U8
Farie St. G73 53 Y16
Farm Ct., Both. 69 HH18
Fallside Rd.
Farm La., Udd. 69 HH17
Myers Cres.

Farm Pk., Lenz. 13 CC6
Farm Rd. G41 50 S14
Farm Rd., Blan. 68 FF19
Farm Rd., Clyde. 5 L5
Farm Rd., Dalm. 4 J6
Farme Cross G73 53 Y15
Farmeloan Rd. G73 53 Y16
Farmington Av. G32 39 CC13
Farmington Gdns. G32 39 CC13
Farmington Gate G32 39 CC13
Farmington Gro. G32 39 CC13
Farne Dr. G44 63 V18
Farnell St. G4 35 V11
Farrier Ct., John. 43 D14
Faskally Av., Bish. 10 X6
Faskin Cres. G53 48 N16
Faskin Pl. G53 48 N16
Faskin Rd. G53 48 N16
Fasque Pl. G15 6 N6
Fastnet St. G33 38 BB12
Faulbswood Cres., Pais. 45 H15
Fauldhouse St. G5 52 W14
Faulds, Bail. 40 FF13
Faulds Gdns., Bail. 40 FF13
Fauldshead Rd., Renf. 17 M10
Fauldspark Cres., Bail. 40 FF13
Fauldswood Cres., Pais. 45 H15
Fauldswood Dr., Pais. 45 H15
Fearnmore Rd. G20 20 T8
Fendoch St. G32 54 BB14
Fenella St. G32 38 BB13
Fennsbank Av. G73 65 Z18
Fenwick Dr., Barr. 59 M19
Fenwick Pl., Giff. 62 S19
Fenwick Rd., Giff. 62 T19
Fereneze Av., Barr. 59 L18
Fereneze Av., Pais. 31 L12
Ferenze Cres. G13 18 P8
Ferenze Dr., Pais. 46 J16
Fergus Ct. G20 21 U10
Fergus Dr. G20 21 U10
Ferguslie, Pais. 45 H14
Ferguslie Pk., Pais. 29 G13
Ferguslie Pk. Av., Pais. 29 H13
Ferguslie Wk., Pais. 45 H14
Ferguson Av., Renf. 17 M10
Ferguson St., John. 43 D14
Ferguson St., Renf. 17 M10
Fergusson Rd., Cumb. 70 NN3
Ferguston Rd., Bear. 7 R6
Fern Av., Bish. 23 Y8
Fern Av., Lenz. 13 CC5
Fern Dr., Barr. 59 L18
Fern Hill Gra. G71 69 HH19
Fernan St. G32 38 AA13
Fernbank Av. G72 67 CC18
Fernbank St. G22 22 X9
Fernbrae Rd. G46 65 Z18
Fernbrae Way G73 65 Y18
Ferncroft Dr. G44 64 W17
Ferndale Ct. G23 20 T8
Rothes Dr.
Ferndale Dr. G23 20 T8
Ferndale Gdns. G23 20 T8
Ferndale Pl. G23 20 T8
Rothes Dr.
Ferness Oval G21 23 Z8
Ferness Pl. G21 23 Z8
Ferness Rd. G21 23 Z9
Ferngrove Av. G12 20 S9
Fernhill Rd. G73 65 Y18
Fernleigh Pl., Chr. 15 GG7
Fernleigh Rd. G43 62 T17
Ferry Rd. G3 34 S12
Ferry Rd., Both. 69 HH19
Ferry Rd., Renf. 17 M10
Ferry Rd., Udd. 68 FF17
Ferryden St. G14 33 R11
Fersit St. G43 62 T17
Fetlar Dr. G44 64 W17
Fettercairn Av. G15 6 N6
Fettercairn Gdns., Bish. 11 Z7
Fettes St. G33 38 AA12
Fidra St. G33 38 AA12
Fielden Pl. G40 37 Y13

Fielden St. G40	37	Y13
Fieldhead Dr. G43	62	S17
Fieldhead Sq. G43	62	S17
Fife Av. G52	48	P14
Fife Cres., Both.	69	HH19
Fifeway, Bish.	23	Z8
Fifth Av. G12	19	R9
Fifth Av. G33	24	BB9
Fifth Av., Lenz.	13	CC7
Fifth Av., Renf.	31	M11
Finart Dr., Pais.	47	L15
Finch Pl., John.	43	C16
Findhorn Av., Renf.	18	N10
Findhorn Cres., Pais.	45	G15
Findhorn St. G33	37	Z12
Findochty St. G33	39	CC11
Fingal La. G20	20	T8
Fingal St.		
Fingal St. G20	20	T8
Fingask St. G32	55	CC14
Finglas Av., Pais.	47	L15
Fingleton Av., Barr.	59	M19
Finhaven St. G32	54	AA14
Finlarig St. G34	40	FF12
Finlas St. G22	22	W10
Finlay Dr. G31	37	Y12
Finnart Sq. G40	52	X14
Finnart St. G40	52	X14
Finnieston Pl. G3	35	U12
Finnieston St.		
Finnieston St. G3	35	U12
Finsbay St. G51	33	R13
Fintry Av., Pais.	46	K16
Fintry Cres., Barr.	59	M19
Fintry Cres., Bish.	11	Z7
Fintry Dr. G44	52	W16
Fir Pl. G72	67	CC17
Caledonian Circuit		
Fir Pl., Bail.	56	EE14
Fir Pl., John.	44	E15
Firbank Ter., Barr.	60	N19
Firdon Cres. G15	6	P7
Firhill Rd. G20	21	V10
Firhill St. G20	21	V10
Firpark Pl. G31	36	X12
Firpark St.		
Firpark Rd., Bish.	23	Y8
Firpark St. G31	36	X12
Firpark Ter. G31	36	X12
Ark La.		
First Av. G33	24	BB10
First Av. G44	63	U19
First Av., Bear.	8	S6
First Av., Lenz.	13	CC7
First Av., Renf.	31	M11
First Av., Udd.	57	GG16
First Gdns. G41	50	S14
First St., Udd.	57	GG16
First Ter., Clyde.	5	L6
Firwood Dr. G44	64	W17
Fischer Gdns., Pais.	29	G13
Fisher Av., Pais.	45	G14
Fisher Ct. G31	36	X12
Fisher Cres., Clyde.	5	L5
Fisher Dr., Pais.	45	G14
Fisher Way, Pais.	45	G14
Fisher Dr.		
Fishers Rd., Renf.	17	M9
Fishescoates Av. G73	65	Z18
Fishescoates Gdns. G73	65	Z17
Fishescoates Rd.		
Fishescoates Rd. G73	65	Z17
Fitzalan Dr., Pais.	31	L13
Fitzalan Rd., Renf.	31	L11
Fitzroy La. G3	35	U12
Claremont St.		
Fitzroy Pl. G3	35	U12
Claremont St.		
Fitzroy Pl. G3	35	U12
Sauchiehall St.		
Flax Rd., Udd.	69	HH17
Fleet Av., Renf.	32	N11
Fleet St. G32	54	BB14
Fleming Av., Chr.	26	FF8
Fleming Av., Clyde.	17	M8

Fleming Rd., Cumb.	70	NN3
Fleming St. G31	37	Y13
Fleming St., Pais.	30	K12
Flemington Rd. G72	67	DD19
Flemington St. G21	22	X10
Fleurs Av. G41	50	S14
Fleurs Rd. G41	50	S14
Floors St., John.	43	D15
Floorsburn Cres., John.	43	D15
Flora Gdns., Bish.	11	Z7
Florence Dr., Giff.	62	T19
Florence Gdns. G73	65	Z18
Florence St. G5	36	W13
Florentine Pl. G12	35	U11
Gibson St.		
Florentine Ter. G12	35	U11
Southpark Av.		
Florida Av. G42	51	V16
Florida Cres. G42	51	V16
Florida Dr. G42	51	V16
Florida Gdns., Bail.	40	EE13
Florida Sq. G42	51	V16
Florida St. G42	51	V16
Flowerdale Pl. G53	60	P19
Waukglen Dr.		
Flures Av., Renf.	16	K8
Flures Cres., Renf.	16	K8
Flures Dr., Renf.	16	K8
Flures Pl., Renf.	16	K8
Fochabers Dr. G52	33	Q13
Fogo Pl. G20	20	T9
Forbes Dr. G40	36	X13
Forbes Pl., Pais.	46	K14
Forbes St. G40	36	X13
Ford Rd. G12	20	T10
Fordneuk St. G40	37	Y13
Fordoun St. G34	40	FF12
Fordyce St. G11	34	S11
Fore St. G14	19	Q10
Forehouse Rd., Kilb.	42	A14
Forest Dr., Udd.	69	HH18
Forest Gdns., Lenz.	12	BB6
Forest Pl., Lenz.	12	BB6
Forest Pl., Pais.	46	K15
Brodie Pk. Av.		
Forest Rd., Cumb.	71	QQ3
Forest Vw., Cumb.	71	QQ2
Foresthall Cres. G21	23	Y10
Foresthall Dr. G21	23	Y10
Forfar Av. G52	48	P14
Forfar Cres., Bish.	23	Z8
Forgan Gdns., Bish.	23	Z8
Forge, The, Giff.	62	T18
Braidpark Dr.		
Forge St. G21	37	Y11
Forglen St. G34	40	EE11
Formby Dr. G23	8	T7
Forres Av. G46	62	T18
Forres Gate, Giff.	62	T19
Forres Av.		
Forres St. G23	9	U7
Tolsta St.		
Forrest St. G40	37	Y13
Forrestfield St. G21	37	Y11
Fortevoit Av., Bail.	40	FF13
Fortevoit Pl., Bail.	40	FF13
Forth Av., Pais.	45	G15
Forth Av., Renf.	31	M11
Third Av.		
Forth Pl., John.	43	C16
Forth Rd. G61	7	Q5
Forth Rd., Bear.	7	Q7
Forth St. G41	51	U14
Fortingall Av. G12	20	T9
Grandtully Dr.		
Fortingall Pl. G12	20	T9
Fortrose St. G11	34	S11
Foswell Pl. G15	6	N5
Fotheringay La. G41	51	U15
Beaton Rd.		
Fotheringay Rd. G41	50	T15
Foulis La. G13	19	R9
Foulis St. G13	19	R9
Foundary St. G21	22	X10

Foundry La., Barr.	59	L19
Main St.		
Foundry Open G31	37	Y13
Fountain St. G31	36	X13
Fountainwell Av. G21	36	W11
Fountainwell Dr. G21	36	W11
Fountainwell Pl. G21	36	W11
Fountainwell Rd. G21	36	W11
Fountainwell Sq. G21	36	X11
Fountainwell Ter. G21	36	X11
Fourth Av. G33	24	BB9
Fourth Av., Lenz.	13	CC7
Fourth Av., Renf.	31	M11
Third Av.		
Fourth Gdns. G41	50	S14
Fourth St., Udd.	57	GG15
Fox La. G1	36	W13
Fox St. G1	35	V13
Foxbar Cres., Pais.	45	G16
Foxbar Dr. G13	18	P9
Foxbar Dr. G78	45	G16
Foxbar Rd., Pais.	45	G16
Foxes Gro. G66	13	DD5
Foxglove Pl. G53	60	P18
Foxhills Pl. G23	9	U7
Foxley St. G32	55	CC15
Foyers Ct. G13	18	P9
Kirkton Av.		
Foyers Ter. G21	23	Y10
Francis St. G5	51	V14
Frankfield Rd. G33	25	DD9
Frankfield St. G33	37	Z11
Frankfort St. G41	51	U15
Franklin St. G40	52	X14
Fraser Av. G73	53	Z16
Fraser Av., John.	44	E15
Fraser St. G72	66	AA17
Fraserbank St. G21	22	W10
Keppochhill Rd.		
Frazer St. G31	37	Z13
Freeland Dr. G53	60	P17
Freeland Dr., Renf.	16	J9
Freelands Ct., Old K.	4	J5
Freelands Pl., Old K.	4	J6
Freelands Rd., Old K.	4	J5
French St. G40	52	X14
French St., Dalm.	4	K6
French St., Renf.	31	L11
Freuchie St. G34	40	EE12
Friar Av., Bish.	11	Y6
Friars Ct. Rd., Chr.	14	EE7
Friars Pl. G13	19	Q8
Friarscourt Av. G13	7	Q7
Friarscourt La. G13	19	Q8
Arrowsmith Av.		
Friarton Rd. G43	63	U17
Friendship Way, Renf.	31	M11
Fruin Pl. G22	22	W10
Fruin Rd. G15	6	N7
Fruin St. G22	22	W10
Fulbar Av., Renf.	17	M10
Fulbar Ct., Renf.	17	M10
Fulbar Av.		
Fulbar Cres., Pais.	45	G15
Fulbar Gdns., Pais.	45	G15
Peacock Dr.		
Fulbar La., Renf.	17	M10
Fulbar Rd. G51	33	Q12
Fulbar Rd., Pais.	45	G14
Fulbar St., Renf.	17	M10
Fullarton Av. G32	54	BB15
Fullarton Rd. G32	54	AA16
Fullerton St., Pais.	30	J12
Fullerton Ter., Pais.	30	K12
Fulmar Ct., Bish.	22	X8
Fulmar Pl., John.	43	C16
Fulton Cres., Kilb.	42	B14
Fulton St. G13	19	Q8
Fulwood Av. G13	18	N8
Fulwood Av., Linw.	28	E13
Fulwood Pl. G13	18	N8
Fyvie Av. G43	62	S17

| Gadie Av., Renf. | 32 | N11 |

Gadie St. G33	37	Z12
Gadloch Av., Lenz.	13	CC7
Gadloch Gdns., Lenz.	13	CC6
Gadloch St. G22	22	W9
Gadlock Vw. G66	13	CC7
Gadsburn Ct. G21	23	Z9
Wallacewell Quad.		
Gadshill St. G21	36	X11
Gailes Pk., Both.	69	GG19
Gailes St. G40	53	Y14
Gairbraid Av. G20	20	T9
Gairbraid Ct. G20	20	T9
Gairbraid Pl. G20	20	T9
Gairbraid Ter., Bail.	41	HH13
Gairn St. G11	34	S11
Castlebank St.		
Gala Av., Renf.	32	N11
Gala St. G33	38	AA11
Galbraith Av. G51	33	R12
Burghead Dr.		
Galbraith Dr. G51	33	Q12
Galbraith St. G51	33	Q12
Moss Rd.		
Galdenoch St. G33	38	BB11
Gallacher Av., Pais.	45	H15
Gallan Av. G23	9	U7
Galloway Dr. G73	65	Y18
Galloway St. G21	22	X9
Gallowflat St. G73	53	Y16
Reid St.		
Gallowgate G1	36	W13
Gallowhill Av., Lenz.	13	CC5
Gallowhill Gro., Lenz.	13	CC5
Gallowhill Rd., Lenz.	13	CC5
Gallowhill Rd., Pais.	30	K13
Galston St. G53	60	N17
Gamrie Dr. G53	48	P16
Gamrie Gdns. G53	48	P16
Gamrie Rd. G53	48	P16
Gannochy Dr., Bish.	11	Z7
Gantock Cres. G33	38	BB12
Gardenside Av. G32	54	BB16
Gardenside Av., Udd.	69	GG17
Gardenside Cres.	54	BB16
G32		
Gardenside Pl. G32	54	BB16
Gardenside St., Udd.	69	GG17
Gardner La., Bail.	56	FF14
Church St.		
Gardner St. G11	34	S11
Gardyne St. G34	40	EE11
Garfield St. G31	37	Y13
Garforth Rd., Bail.	55	DD14
Gargrave Av., Bail.	55	DD14
Garion Dr. G13	18	P9
Talbot Dr.		
Garlieston Rd. G33	39	DD13
Garmouth Ct. G51	33	R12
Garmouth St.		
Garmouth Gdns. G51	33	R12
Garmouth St. G51	33	R12
Garnet La. G3	35	V11
Garnet St.		
Garnet St. G3	35	V11
Garnethill St. G3	35	V11
Garngaber Av., Lenz.	13	CC5
Garngaber Ct. G66	13	DD5
Woodilee Rd.		
Garnie Av., Renf.	16	J8
Garnie Cres., Renf.	4	J7
Garnie La., Renf.	4	J7
Garnie Oval, Renf.	4	J7
Garnie Pl., Renf.	4	J7
Garnieland Rd., Renf.	4	J7
Garnkirk La. G33	25	DD9
Garnkirk St. G21	36	X11
Garnock St. G21	36	X11
Garrell Way, Cumb.	70	NN3
Garrioch Cres. G20	20	T9
Garrioch Dr. G20	20	T9
Garrioch Gate G20	20	T9
Garrioch Quad. G20	20	T9
Garrioch Rd. G20	20	T10
Garriochmill Rd. G20	21	U10
Raeberry St.		

Garriochmill Way G20	21	U10
Woodside Rd.		
Garrowhill Dr., Bail.	55	DD14
Garry Av., Bear.	8	S7
Garry Dr., Pais.	45	H15
Garry St. G44	51	V16
Garscadden G13	18	P8
Garscadden Rd. G15	6	P7
Garscadden Vw., Clyde.	5	M6
Kirkoswald Dr.		
Garscube Rd. G20	21	V10
Gartartan Rd., Pais.	32	N13
Gartcarron Hill, Cumb.	70	MM2
Dunbrach Rd.		
Gartconnel Dr., Bear.	7	R5
Gartconnel Gdns., Bear.	7	R5
Gartconnel Rd., Bear.	7	R5
Gartcosh Rd., Bail.	41	HH12
Gartcraig Rd. G33	38	AA12
Gartferry Av., Chr.	15	GG7
Gartferry Rd., Chr.	15	GG7
Gartferry St. G21	23	Y10
Garth St. G1	36	W12
Garthamlock Rd. G33	39	DD11
Garthland Dr. G31	37	Y12
Garthland La., Pais.	30	K13
Gartliston Ter., Bail.	41	HH13
Gartloch Cotts., Chr.	26	EE9
Gartloch Cotts., Gart.	27	GG10
Gartloch Rd. G33	38	AA11
Gartly St. G44	63	U18
Clarkston Rd.		
Gartmore Gdns., Udd.	57	GG16
Gartmore La., Chr.	15	HH7
Gartmore Rd., Pais.	47	M14
Gartmore Ter. G72	66	AA18
Gartness St. G31	37	Y12
Gartocher Rd. G32	39	CC13
Gartons Rd. G21	23	Z10
Gartshore Rd.,	15	GG5
Drumbreck		
Garturk St. G42	51	V15
Garvald Ct. G40	53	Y14
Baltic St.		
Garvald St. G40	53	Y14
Garve Av. G44	63	V18
Garvel Cres. G33	39	DD13
Garvel Rd. G33	39	DD13
Garvock Dr. G43	62	S17
Gas St., John.	44	E14
Gask Pl. G13	18	N8
Gatehouse St. G32	38	BB13
Gateside Av. G72	67	CC17
Gateside Cres., Barr.	59	L19
Gateside Pl., Kilb.	42	B14
Gateside Rd., Barr.	59	L19
Gateside St. G31	37	Y13
Gauldry Av. G52	49	Q14
Gauze St., Pais.	30	K13
Gavins Rd., Clyde.	5	L5
Gavinton St. G44	63	U18
Gear Ter. G40	53	Y15
Geary St. G23	8	T7
Torrin Rd.		
Geddes Rd. G21	23	Z8
Gelston St. G32	54	BB14
General Terminus Quay	35	U13
G51		
Generals Gate, Udd.	69	GG17
Cobbleriggs Way		
Gentle Row, Clyde.	4	K5
George Av., Clyde.	5	M6
Robert Burns Av.		
George Cres., Clyde.	5	M6
George Gray St. G73	53	Z16
George Mann Ter. G73	65	Y17
George Pl., Pais.	46	K14
George Reith Av. G12	19	R9
George Sq. G2	36	W12
George St. G1	36	W12
George St., Bail.	56	EE14
George St., Barr.	59	L18
George St., John.	43	D14
George St., Pais.	46	J14

Gertrude Pl., Barr.	59	L19
Gibb St. G21	36	X11
Royston Rd.		
Gibson Cres., John.	43	D15
Gibson Rd., Renf.	31	L11
Gibson St. G12	35	U11
Gibson St. G40	36	X13
Giffnock Pk. Av., Giff.	62	T18
Gifford Dr. G52	32	P13
Gilbert St. G3	34	T12
Gilbertfield Pl. G33	38	BB11
Gilbertfield Rd. G72	67	CC18
Gilbertfield St. G33	38	BB11
Gilfillan Way, Pais.	45	G16
Ashton Way		
Gilhill St. G20	20	T8
Gilia St. G72	66	AA17
Gillies La., Bail.	56	FF14
Bredisholm Rd.		
Gills Ct. G31	37	Y13
Gilmerton St. G32	54	BB14
Gilmour Av., Clyde.	5	L5
Gilmour Cres. G73	52	X16
Gilmour Pl. G5	52	W14
Gilmour St., Clyde.	5	M6
Gilmour St., Pais.	30	K13
Girthon St. G32	55	CC14
Girvan St. G33	37	Z11
Gladney Av. G13	18	N8
Gladsmuir Rd. G52	32	P13
Gladstone Av., Barr.	59	L19
Gladstone St. G4	35	V11
Gladstone St., Dalm.	4	K7
Glaive Rd. G13	7	Q7
Glamis Av., John.	44	E15
Glamis Gdns., Bish.	11	Y6
Glamis Pl. G31	53	Z14
Glamis Rd.		
Glamis Rd. G31	53	Z14
Glanderston Av., Barr.	60	N19
Glanderston Dr. G13	18	P8
Glaselune St. G34	40	FF12
Lochdochart Rd.		
Glasgow Rd. G72	66	AA17
Glasgow Rd. G72	66	AA19
Glasgow Rd. G73	52	X15
Glasgow Rd., Bail.	55	DD14
Glasgow Rd., Barr.	59	M18
Glasgow Rd., Blan.	68	FF19
Glasgow Rd., Clyde.	5	L5
Glasgow Rd., Clyde.	17	L8
Glasgow Rd., Cumb.	71	PP2
Glasgow Rd., Cumb.	70	MM4
Glasgow Rd., E.K.	66	AA19
Glasgow Rd., Pais.	31	L13
Glasgow Rd., Renf.	18	N10
Glasgow Rd., Udd.	56	FF16
Glasgow St. G12	21	U10
Glassel Rd. G34	40	FF11
Glasserton Pl. G43	63	U17
Glasserton Rd. G43	63	U17
Glassford St. G1	36	W12
Glebe, The, Both.	69	HH19
Green St.		
Glebe Av. G71	69	HH19
Glebe Ct. G4	36	W12
Glebe Hollow G71	69	HH19
Glebe Wynd		
Glebe Pl. G72	66	BB17
Glebe Pl. G73	52	X16
Glebe St. G4	36	W11
Glebe St., Renf.	17	M10
Glebe Wynd G71	69	HH19
Gleddoch Rd. G52	32	N13
Glen Affric Av. G53	61	Q18
Glen Affric Dr. G53	61	Q18
Glen Affric Pl. G53	61	Q18
Glen Alby Pl. G53	61	Q18
Glen Av. G32	38	BB13
Glen Av., Chr.	15	GG7
Glen Clunie Av. G53	61	Q18
Glen Clunie Dr. G53	61	Q18
Glen Clunie Pl. G53	61	Q18
Glen Cona Dr. G53	61	Q17
Glen Cres. G13	18	N8

Name	Page	Grid
Glen Esk Dr. G53	61	Q18
Glen Fyne Rd., Cumb.	70	MM2
Glen Gdns., John.	44	F14
Glen La., Pais.	30	K13
Glen Lednock Dr., Cumb.	70	MM2
Glen Fyne Rd.		
Glen Livet Pl. G53	61	Q18
Glen Loy Pl. G53	61	Q18
Glen Mallie Dr. G53	61	Q18
Glen Markie Dr. G53	61	Q18
Glen Moriston Rd., Thorn.	61	Q18
Glen Nevis Pl. G73	65	Z19
Glen Ogle St. G32	55	CC14
Glen Orchy Dr. G53	61	Q18
Glen Orchy Pl. G53	61	Q18
Glen Pk. Av., Thorn.	61	R19
Glen Rd. G32	38	BB12
Glen Sax Dr., Renf.	32	N11
Glen Sq. G33	24	BB10
Glen St. G72	67	CC18
Glen St., Barr.	59	M18
Glen St., Pais.	30	K13
Glen Vw., Cumb.	71	QQ2
Glenacre Cres., Udd.	57	GG16
Glenacre Dr. G45	64	W18
Glenacre Quad. G45	64	W18
Glenacre Rd., Cumb.	70	NN4
Glenacre St. G45	64	W18
Glenacre Ter. G45	64	W18
Glenallan Way, Pais.	45	G16
Glenalmond Rd. G73	65	Z18
Glenalmond St. G32	54	BB14
Glenapp Av., Pais.	47	L15
Glenapp Rd., Pais.	47	L15
Glenapp St. G41	51	U14
Glenarklet Dr., Pais.	47	L15
Glenartney Row, Chr.	14	FF7
Glenashdale Way, Pais.	47	L15
Glenbrittle Dr.		
Glenavon Av. G73	65	Z18
Glenavon Rd. G20	20	T8
Thornton St.		
Glenavon Ter. G11	34	S11
Crow Rd.		
Glenbank Av., Lenz.	13	CC6
Glenbank Dr., Thorn.	61	R19
Glenbank Rd., Lenz.	13	CC6
Glenbarr St. G21	36	X11
Glenbervie Pl. G23	8	T7
Glenbrittle Dr., Pais.	47	L15
Glenbrittle Way, Pais.	46	K15
Glenbuck Av. G33	24	AA9
Glenbuck Dr. G33	24	AA9
Glenburn Av. G73	65	Z17
Glenburn Av., Bail.	40	FF13
Glenburn Cres., Chr.	15	GG7
Glenburn Cres., Pais.	46	J16
Glenburn Gdns., Bish.	10	X7
Glenburn Rd., Bear.	7	Q5
Glenburn Rd., Giff.	62	S19
Glenburn Rd., Pais.	45	H16
Glenburn St. G20	21	U8
Glenburnie Pl. G34	40	EE12
Glencairn Dr. G41	50	T15
Glencairn Dr. G73	52	X16
Glencairn Dr., Chr.	15	GG7
Glencairn Gdns. G41	51	U15
Glencairn Dr.		
Glencairn Rd., Cumb.	71	QQ3
Glencairn Rd., Pais.	31	L12
Glencally Av., Pais.	47	L15
Glencart Gro., John.	43	C15
Milliken Pk. Rd.		
Glenclora Dr., Pais.	47	L15
Glencloy St. G20	20	T8
Glencoats Cres., Pais.	29	H13
Glencoats Dr., Pais.	29	H13
Glencoe Pl. G13	19	R8
Glencoe Rd. G73	65	Z18
Glencoe St. G13	19	R8
Glencorse Rd., Pais.	46	J15
Glencorse St. G32	38	AA12
Glencroft Av., Udd.	57	GG16
Glencroft Rd. G44	64	W17
Glencryan Rd., Cumb.	71	PP4
Glendale Cres., Bish.	23	Z8
Glendale Dr., Bish.	23	Z8
Glendale Pl. G31	37	Y13
Glendale St.		
Glendale Pl. G64	23	Z8
Glendale St. G31	37	Y13
Glendaruel Av., Bear.	8	S6
Glendaruel Rd. G73	66	AA19
Glendee Gdns., Renf.	31	M11
Glendee Rd., Renf.	31	M11
Glendenning Rd. G13	7	R7
Glendevon Pl., Dalm.	4	K6
Glendevon Sq. G33	38	BB11
Glendore St. G14	33	R11
Glendower Way, Pais.	45	G16
Spencer Dr.		
Glenduffhill Rd., Bail.	39	DD13
Gleneagles Av., Cumb.	71	PP1
Muirfield Rd.		
Gleneagles Cotts. G14	19	Q10
Dumbarton Rd.		
Gleneagles Dr., Bish.	11	Y6
Gleneagles Gdns., Bish.	11	Y6
Gleneagles La. N. G14	19	Q10
Dunglass Av.		
Gleneagles Pk., Both.	69	GG19
Gleneagles Ter. G14	19	Q10
Dumbarton Rd.		
Glenelg Quad. G34	40	FF11
Glenetive Pl. G73	66	AA19
Glenfarg Cres., Bear.	8	S6
Glenfarg Rd. G73	65	Y18
Glenfarg St. G20	35	V11
Glenfield Cres., Pais.	58	J17
Glenfield Rd., Pais.	58	J17
Glenfinnan Dr. G20	20	T9
Glenfinnan Dr., Bear.	8	T6
Glenfinnan Pl. G20	20	T9
Glenfinnan Rd. G20	20	T9
Glenfruin Dr., Pais.	47	L15
Glengarry Dr. G52	33	Q13
Glengavel Cres. G33	24	AA9
Glengyre St. G34	40	FF11
Glenhead Cres. G22	22	W9
Glenhead Rd., Dalm.	5	L5
Glenhead Rd., Lenz.	13	CC6
Glenhead St. G22	22	W9
Glenholme, Pais.	45	H15
Glenhove Rd., Cumb.	71	PP3
Gleniffer Av. G13	18	P9
Gleniffer Cres., John.	44	F15
Gleniffer Dr., Barr.	59	L17
Gleniffer Rd., Pais.	45	H16
Gleniffer Rd., Renf.	31	L11
Gleniffer Vw., Clyde.	5	M6
Kirkoswald Dr.		
Glenisa Av., Chr.	15	HH6
Glenisla St. G31	53	Z14
Glenkirk Dr. G15	6	P7
Glenlee Cres. G52	48	N14
Glenlora Dr. G53	48	P16
Glenlora Ter. G53	48	P16
Glenluce Dr. G32	55	CC14
Glenlui Av. G73	65	Y17
Glenlyon Pl. G73	65	Z18
Glenmalloch Pl., John.	44	F14
Glenmanor Av., Chr.	15	GG7
Glenmore Av. G42	52	X16
Glenmuir Dr. G53	60	P17
Glenpark Rd. G31	37	Y13
Glenpark St. G31	37	Y13
Glenpark Ter. G72	54	AA16
Glenpatrick Bldgs., John.	44	F15
Glenpatrick Rd., John.	44	F15
Glenraith Rd. G33	24	BB10
Glenraith Sq. G33	24	BB10
Glenraith Wk. G33	25	CC10
Glenshee St. G31	53	Z14
Glenshiel Av., Pais.	47	L15
Glenside Av. G53	48	P15
Glenside Dr. G73	65	Z17
Glenspean Pl. G43	62	T17
Glenspean St.		
Glenspean St. G43	62	T17
Glentanar Pl. G22	21	V8
Glentarbert Rd. G73	65	Z18
Glenturret St. G32	54	BB14
Glentyan Av., Kilb.	42	B14
Glentyan Dr. G53	60	P17
Glentyan Ter. G53	48	P16
Glenview Cres., Chr.	15	HH6
Glenview Pl., Blan.	68	FF19
Glenville Av., Giff.	62	S18
Glenwood Ct., Kirk.	12	BB5
Glenwood Dr., Thorn.	61	R19
Glenwood Gdns., Kirk.	12	BB5
Glenwood Pl., Kirk.	12	BB5
Glenwood Rd., Kirk.	12	BB5
Gloucester Av. G73	65	Z17
Gloucester St. G5	35	V13
Gockston Rd., Pais.	30	J12
Gogar Pl. G33	38	AA12
Gogar St. G33	38	AA12
Goldberry Av. G14	18	P9
Goldie Rd., Udd.	69	HH18
Golf Ct. G44	63	U19
Golf Dr. G15	6	N7
Golf Dr., Pais.	47	M14
Golf Rd. G73	65	Y18
Golf Vw., Bear.	6	P5
Golf Vw., Dalm.	4	K6
Golfhill Dr. G31	37	Y12
Golfhill La. G31	37	Y12
Whitehill St.		
Golfhill Ter. G31	36	X12
Firpark St.		
Golspie St. G51	34	S12
Goosedubbs G1	36	W13
Stockwell St.		
Gopher Av., Udd.	57	HH16
Myrtle Rd.		
Gorbals Cross G5	36	W13
Gorbals La. G5	35	V13
Oxford St.		
Gorbals St. G5	35	V13
Gordon Av. G44	63	U19
Gordon Av., Bail.	39	DD13
Gordon Dr. G44	63	U18
Gordon La. G1	35	V12
Gordon St.		
Gordon Rd. G44	63	U19
Gordon St. G1	35	V12
Gordon St., Pais.	46	K14
Gordon Ter., Blan.	68	FF19
Gorebridge St. G32	38	AA12
Gorget Av. G13	7	Q7
Gorget Pl. G13	7	Q7
Gorget Quad. G15	6	P7
Gorget Av.		
Gorse Dr., Barr.	59	L18
Gorse Pl., Udd.	57	HH16
Myrtle Rd.		
Gorsewood, Bish.	10	X7
Gorstan Pl. G20	20	T9
Wyndford Rd.		
Gorstan St. G23	20	T8
Gosford La. G14	18	N9
Dumbarton Rd.		
Goudie St., Pais.	30	J12
Gough St. G33	37	Z12
Gourlay Path G21	22	W10
Endrick St.		
Gourlay St. G21	22	W10
Gourock St. G5	51	V14
Govan Cross G51	34	S12
Govan Rd. G51	33	R12
Govanhill St. G42	51	V15
Gowanbank Gdns., John.	43	D15
Floors St.		
Gowanbrae, Lenz.	13	CC5
Gallowhill Rd.		
Gowanlea Av. G15	6	P7
Gowanlea Dr., Giff.	62	T18
Gowanlea Ter., Udd.	57	HH16
Gower La. G51	34	T13
Gower St.		
Gower St. G41	50	T14
Gower Ter. G41	34	T13

Street	Page	Grid
Goyle Av. G15	7	Q6
Grace Av., Bail.	41	GG13
Grace St. G3	35	U12
Graffham Av., Giff.	62	T18
Grafton Pl. G4	36	W12
Graham Av. G72	67	CC17
Graham Av., Clyde.	5	L6
Graham Sq. G31	36	X13
Graham St., Barr.	59	L18
Graham St., John.	43	D15
Graham Ter., Bish.	23	Y8
Grahamston Ct., Pais.	47	M16
Grahamston Cres., Pais.	47	M16
Grahamston Pk., Barr.	59	L17
Grahamston Pl., Pais.	47	M16
Grahamston Rd.		
Grahamston Rd., Barr.	59	L17
Graighead Av. G33	23	Z10
Graignestock Pl. G40	36	X13
London Rd.		
Grainger Rd., Bish.	11	Z7
Grampian Av., Pais.	46	J16
Grampian Cres. G32	54	BB14
Grampian Pl. G32	54	BB14
Grampian St. G32	54	BB14
Grampian Way, Barr.	59	M19
Gran St., Clyde.	18	N8
Granby La. G12	20	T10
Great George St.		
Granby Pl. G12	20	T10
Great George St.		
Grandtully Dr. G12	20	T9
Grange Gdns. G71	69	HH19
Blairston Av.		
Grange Rd. G42	51	V16
Grange Rd., Bear.	7	R5
Grangeneuk Gdns., Cumb.	70	MM3
Grant St. G3	35	U11
Grantlea Gro. G32	55	CC14
Grantlea Ter. G32	55	CC14
Grantley Gdns. G41	50	T16
Grantley St. G41	50	T16
Granton St. G5	52	X15
Granville St. G3	35	U12
Granville St., Clyde.	5	L6
Gray Dr., Bear.	7	R6
Gray St. G3	34	T11
Great Dovehill G1	36	W13
Great George La. G12	20	T10
Great George St.		
Great George St. G12	20	T10
Great Hamilton St., Pais.	46	K15
Great Kelvin La. G12	21	U10
Glasgow St.		
Great Western Rd. G12	20	T10
Great Western Ter. G12	20	T10
Green, The G40	36	X13
Green Fm. Rd., Linw.	28	E13
Green Lo. Ter. G40	52	X14
Greenhead St.		
Green Pk., Both.	69	HH19
Green St.		
Green Rd. G73	53	Y16
Green Rd., Pais.	45	H14
Green St. G40	36	X13
Green St., Both.	69	HH19
Green St., Clyde.	5	L6
Greenan Av. G42	52	X16
Greenbank Dr., Pais.	46	J16
Greenbank Rd., Cumb.	70	MM3
Greenbank St. G43	62	S17
Harriet St.		
Greenbank St. G73	53	Y16
Greendyke St. G1	36	W13
Greenend Av., John.	43	C15
Greenend Pl. G32	39	CC12
Greenfaulds Cres., Cumb.	71	PP4
Greenfaulds Rd., Cumb.	70	NN4
Greenfield Av. G32	38	BB12
Greenfield Pl. G32	38	BB13
Budhill Av.		
Greenfield Rd. G32	39	CC13
Greenfield St. G51	33	R12
Greengairs Av. G51	33	Q12
Greenhaugh St. G51	34	S12
Greenhead Rd., Bear.	7	R6
Greenhead Rd., Renf.	16	J8
Greenhead St. G40	52	X14
Greenhill, Bish.	11	Y7
Greenhill Av., Gart.	27	GG8
Greenhill Av., Giff.	62	S19
Greenhill Ct. G73	53	Y16
Greenhill Cres., John.	44	F15
Greenhill Cres., Linw.	28	F13
Greenhill Dr., Linw.	28	F13
Greenhill Rd. G73	53	Y16
Greenhill Rd., Pais.	30	J13
Greenhill St. G73	53	Y16
Greenholm Av., Udd.	57	GG16
Greenholme St. G40	63	V17
Holmlea Rd.		
Greenknowe Rd. G43	62	S17
Greenlaw Av., Pais.	31	L13
Greenlaw Cres., Pais.	31	L13
Greenlaw Dr.		
Greenlaw Dr., Pais.	31	L13
Greenlaw Rd. G14	18	N9
Greenlaw Ter., Pais.	31	L13
Greenlaw Av.		
Greenlea Rd., Chr.	26	EE8
Greenlea St. G13	19	R9
Greenlees Gdns. G72	66	AA18
Greenlees Pk. G72	66	BB18
Greenlees Rd. G72	66	BB17
Greenloan Av. G51	33	Q12
Greenmount G22	21	V8
Greenock Av. G44	63	V17
Greenock Rd., Pais.	30	J12
Greenock Rd., Renf.	16	J9
Greenrig St. G33	23	Z10
Greenrig St., Udd.	69	GG17
Greenrigg Rd., Cumb.	71	PP3
Greenshields Rd., Bail.	40	EE13
Greenside Cres. G33	24	AA10
Greenside St. G33	24	AA10
Greentree Dr., Bail.	55	DD14
Greenview St. G43	50	T16
Greenways Av., Pais.	45	H15
Greenways Ct., John.	45	H15
Greenwell Pl. G51	34	S12
Greenwell St. G51	34	S12
Govan Rd.		
Greenwood Av. G72	67	DD17
Greenwood Av., Chr.	15	GG7
Greenwood Dr., Bear.	8	S6
Greenwood Quad., Clyde.	5	M7
Greer Quad., Clyde.	5	L6
Grenville Dr. G72	66	AA18
Greran Dr., Renf.	17	L10
Gretna St. G40	53	Y14
Greyfriars St. G32	38	AA12
Greystone Av. G73	65	Z17
Greywood St. G13	19	R8
Grier Path G31	37	Z13
Grierson La. G33	37	Z12
Lomax St.		
Grierson St. G33	37	Z12
Grieve Rd., Cumb.	71	PP2
Griqua Ter. G71	69	HH19
Grogarry Rd. G15	6	P6
Springside Pl.		
Grosvenor Cres. G12	20	T10
Observatory Rd.		
Grosvenor Cres. La. G12	20	T10
Byres Rd.		
Grosvenor La. G12	20	T10
Byres Rd.		
Grosvenor Mans. G12	20	T10
Observatory Rd.		
Grosvenor Ter. G12	20	T10
Grove, The Kilb.	42	B14
Grove Pk., Lenz.	13	CC6
Groveburn Av., Thorn.	62	S18
Grovepark Gdns. G20	35	V11
Grovepark Pl. G20	21	V10
Grovepark St. G20	21	V10
Groves, The, Bish.	23	Z8
Woodhill Rd.		
Grudie St. G34	40	EE12
Gryffe Av., Renf.	17	L10
Gryffe Cres., Pais.	45	G15
Gryffe St. G44	63	V17
Guildford St. G33	39	CC11
Gullane Cres., Cumb.	70	NN1
Gullane St. G11	34	S11
Purdon St.		
Guthrie St. G20	20	T9
Haberlea Av. G53	61	Q18
Haberlea Gdns. G53	61	Q19
Hagg Cres., John.	43	D14
Hagg Pl., John.	43	D14
Hagg Rd., John.	43	D15
Haggs Rd. G41	50	T15
Haggs Wd. Av. G41	50	T15
Haghill Rd. G31	37	Z12
Haig Dr., Bail.	55	DD14
Haig St. G21	23	Y10
Hailes Av. G32	39	CC13
Haining Rd., Renf.	17	M10
Hairmyres St. G42	51	V15
Govanhill St.		
Hairst St., Renf.	17	M10
Halbeath Av. G15	6	N6
Halbert St. G41	51	U15
Haldane La. G14	19	Q10
Haldane St.		
Haldane St. G14	19	Q10
Halgreen Av. G15	6	N6
Halifax Way, Renf.	31	M11
Britannia Way		
Hall St., Clyde.	5	L7
Hallbrae St. G33	38	AA11
Halley Dr. G13	18	N8
Halley Pl. G13	18	N9
Halley Sq. G13	18	N8
Halley St. G13	18	N8
Hallhill Cres. G33	39	DD13
Hallhill Rd. G32	38	BB13
Hallhill Rd., John.	43	C16
Hallidale Cres., Renf.	32	N11
Hallrule Dr. G52	33	Q13
Hallside Av. G72	67	DD17
Hallside Cres. G72	67	DD17
Hallside Dr. G72	67	DD17
Hallside Rd. G72	67	DD18
Hallside St. G5	52	W14
Hallydown Dr. G13	19	Q9
Halton Gdns., Bail.	55	DD14
Hamilton Av. G41	50	S14
Hamilton Cres. G72	67	CC18
Hamilton Cres., Renf.	17	M9
Hamilton Dr. G12	21	U10
Hamilton Dr. G72	66	BB17
Hamilton Dr., Both.	69	HH19
Hamilton Dr., Giff.	62	T19
Hamilton Pk. Av. G12	21	U10
Hamilton Rd. G32	55	DD15
Hamilton Rd. G72	66	BB17
Hamilton Rd. G73	53	Y16
Hamilton Rd., Blan.	67	DD18
Hamilton Rd., Both.	69	HH19
Hamilton St. G42	52	W15
Hamilton St., Clyde.	17	M8
Hamilton St., Pais.	30	K13
Hamilton Ter., Clyde.	17	M8
Hamilton Vw., Udd.	57	HH16
Hamiltonhill Cres. G22	21	V10
Hamiltonhill Rd.		
Hamiltonhill Rd. G22	21	V10
Hampden Dr. G42	51	V16
Cathcart Rd.		
Hampden La. G42	51	V16
Cathcart Rd.		
Hampden Ter. G42	51	V16
Cathcart Rd.		
Hampden Way, Renf.	31	M11
Lewis Av.		
Hangingshaw Pl. G42	52	W16
Haning, The, Renf.	31	M11
Hanover St. G1	36	W12
Hanson St. G31	36	X12

Street	Page	Grid
Hapland Av. G53	49	Q15
Hapland Rd. G53	49	Q15
Harbour La., Pais.	30	K13
Harbour Rd., Pais.	30	K12
Harburn Pl. G23	9	U7
Harbury Pl. G14	18	N9
Harcourt Dr. G31	37	Y12
Hardgate Dr. G51	33	Q12
Hardgate Gdns. G51	33	Q12
Hardgate Pl. G51	33	Q12
Hardgate Rd. G51	33	Q12
Hardie Av. G73	53	Z16
Hardridge Av. G52	49	Q15
Hardridge Rd.		
Hardridge Pl. G52	49	R15
Hardridge Rd. G52	49	Q15
Harefield Dr. G14	18	P9
Harelaw Av. G44	63	U18
Harelaw Av., Barr.	59	M19
Harelaw Cres., Pais.	46	J16
Harhill St. G51	33	R12
Harland Cotts. G14	33	Q11
South St.		
Harland St. G14	19	Q10
Harlaw Gdns. G64	11	Z7
Harley St. G51	34	T13
Harmetray St. G22	22	W9
Harmony Pl. G51	34	S12
Harmony Row G51	34	S12
Harmony Sq. G51	34	S12
Harmsworth St. G11	33	R11
Harport St. G46	61	R18
Harriet St. G73	53	Y16
Harris Rd. G23	9	U7
Harris Rd., Old K.	4	J5
Harrison Dr. G51	34	S13
Harrow Ct. G15	6	N6
Linkwood Dr.		
Harrow Pl. G15	6	N6
Hart St. G31	38	AA13
Hart St., Linw.	28	E13
Hartfield Ter., Pais.	47	L15
Hartlaw Cres. G52	32	P13
Hartree Av. G13	18	N8
Hartstone Pl. G53	48	P16
Hartstone Rd. G53	48	P16
Hartstone Ter. G53	48	P16
Harvey St. G4	36	W11
Harvie St. G51	34	T13
Harwood St. G32	38	AA12
Hastie St. G3	34	T11
Old Dumbarton Rd.		
Hatfield Dr. G12	19	R9
Hathaway Dr., Giff.	62	S19
Hathaway La. G20	21	U9
Avenuepark St.		
Hathaway St. G20	21	U9
Hathersage Av., Bail.	40	EE13
Hathersage Dr., Bail.	40	EE13
Hathersage Gdns., Bail.	40	EE13
Hatters Row G40	52	X14
Dalmarnock Rd.		
Hatton Dr. G52	48	P14
Hatton Gdns. G52	48	P14
Haugh Rd. G3	34	T12
Haughburn Pl. G53	48	P16
Haughburn Rd. G53	48	P16
Haughburn Ter. G53	49	Q16
Havelock La. G11	34	T11
Dowanhill St.		
Havelock St. G11	34	T11
Hawick Av. G78	45	H15
Hawick St. G13	18	N8
Hawkhead Av., Pais.	47	L15
Hawkhead Rd., Pais.	47	L14
Hawthorn Av., Bish.	23	Y8
Hawthorn Av., Lenz.	13	CC5
Hawthorn Av., Renf.	16	K8
Hawthorn Cres., Renf.	4	K7
Hawthorn Quad. G22	22	W9
Hawthorn Rd., Renf.	16	K8
Hawthorn St. G22	22	W9
Hawthorn St., Clyde.	5	L6
Hawthorn Ter., Udd.	57	HH16
Douglas St.		
Hawthorn Wk. G72	65	Z17
Hawthorn Wk., Bish.	23	Z8
Letham Dr.		
Hawthornden Gdns. G23	9	U7
Hawthorne Av., John.	44	E15
Hay Dr., John.	44	E14
Hayburn Ct. G11	34	S11
Hayburn Cres. G11	20	S10
Hayburn La. G12	20	S10
Queensborough Gdns.		
Hayburn St. G11	34	S11
Hayfield St. G5	52	W14
Hayhill Cotts., Gart.	27	HH9
Hayle Gdns., Chr.	15	GG6
Haylynn St. G14	33	R11
Haymarket St. G32	38	AA12
Haystack Pl., Lenz.	13	CC6
Hayston Cres. G22	21	V9
Hayston St. G22	21	V9
Haywood St. G22	21	V9
Hazel Av. G44	63	U18
Clarkston Rd.		
Hazel Av., John.	44	E15
Hazel Av., Lenz.	13	CC5
Hazel Dene, Bish.	11	Y7
Hazel Gro., Lenz.	13	CC5
Hazel Rd., Cumb.	71	QQ2
Hazel Ter., Udd.	57	HH16
Douglas St.		
Hazelden Gdns. G44	63	U18
Hazellea Dr., Giff.	62	T18
Hazelwood Av. G78	45	G16
Hazelwood Gdns. G73	65	Z18
Hazelwood Rd. G41	50	T14
Hazlitt St. G20	21	V9
Heath Av., Bish.	23	Y8
Heath Av., Lenz.	13	CC6
Heathcliffe Av., Blan.	68	FF19
Heathcot Av. G15	6	N7
Heathcot Pl. G15	6	N7
Heathcot Av.		
Heather Av., Barr.	59	L17
Heather Dr., Lenz.	12	BB6
Heather Gdns., Lenz.	12	BB6
Heather Pl., John.	44	E15
Heather Pl., Lenz.	12	BB5
Heather St. G41	35	U13
Scotland St.		
Heatherbrae, Bish.	10	X7
Heatheryknowe Rd., Bail.	41	GG12
Heathfield Av., Chr.	15	GG7
Heathfield St. G33	39	CC12
Heathfield Ter. G21	22	X9
Broomfield Rd.		
Heathside Rd., Giff.	62	T18
Heathwood Dr., Thorn.	62	S18
Hecla Av. G15	6	N6
Hecla Pl. G15	6	N6
Hector Rd. G41	50	T16
Heddle Pl. G2	35	V12
Cadogan St.		
Heggie Ter. G14	19	Q10
Dumbarton Rd.		
Helen St. G52	33	R13
Helensburgh Dr. G13	19	Q9
Helenslea G72	67	CC18
Helenvale Ct. G31	37	Z13
Helenvale St.		
Helenvale St. G31	53	Z14
Helmsdale Av., Blan.	68	FF18
Helmsdale Ct. G72	67	CC17
Hemlock St. G13	19	R8
Henderland Rd., Bear.	7	R7
Henderson Av. G72	67	CC17
Henderson St. G20	21	U10
Henderson St., Clyde.	18	N8
Henderson St., Pais.	30	J13
Henrietta St. G14	19	Q10
Henry St., Barr.	59	L18
Hepburn Rd. G52	32	P12
Herald Av. G13	7	Q7
Herald Way, Renf.	31	M11
Viscount Av.		
Herbert St. G20	21	U10
Herbertson St. G5	35	V13
Eglinton St.		
Hercla Av. G15	6	N6
Hercla Pl. G15	6	N6
Hercla Sq. G15	6	N7
Hercules Way, Renf.	31	M11
Friendship Way		
Herichell St. G13	19	R9
Foulis La.		
Heriot Av., Pais.	45	G16
Heriot Cres., Bish.	11	Y6
Heriot Rd., Lenz.	13	CC6
Herma St. G23	21	U8
Hermiston Av. G32	39	CC13
Hermiston Pl. G32	39	CC13
Hermiston Rd. G32	38	BB12
Hermitage Av. G13	19	Q9
Heron Ct., Clyde.	5	L5
Heron Pl., John.	43	C16
Heron St. G40	52	X14
Heron Way, Renf.	31	M11
Britannia Way		
Herries Rd. G41	50	T15
Herriet St. G41	51	U14
Herschell St. G13	19	R9
Foulis La.		
Hertford Av. G12	20	S9
Hexham Gdns. G41	50	T15
Heys St., Barr.	59	M19
Hickman St. G42	51	V15
Hickory St. G22	22	X9
High Barholm, Kilb.	42	B14
High Calside, Pais.	46	J14
High Craighall Rd. G4	35	V11
High Parksail, Renf.	16	J8
High St., Pais.	46	J14
High St. G1	36	W13
High St. G73	53	Y16
High St., John.	43	D14
High St., Pais.	46	J14
High St., Renf.	17	M10
Highburgh Dr. G73	65	Y17
Highburgh Rd. G12	34	T11
Highburgh Ter. G12	34	T11
Highburgh Rd.		
Highcraig Av., John.	43	C15
Highcroft Av. G44	64	W17
Highfield Av., Pais.	46	J16
Highfield Cres., Pais.	46	J16
Highfield Dr. G12	20	S9
Highfield Dr. G73	65	Z18
Highfield Pl. G12	20	S9
Highkirk Vw., John.	43	D15
Highland La. G51	34	T12
Hilary Av. G73	65	Z17
Hilary Dr., Bail.	39	DD13
Hilda Cres. G33	24	AA10
Hill Pk., Clyde.	5	L5
Hill Path G52	32	P13
Hill Pl. G52	32	P13
Hill Rd., Cumb.	70	NN3
Hill St. G3	35	V11
Hillcrest, Chr.	26	FF8
Hillcrest Av. G32	54	BB16
Hillcrest Av. G44	63	U18
Hillcrest Av., Cumb.	70	NN3
Hillcrest Av., Pais.	58	J17
Hillcrest Ct., Cumb.	70	NN3
Hillcrest Rd. G32	55	CC16
Hillcrest Rd., Bear.	7	R6
Hillcrest Rd., Udd.	57	HH16
Hillcrest Ter., Both.	69	HH18
Churchill Cres.		
Hillcroft Ter., Bish.	22	X8
Hillend Cres., Clyde.	4	K5
Hillend Rd. G22	21	V8
Hillend Rd. G73	65	Y17
Hillfoot Av. G73	53	Y16
Hillfoot Av., Bear.	7	R5
Hillfoot Dr., Bear.	7	R5
Hillfoot Gdns., Udd.	57	GG16
Hillfoot St. G31	37	Y12
Hillfoot Ter., Bear.	8	S5
Milngavie Rd.		
Hillhead Av. G73	65	Y18

Hillhead Av., Chr. 15 GG7
Hillhead Gdns. G12 34 T11
Hillhead St.
Hillhead Pl. G12 35 U11
Bank St.
Hillhead St. G12 34 T11
Hillhouse St. G21 23 Y10
Hillington Gdns. G52 49 Q14
Hillington Ind. Est. G52 32 N12
Hillington Pk. Cres. G52 33 Q13
Hillington Quad. G52 32 P13
Hillington Rd. G52 32 N11
Hillington Rd. S., Renf. 32 P13
Hillington Ter. G52 32 P13
Hillkirk Pl. G21 22 X10
Hillkirk St. G21 22 X10
Hillkirk St. La. G21 22 X10
Hillkirk St.
Hillneuk Av., Bear. 7 R5
Hillneuk Dr., Bear. 8 S5
Hillpark Av., Pais. 46 J15
Hillpark Dr. G43 62 T17
Hillsborough Rd., Bail. 39 DD13
Hillsborough Sq. G12 34 T11
Hillhead St.
Hillsborough Ter. G12 21 U10
Bower St.
Hillside Av., Bear. 7 R5
Hillside Ct., Thorn. 61 R18
Hillside Dr., Barr. 59 L18
Hillside Dr., Bear. 8 S5
Hillside Dr., Bish. 11 Y7
Hillside Gdns. G11 20 S10
Turnberry Rd.
Hillside Gdns. La. G11 20 S10
North Gardner St.
Hillside Gro., Barr. 59 L18
Hillside Quad. G43 62 S17
Hillside Rd. G43 62 S17
Hillside Rd., Barr. 59 L18
Hillside Rd., Pais. 47 L15
Hillswick Cres. G22 21 V8
Hilltop Rd., Chr. 15 GG7
Eastwood Rd.
Hillview Cres., Udd. 57 GG16
Hillview Dr., Blan. 68 FF19
Hillview Rd., John. 44 F15
Hillview St. G32 38 AA13
Hilton Gdns. G13 19 R8
Hilton Gdns. La. G13 19 R8
Fulton St.
Hilton Pk., Bish. 10 X6
Hilton Rd., Bish. 10 X6
Hilton Ter. G13 19 R8
Hilton Ter. G72 66 AA18
Hilton Ter., Bish. 10 X6
Hinshaw St. G20 21 V10
Hinshelwood Dr. G51 34 S13
Hinshelwood Pl. G51 34 S13
Edmiston Dr.
Hirsel Pl., Udd. 69 HH18
Lomond Dr.
Hobart Cres., Dalm. 4 J5
Hobart St. G22 21 V10
Hobden St. G21 23 Y10
Hoddam Av. G45 64 X18
Hoddam Ter. G45 65 Y18
Hoey St. G51 34 T12
Hogan Ct., Clyde. 4 K5
Dalgleish Av.
Hogarth Av. G32 37 Z12
Hogarth Cres. G32 37 Z12
Hogarth Dr. G32 37 Z12
Hogarth Gdns. G32 37 Z12
Hogg Av., John. 43 D15
Hogganfield St. G33 37 Z11
Holburn Av., Pais. 29 H13
Hole Brae, Cumb. 71 PP2
Holeburn Rd. G43 62 T17
Holehouse Dr. G13 18 P9
Holland St. G2 35 V12
Hollinwell Rd. G23 21 U8
Hollowglen Rd. G32 38 BB13
Hollows Av., Pais. 45 G16
Hollows Cres., Pais. 45 G16

Holly Dr. G21 23 Y10
Holly Pl., John. 44 E16
Holly St., Clyde. 5 L6
Hollybank Pl. G72 66 BB18
Hollybank St. G21 37 Y11
Hollybrook St. G42 51 V15
Hollybush Av., Pais. 45 H16
Hollybush Rd. G52 32 N13
Hollymount, Bear. 7 R7
Holm Av., Pais. 46 K15
Holm Av., Udd. 57 GG16
Holm Pl., Linw. 28 E12
Holm St. G2 35 V12
Holmbank Av. G41 50 T16
Holmbrae Av., Udd. 57 GG16
Holmbrae Rd., Udd. 57 GG16
Holmbyre Rd. G45 64 W19
Holmbyre Ter. G45 64 W19
Holmes Av., Renf. 31 M11
Holmfauldhead Dr. G51 33 R12
Holmfauldhead Pl. G51 33 R12
Govan Rd.
Holmhead Cres. G44 63 V17
Holmhead Pl. G44 63 V17
Holmhead Rd. G44 63 V17
Holmhill Av. G72 66 BB18
Holmhills Dr. G72 66 AA18
Holmhills Gdns. G72 66 AA18
Holmhills Gro. G72 66 AA18
Holmhills Pl. G72 66 AA18
Holmhills Rd. G72 66 AA18
Holmhills Ter. G72 66 AA18
Holmlea Rd. G44 51 V16
Holms Pl., Gart. 27 GG8
Holmswood Av., Blan. 68 FF19
Holmwood Av., Udd. 57 GG16
Holmwood Gdns., Udd. 69 GG17
Holyrood Cres. G20 35 U11
Holyrood Quad. G20 35 U11
Holywell St. G31 37 Y13
Homeston Av., Udd. 69 HH18
Honeybog Rd. G52 32 N13
Hood St., Clyde. 5 M7
Hope St. G2 35 V12
Hopefield Av. G12 20 T9
Hopehill Pl. G20 21 V10
Hopehill Rd.
Hopehill Rd. G20 21 V10
Hopeman Av. G46 61 R18
Hopeman Dr. G46 61 R18
Hopeman Path, Thorn. 61 R18
Kennishead Pl.
Hopeman Rd. G46 61 R18
Hopeman St. G46 61 R18
Hopetoun Pl. G23 9 U7
Hopetoun Ter. G21 23 Y10
Foresthall Dr.
Hornal Rd., Udd. 69 HH18
Hornbeam Dr., Dalm. 5 L6
Hornbeam Rd., Udd. 57 HH16
Myrtle Rd.
Horndean Ct., Bish. 11 Y6
Horndean Cres. G33 39 CC11
Horne St. G22 22 X9
Hawthorn St.
Hornshill Rd. G33 25 DD8
Hornshill St. G21 23 Y10
Horsburgh St. G33 39 CC11
Horse Shoe La., Bear. 7 R6
Horse Shoe Rd., Bear. 7 R5
Horslethill Rd. G12 20 T10
Hospital St. G5 51 V14
Hotspur St. G20 21 U10
Houldsworth La. G3 35 U12
Finnieston St.
Houldsworth St. G3 35 U12
Househillmuir Cres. 49 Q16
G53
Househillmuir La. G53 49 Q16
Househillmuir Pl. G53 49 Q16
Househillmuir Rd. G53 60 P17
Househillwood Cres. 48 P16
G53
Househillwood Rd. G53 60 P17
Housel Av. G13 18 P8

Houston Pl. G5 35 U13
Houston Pl., John. 44 F15
Houston Sq., John. 43 D14
Houston St. G5 35 U13
Houston St., Renf. 17 M10
Howard St. G1 35 V13
Howard St., Pais. 47 L14
Howat St. G51 34 S12
Howden Dr., Linw. 28 E13
Howe St., Pais. 45 G14
Howford Rd. G52 48 P14
Howgate Av. G15 6 N6
Howieshill Av. G72 66 BB17
Howieshill Rd. G72 66 BB18
Howth Dr. G13 19 R8
Howth Ter. G13 19 R8
Howwood St. G41 35 U13
Hoylake Pk., Both. 69 GG19
Hoylake Pl. G23 9 U7
Hozier Cres., Udd. 57 GG16
Hozier St. G40 52 X14
Hubbard Dr. G11 33 R11
Hugh Murray Gro. G72 67 CC17
Hughenden Dr. G12 20 S10
Hughenden Gdns. G12 20 S10
Hughenden La. G12 20 S10
Hughenden Rd. G12 20 S10
Hughenden Ter. G12 20 S10
Hughenden Rd.
Hugo St. G20 21 U9
Hume Dr., Both. 69 HH18
Hume Dr., Udd. 57 GG16
Hume Rd., Cumb. 71 PP2
Hume St., Clyde. 5 L7
Hunter Pl. G78 42 B15
Hunter Rd. G73 53 Z15
Hunter St. G4 36 X13
Hunter St., Pais. 30 K13
Hunterfield Dr. G72 66 AA17
Hunterhill Av., Pais. 46 K14
Hunterhill Rd.
Hunterhill Rd., Pais. 46 K14
Huntersfield Rd., John. 43 C15
Huntershill Rd., Bish. 22 X8
Huntershill St. G21 22 X9
Huntershill Way, Bish. 22 X8
Crowhill Rd.
Huntingdon Sq. G21 36 X11
Huntingdon Rd.
Huntington Rd. G21 36 X11
Huntingtower Rd., Bail. 56 EE14
Huntley Rd. G52 32 N12
Huntly Av., Giff. 62 T19
Huntly Dr. G72 66 BB18
Huntly Gdns. G12 20 T10
Huntly Path, Chr. 15 HH7
Burnbrae Av.
Huntly Rd. G12 20 T10
Huntly Ter., Pais. 47 L15
Hurlet Rd., Pais. 47 M15
Hurley Hawkin, Bish. 23 Z8
Hurlford Av. G13 18 N8
Hutcheson Rd., Thorn. 62 S19
Hutcheson St. G1 36 W12
Hutchinson Ct. G2 35 V12
Hope St.
Hutchinson Pl. G72 67 DD18
Hutchison Ct., Giff. 62 S18
Berryhill Rd.
Hutchison Dr., Bear. 8 S7
Hutton Dr. G51 33 R12
Huxley St. G20 21 U9
Hydepark Pl. G21 22 X9
Springburn Rd.
Hydepark St. G3 35 U12
Hyndal Av. G53 49 Q15
Hyndford St. G51 34 S12
Hyndland Av. G11 34 S11
Hyndland Rd. G12 20 S10
Hyndland St. G11 34 T11
Hyndlee Dr. G52 33 Q13
Hyslop Pl., Clyde. 5 L6
Albert Rd.

Iain Dr., Bear.	7	Q5
Iain Rd., Bear.	7	Q5
Ibrox St. G51	34	T13
Ibrox Ter. G51	34	S13
Ibrox Ter. La. G51	34	S13
Ibroxholm La. G51	34	T13
Paisley Rd. W.		
Ibroxholm Oval G51	34	S13
Ibroxholm Pl. G51	34	T13
Ilay Av., Bear.	19	R8
Ilay Ct., Bear.	20	S8
Ilay Rd., Bear.	20	S8
Inchbrae Rd. G52	49	Q14
Inchfad Dr. G15	6	N6
Inchholm St. G11	33	R11
Inchinnan Rd., Pais.	30	K12
Inchinnan Rd., Renf.	17	L10
Inchkeith Pl. G32	38	BB12
Inchlee St. G14	33	R11
Inchmurrin Dr. G73	65	Z19
Inchmurrin Gdns. G73	65	Z19
Inchmurrin Pl. G73	65	Z19
Inchoch St. G33	39	DD11
Inchrory Pl. G15	6	N6
Incle St., Pais.	30	K13
India Dr., Renf.	16	J9
India St. G2	35	V12
Inga St. G20	21	U8
Ingerbreck Av. G73	65	Z18
Ingleby Dr. G31	37	Y12
Inglefield St. G42	51	V15
Ingleneuk Av. G33	24	BB9
Inglestone Av., Thorn.	62	S19
Inglis St. G31	37	Y13
Ingram St. G1	36	W12
Inishail Rd. G33	39	CC11
Inkerman Rd. G52	32	N13
Innerwick Dr. G52	32	P13
Inver Rd. G33	39	DD12
Inveraray Dr., Bish.	11	Y6
Invercanny Dr. G15	6	N6
Invercanny Pl. G15	6	P6
Inverclyde Gdns. G11	19	R10
Broomhill Dr.		
Inverclyde Gdns. G73	66	AA18
Inveresk Cres. G32	38	BB13
Inveresk St. G32	38	BB13
Inverewe Av. G46	61	Q18
Inverewe Dr. G46	61	Q19
Inverewe Gdns. G46	61	Q19
Inverewe Pl. G46	61	Q18
Invergarry Av. G46	61	Q19
Invergarry Ct. G46	61	Q19
Invergarry Dr. G46	61	Q19
Invergarry Gdns. G46	61	Q19
Invergarry Gro. G46	61	Q19
Invergarry Pl. G46	61	Q19
Invergarry Quad. G46	61	R19
Invergarry Vw. G46	61	R19
Inverglas Av., Renf.	32	N11
Morriston Cres.		
Invergordon Av. G43	51	U16
Invergyle Dr. G52	32	P13
Inverkar Dr., Pais.	45	H15
Inverkip St. G5	36	W13
Inverlair Av. G43	63	U17
Inverleith St. G32	37	Z13
Inverlochy St. G33	39	CC11
Inverness St. G51	33	Q13
Inveroran Dr., Bear.	8	S6
Invershiel Rd. G23	8	T7
Invershin Dr. G20	20	T9
Wyndford Rd.		
Inverurie St. G21	22	W10
Inzievar Ter. G32	54	BB15
Iona Ct. G51	34	S12
Iona Cres., Old K.	4	J5
Iona Dr., Old K.	4	J5
Iona Dr., Pais.	46	J16
Iona Gdns., Old K.	4	J5
Iona La., Chr.	15	HH7
Heathfield Av.		
Iona Pl., Old K.	4	J5
Iona Rd. G73	66	AA18
Iona Rd., Renf.	31	M11
Iona St. G51	34	S12
Iris Av. G45	65	Y18
Irongray St. G31	37	Z12
Irvine Dr., Linw.	28	E13
Irvine St. G40	53	Y14
Irving Av., Clyde.	5	L5
Stewart Dr.		
Irving Quad., Clyde.	5	L5
Stewart Dr.		
Iser La. G41	51	U16
Island Rd., Cumb.	70	MM4
Islay Av. G73	66	AA18
Islay Cres., Old K.	4	J5
Islay Cres., Pais.	46	J16
Islay Dr., Old K.	4	J5
Ivanhoe Rd. G13	19	Q8
Ivanhoe Rd., Cumb.	70	NN4
Ivanhoe Rd., Pais.	45	G15
Ivanhoe Way, Pais.	45	G15
Ivanhoe Rd.		
Ivybank Av. G72	67	CC18
Jacks Rd., Udd.	69	HH17
Jagger Gdns., Bail.	55	DD14
Jamaica St. G1	35	V13
James Dunlop Gdns., Bish.	23	Y8
Graham Ter.		
James Gray St. G41	51	U16
James Morrison St. G1	36	W13
St. Andrews Sq.		
James Nisbet St. G21	36	X12
James St. G40	52	X14
James Watt La. G2	35	V12
James Watt St.		
James Watt St. G2	35	V12
Jamieson Ct. G42	51	V15
Jamieson Path G42	51	V15
Jamieson St.		
Jamieson St. G42	51	V15
Janebank Av. G72	67	CC18
Janefield Av., John.	43	D15
Janefield St. G31	37	Y13
Janes Brae, Cumb.	70	NN4
Janetta St., Clyde.	5	L6
Jardine St. G20	21	U10
Jardine Ter., Gart.	27	GG9
Jasgray St. G42	51	U15
Jean Armour Dr., Clyde.	5	M6
Jedburgh Av. G73	53	Y16
Jedburgh Dr., Pais.	45	H15
Jedburgh Gdns. G20	21	U10
Jedworth Av. G15	6	P6
Jellicoe St., Dalm.	4	K6
Jennys Well Rd., Pais.	47	L15
Jerviston Rd. G33	39	CC11
Jessie St. G42	52	W15
Jessiman Sq., Renf.	31	L11
John Brown Pl., Chr.	26	FF8
John Knox La. G4	36	X12
Drygate		
John Knox St. G4	36	X12
John Knox St., Clyde.	17	M8
John Lang St., John.	44	E14
John St. G1	36	W12
John St., Barr.	59	L18
John St., Pais.	46	J14
Johnshaven St. G43	50	T16
Bengal St.		
Johnston Rd., Gart.	27	HH9
Johnston St., Pais.	46	K14
Gordon St.		
Johnstone Av. G52	32	P13
Johnstone Av., Clyde.	17	M8
Johnstone Dr. G72	66	BB17
Johnstone Dr. G73	53	Y16
Joppa St. G33	38	AA12
Jordan St. G14	33	Q11
Jordanhill Cres. G13	19	Q9
Jordanhill Dr. G13	19	Q9
Jordanhill La. G13	19	R9
Austen Rd.		
Jordanvale Av. G14	33	Q11
Jowitt Av., Clyde.	5	M7
Joycelyn Sq. G1	36	W13
Jubilee Bk., Lenz.	13	CC6
Heriot Rd.		
Jubilee Path, Bear.	7	R6
Jubilee Ter., John.	43	C15
Julian Av. G12	20	T10
Julian La. G12	20	T10
Julian Av.		
Juniper Ct., Lenz.	12	BB5
Juniper Pl. G32	55	DD14
Juniper Pl., John.	44	E16
Juniper Ter. G32	55	DD14
Jura Av., Renf.	31	M11
Jura Ct. G52	33	R13
Jura Dr., Blan.	68	FF18
Jura Dr., Old K.	4	J5
Jura Rd.		
Jura Gdns., Old K.	4	J5
Jura Rd.		
Jura Pl., Old K.	4	J5
Jura Rd.		
Jura Rd., Old K.	4	J5
Jura Rd., Pais.	46	J16
Jura St. G52	33	R13
Kaim Dr. G53	61	Q17
Kames St. G5	51	V14
Karol Path G4	35	V11
St. Peters St.		
Katewell Av. G15	6	N6
Katrine Av., Bish.	11	Y7
Katrine Dr., Pais.	45	G15
Katrine Pl. G72	66	BB17
Kay St. G21	22	X10
Kaystone Rd. G15	6	P7
Keal Av. G15	18	P8
Keal Cres. G15	18	P8
Keal Dr. G15	18	P8
Keal Pl. G15	18	P8
Kearn Av. G15	6	P7
Kearn Pl. G15	6	P7
Keats Pk., Udd.	69	HH18
Keir Dr., Bish.	10	X7
Keir St. G41	51	U14
Keirhill Rd., Cumb.	70	MM3
Woodburn Rd.		
Keirs Wk. G72	66	BB17
Keith Av., Giff.	62	T18
Keith Ct. G11	34	T11
Keith St.		
Keith St. G11	34	T11
Kelbourne St. G20	21	U10
Kelburn St., Barr.	59	L19
Kelburne Dr., Pais.	31	L13
Kelburne Gdns., Bail.	56	EE14
Kelburne Gdns., Pais.	31	L13
Kelburne Oval, Pais.	31	L13
Kelhead Av. G52	32	N13
Kelhead Dr. G52	32	N13
Kelhead Path G52	32	P13
Kelhead Pl. G52	32	N13
Kellas St. G51	34	S13
Kells Pl. G15	6	N6
Kelso Av. G73	53	Y16
Kelso Av., Pais.	45	H15
Kelso Pl. G14	18	N9
Kelso St. G13	18	N9
Kelton St. G32	54	BB14
Kelty Pl. G5	35	V13
Bedford St.		
Kelty St. G5	51	V14
Eglinton St.		
Kelvin Av. G52	32	N11
Kelvin Ct. G12	19	R9
Kelvin Cres., Bear.	7	R7
Kelvin Dr. G20	20	T10
Kelvin Dr., Barr.	59	M19
Kelvin Dr., Bish.	11	Y7
Kelvin Dr., Chr.	15	GG7
Kelvin Rd., Cumb.	71	PP4
Kelvin Rd., Udd.	57	GG16
Kelvin Way G3	34	T11
Kelvin Way, Udd.	69	HH18
Bracken Ter.		

Street	Grid	Page	Ref
Kelvindale Bldgs. G12	20	T9	
Kelvindale Rd.			
Kelvindale Cotts. G12	20	T9	
Kelvindale Rd.			
Kelvindale Gdns. G20	20	T9	
Kelvindale Glen G12	20	T9	
Kelvindale Rd.			
Kelvindale Pl. G20	20	T9	
Kelvindale Rd. G12	20	T9	
Kelvingrove St. G3	35	U12	
Kelvingrove Ter. G3	35	U12	
Kelvingrove St.			
Kelvinhaugh Pl. G3	34	T12	
Kelvinhaugh St.			
Kelvinhaugh St. G3	34	T12	
Kelvinside Av. G20	21	U10	
Queen Margaret Dr.			
Kelvinside Dr. G20	21	U10	
Kelvinside Gdns. G20	21	U10	
Kelvinside Gdns. E. G20	21	U10	
Kelvinside Ter. S. G20	21	U10	
Kelvinside Ter. W. G20	21	U10	
Kemp Av., Renf.	31	L11	
Kemp St. G21	22	X10	
Kempock St. G31	53	Z14	
Kempsthorn Cres. G53	48	P15	
Kempsthorn Path G53	48	P15	
Kempsthorn Rd. G53	48	P15	
Kendal Av., Giff.	62	T18	
Kendal Dr. G12	20	S9	
Kendal Ter. G12	20	S9	
Kendoon Av. G15	6	N6	
Kenilworth Av. G41	50	T16	
Kenilworth Cres., Bear.	7	Q5	
Kenilworth Way, Pais.	45	G16	
Kenmar Gdns., Udd.	56	FF16	
Kenmore Gdns., Bear.	8	S5	
Kenmore Rd., Cumb.	71	PP3	
Kenmore St. G32	38	BB13	
Kenmuir Av. G32	55	DD14	
Kenmuir Rd. G32	55	CC16	
Kenmuirhill Rd. G32	55	CC15	
Kenmure Av., Bish.	10	X7	
Kenmure Cres., Bish.	10	X7	
Kenmure Dr., Bish.	10	X7	
Kenmure Gdns., Bish.	10	X7	
Kenmure Row G22	9	V7	
Kenmure St. G41	51	U14	
Kenmure Way G73	65	Y18	
Kennedar Dr. G51	33	R12	
Kennedy Ct., Giff.	62	T18	
Braidholm Cres.			
Kennedy St. G4	36	W12	
Kennet St. G21	37	Y11	
Kennishead Av. G46	61	R17	
Kennishead Path, Thorn.	61	R17	
Kennishead Pl.			
Kennishead Pl. G46	61	R17	
Kennishead Rd. G46	61	R17	
Kennishead Rd. G53	61	Q18	
Kennisholm Av. G46	61	R17	
Kennisholm Path, Thorn.	61	R18	
Kennisholm Av.			
Kennisholm Pl. G46	61	R17	
Kennoway Dr. G11	33	R11	
Kennoway La. G11	33	R11	
Thornwood Dr.			
Kennyhill Sq. G31	37	Y12	
Kensington Dr., Giff.	62	T19	
Kensington Gate G12	20	T10	
Kensington Rd.			
Kensington Rd. G12	20	T10	
Kent Dr. G73	65	Z17	
Kent Rd. G3	35	U12	
Kent St. G40	36	X13	
Kentallen Rd. G33	39	DD13	
Kentigern Ter., Bish.	23	Y8	
Keppel Dr. G44	52	X16	
Keppoch St. G21	22	W10	
Keppochhill Rd. G22	22	W10	
Kerfield Pl. G15	6	N6	
Kerr St. G40	36	X13	
Kerr St., Barr.	59	L19	
Kerr St., Pais.	30	J13	
Kerrera Pl. G33	39	CC13	
Kerrera Rd. G33	39	CC13	
Kerry Pl. G15	6	N6	
Kerrycroy Av. G42	52	W16	
Kerrycroy Pl. G42	52	W16	
Kerrycroy Av.			
Kerrycroy St. G42	52	W16	
Kerrydale St. G40	53	Y14	
Kerrylamont Av. G42	52	X16	
Kersland La. G12	20	T10	
Kersland St.			
Kersland St. G12	20	T10	
Kessington Dr., Bear.	8	S6	
Kessington Rd., Bear.	8	S6	
Kestral Ct., Clyde.	5	L5	
Kestrel Pl., John.	43	C16	
Kestrel Rd. G13	19	Q9	
Kew Gdns. G12	20	T10	
Ruthven St.			
Kew Gdns., Udd.	57	HH16	
Kew La. G12	20	T10	
Saltoun St.			
Kew Ter. G12	20	T10	
Keyden St. G41	35	U13	
Kibbleston Rd., Kilb.	42	B14	
Kidston St. G5	52	W14	
Kierhill Rd., Cumb.	70	MM3	
Kilbarchan Rd., John.	43	C15	
Kilbarchan St. G5	35	V13	
Bedford St.			
Kilbeg Ter. G46	61	Q18	
Kilberry St. G21	37	Y11	
Kilbirnie St. G5	51	V14	
Kilbowie Ct., Clyde.	5	L6	
Crown Av.			
Kilbowie Rd., Clyde.	5	L5	
Kilbowie Rd., Cumb.	71	PP3	
Kilbrennan Rd., Linw.	28	E13	
Kilbride St. G5	52	W15	
Kilbride Vw., Udd.	57	HH16	
Hamilton Vw.			
Kilburn Gro., Blan.	68	FF19	
Kilburn Pl. G13	18	P9	
Kilchattan Dr. G44	52	W16	
Kilchoan Rd. G33	39	CC11	
Kilcloy Av. G15	6	P6	
Kildale St. G73	52	X16	
Kildale Way G73	52	X16	
Kildary Av. G44	63	V17	
Kildary Rd. G44	63	V17	
Kildermorie Rd. G34	40	EE12	
Kildonan Dr. G11	34	S11	
Kildonan Ter. G51	34	S13	
Copland Rd.			
Kildrostan St. G41	51	U15	
Terregles Av.			
Kildrum Rd., Cumb.	71	PP2	
Kilearn Rd., Pais.	31	L12	
Kilfinan St. G22	21	V8	
Kilkerran Dr. G33	24	AA9	
Killarn Way, Pais.	31	L12	
Killearn Dr., Pais.	48	N14	
Killearn St. G22	21	V10	
Killermont Av., Bear.	8	S7	
Killermont Ct., Bear.	8	S6	
Killermont Meadows, Both.	69	GG19	
Killermont Rd., Bear.	8	S6	
Killermont St. G1	36	W12	
Killermont Vw. G20	8	S7	
Killiegrew Rd. G41	50	T15	
Killin St. G32	54	BB14	
Killoch Av., Pais.	29	H13	
Killoch Dr. G13	18	P8	
Killoch Dr., Barr.	59	M19	
Killoch Rd., Pais.	29	H13	
Kilmailing Rd. G44	63	V17	
Kilmair Pl. G20	20	T9	
Wyndford Rd.			
Kilmaluag Ter. G46	61	Q18	
Kilmany Dr. G32	38	AA13	
Kilmany Gdns. G32	38	AA13	
St. Mark St.			
Kilmardinny Av., Bear.	7	R5	
Kilmardinny Cres., Bear.	7	R5	
Kilmardinny Dr., Bear.	7	R5	
Kilmardinny Gate, Bear.	7	R5	
Kilmardinny Av.			
Kilmardinny Gro., Bear.	7	R5	
Kilmarnock Rd. G43	62	T17	
Kilmartin Pl., Thorn.	61	R18	
Kilmaurs Dr., Giff.	63	U18	
Kilmaurs St. G51	33	R13	
Kilmorie Dr. G73	52	X16	
Kilmory Av., Udd.	57	HH16	
Spindlehowe Rd.			
Kilmuir Cres. G46	61	Q18	
Kilmuir Dr. G46	61	R18	
Kilmuir Rd. G46	61	R18	
Kilmuir Rd., Udd.	57	GG15	
Kilmun La. G20	20	T8	
Kilmun St.			
Kilmun Pl. G20	20	T8	
Kilmun St.			
Kilmun St. G20	20	T8	
Kilnside Rd., Pais.	30	K13	
Kiloran St. G46	61	R18	
Kilpatrick Av., Pais.	45	H15	
Kilpatrick Cres., Pais.	46	J15	
Kiltearn Rd. G33	39	DD12	
Kilvaxter Dr. G46	61	R18	
Kilwynet Way, Pais.	31	L12	
Kimberley St., Dalm.	4	J5	
Kinalty Rd. G44	63	V17	
Kinarvie Cres. G53	48	N16	
Kinarvie Gdns. G53	48	N16	
Kinarvie Rd.			
Kinarvie Pl. G53	48	N16	
Kinarvie Rd. G53	48	N16	
Kinarvie Ter. G53	48	N16	
Kinbuck St. G22	22	W10	
Kincaid Gdns. G72	66	BB17	
Kincardine Cres., Bish.	23	Y8	
Graham Ter.			
Kincardine Dr., Bish.	23	Y8	
Kincardine Pl., Bish.	23	Z8	
Kincardine Sq. G33	39	CC11	
Kincath Av. G73	65	Z18	
Kinclaven Av. G15	6	P6	
Kincraig St. G51	33	Q13	
Kinellan Rd., Bear.	7	R7	
Kinellar Dr. G14	18	P9	
Kinfauns Dr. G15	6	N6	
Kinfauns Ter. G51	34	S13	
Copland Rd.			
King Edward Rd. G13	19	R9	
King George V Bri. G5	35	V13	
King St. G1	36	W13	
King St. G73	53	Y16	
King St., Clyde.	17	M8	
King St., Pais.	30	J13	
Kingarth St. G42	51	V15	
Kinghorn Dr. G44	52	W16	
Kinglas Rd., Bear.	7	Q7	
Kings Cres. G72	66	BB17	
Kings Cres., John.	44	F14	
Kings Cross G31	36	X12	
Kings Dr. G40	52	X14	
Kings Dr., Cumb.	70	NN1	
Kings Inch Rd., Renf.	17	M9	
Kings La. W., Renf.	17	M10	
Bell St.			
Kings Pk. Av. G44	64	W17	
Kings Pk. Rd. G44	51	V16	
Kings Pl. G22	21	V8	
Kingsacre Rd. G44	52	W16	
Kingsbarns Dr. G44	51	V16	
Kingsborough Gdns. G12	20	S10	
Kingsborough Gate G12	20	S10	
Prince Albert Rd.			
Kingsborough Ter. G12	20	S10	
Hyndland Rd.			
Kingsbrae Dr. G44	52	W16	
Kingsbridge Cres. G44	64	W17	
Kingsbridge Dr. G44	64	W17	
Kingsburgh Dr., Pais.	31	L13	
Kingsburn Dr. G73	65	Y17	
Kingsburn Gro. G73	65	Y17	
Kingscliffe Av. G44	64	W17	
Kingscourt Av. G44	64	W17	

Street	Page	Grid
Kingsdale Av. G44	52	W16
Kingsdyke Av. G44	52	W16
Kingsford Av. G44	63	U18
Kingsheath Av. G73	64	X17
Kingshill Dr. G44	64	W17
Kingshouse Av. G44	64	W17
Kingshurst Av. G44	52	W16
Kingsknowe Dr. G73	64	X17
Kingsland Cres. G52	32	P13
Kingsland Dr. G52	32	P13
Kingsley Av. G42	51	V15
Kingsley Ct., Udd.	57	HH16
Kingslynn Dr. G44	64	W17
Kingslynn La. G44	64	W17
Kingslynn Dr.		
Kingsmuir Dr. G73	64	X17
Kingston Bri. G3	35	U13
Kingston Pl., Dalm.	4	J6
Kingston St. G5	35	V13
Kingsway G14	18	P9
Kingsway Ct. G14	18	P9
Kingswood Dr. G44	64	W17
Kingussie Dr. G44	64	W17
Kiniver Dr. G15	6	P7
Kinloch Av. G72	66	BB18
Kinloch Av., Linw.	28	E13
Pentland Dr.		
Kinloch Rd., Renf.	31	L11
Kinloch St. G40	53	Z14
Kinmount Av. G44	51	V16
Kinmount La. G44	51	V16
Kinmount Av.		
Kinnaird Cres., Bear.	8	S6
Kinnaird Dr., Linw.	28	E13
Kinnaird Pl. G64	23	Y8
Kinnear Rd. G40	53	Y14
Kinnell Av. G52	49	Q14
Kinnell Cres. G52	49	Q14
Kinnell Path G52	49	Q14
Kinnell Cres.		
Kinnell Pl. G52	49	R15
Mosspark Dr.		
Kinnell Sq. G52	49	Q14
Kinning St. G5	35	U13
Kinnoul La. G12	20	T10
Dowanhill St.		
Kinpurnie Rd., Pais.	31	M13
Kinross Av. G52	48	P14
Kinsail Dr. G52	32	N13
Kinstone Av. G14	18	P9
Kintessack Pl., Bish.	11	Z7
Kintore Rd. G43	63	U17
Kintra St. G51	34	S13
Kintyre Av., Linw.	28	E13
Kintyre St. G21	37	Y11
Kippen St. G22	22	W9
Kippford St. G32	55	CC14
Kirk La. G43	50	T16
Riverbank St.		
Kirk Pl., Udd.	69	GG17
Kirk Rd., Bear.	7	R5
Kirkaig Av., Renf.	32	N11
Kirkbean Av. G73	65	Y18
Kirkburn Av. G72	66	BB18
Kirkcaldy Rd. G41	50	T15
Kirkconnel Av. G13	18	N9
Kirkconnel Dr. G73	64	X17
Kirkdale Dr. G52	49	R14
Kirkfield Rd., Udd.	69	HH18
Kirkford Rd., Chr.	15	GG7
Bridgeburn Dr.		
Kirkhill Av. G72	66	BB18
Kirkhill Dr. G20	20	T9
Kirkhill Gdns. G72	66	BB18
Kirkhill Gro. G72	66	BB18
Kirkhill Pl. G20	20	T9
Kirkhill Rd., Gart.	27	GG9
Kirkhill Rd., Udd.	57	GG16
Kirkhill Ter. G72	66	BB18
Kirkhope Dr. G15	6	P7
Kirkinner Rd. G32	55	CC14
Kirkintilloch Rd., Bish.	22	X8
Kirkintilloch Rd., Lenz.	13	CC5
Kirkland St. G20	21	U10
Kirklandneuk Rd., Renf.	17	L10
Kirklands Cres., Udd.	69	HH18
Kirklea Av., Pais.	29	H13
Kirklee Circ. G12	20	T10
Kirklee Gdns. G12	20	T9
Bellshaugh Rd.		
Kirklee Gdns. La. G12	20	T9
Bellshaugh Rd.		
Kirklee Pl. G12	20	T10
Kirklee Quad. G12	20	T10
Kirklee Quad. La. G12	20	T10
Kirklee Quad.		
Kirklee Rd. G12	20	T10
Kirklee Ter. G12	20	T10
Kirklee Ter. La. G12	20	T10
Kirklee Ter.		
Kirkliston St. G32	38	AA13
Kirkmuir Av., Renf.	31	L11
Kirkmuir Dr. G73	65	Y18
Kirknewton St. G32	38	BB13
Kirkoswald Dr., Clyde.	5	M6
Kirkoswald Rd. G43	62	T17
Kirkpatrick St. G40	37	Y13
Kirkriggs Av. G73	65	Y17
Kirkriggs Gdns. G73	65	Y17
Kirkriggs Way, Ruth.	65	Y17
Kirkstall Gdns., Bish.	11	Y6
Kirkstonside, Barr.	59	L19
Kirkton Av. G13	18	P9
Kirkton Cres. G13	18	P9
Kirkton Rd. G72	66	BB17
Kirkview Gdns., Udd.	57	GG16
Glencroft Av.		
Kirkville Pl. G15	6	P7
Kirkwall, Cumb.	71	PP1
Kirkwall Av., Blan.	68	FF18
Kirkwell Rd. G44	63	V17
Kirkwood Av., Clyde.	5	M7
Kirkwood Quad., Clyde.	5	M7
Kirkwood Av.		
Kirkwood Rd., Udd.	57	GG15
Newlands Rd.		
Kirkwood St. G51	34	T13
Kirkwood St. G73	53	Y16
Kirn St. G20	20	T8
Kilmun St.		
Kirriemuir Av. G52	49	Q14
Kirriemuir Gdns., Bish.	11	Z7
Kirriemuir Rd., Bish.	11	Z7
Kirtle Dr., Renf.	32	N11
Kirton Av., Barr.	59	L19
Kishorn Pl. G33	39	CC11
Knapdale St. G22	21	V8
Knightsbridge Rd. G13	19	Q9
Knightscliffe Av. G13	19	Q8
Knightswood Cross G13	19	Q8
Knightswood Rd. G13	7	Q7
Knightswood Ter., Blan.	69	GG19
Knock Way, Pais.	31	L12
Knockburnie Rd., Udd.	69	HH18
Knockhall St. G33	39	CC11
Knockhill Dr. G44	51	V16
Knockhill La. G44	51	V16
Mount Annan Dr.		
Knockhill Rd., Renf.	31	L11
Knockside Av., Pais.	46	J16
Knowe Rd., Chr.	26	FF8
Knowe Rd., Pais.	31	L12
Knowe Ter. G22	21	V8
Hillend Rd.		
Knowehead Dr., Udd.	69	GG17
Knowehead Gdns. G41	51	U14
Knowehead Ter.		
Knowehead Gdns., Udd.	69	GG17
Knowehead Ter. G41	51	U14
Knowetap St. G20	21	U8
Knox St., Pais.	45	H14
Kyle Dr., Giff.	62	T18
Kyle Rd., Cumb.	71	PP2
Kyle Sq. G73	65	Y17
Kyle St. G4	36	W11
Kyleakin Gdns., Blan.	68	EE19
Kyleakin Rd. G46	61	Q18
Kyleakin Ter. G46	61	Q18
Kylepark Av., Udd.	68	FF17
Kylepark Cres., Udd.	56	FF16
Kylepark Dr., Udd.	56	FF16
Kylerhea Rd. G46	61	Q18
La Belle Pl. G3	35	U11
Laburnum Gdns., Lenz.	12	BB5
Laburnum Gro.		
Laburnum Gro., Lenz.	12	BB5
Laburnum Pl., John.	44	E16
Laburnum Rd. G41	50	T14
Laburnum Rd., Cumb.	71	QQ3
Lacrosse Ter. G12	21	U10
Lacy St., Pais.	31	L13
Lade Ter. G52	48	P14
Ladeside Dr., John.	43	C15
Ladhope Pl. G13	18	N8
Lady Anne St. G14	18	N9
Lady Isle Cres., Udd.	69	GG17
Lady Jane Gate, Both.	69	GG18
Lady La., Pais.	46	J14
Ladybank Dr. G52	49	R14
Ladyburn St., Pais.	47	L14
Ladyhill Dr., Bail.	56	EE14
Ladykirk Cres. G52	32	P13
Ladykirk Cres., Pais.	46	K14
Ladykirk Dr. G52	32	P13
Ladyloan Av. G15	6	N6
Ladyloan Pl. G15	6	N6
Ladymuir Cres. G53	49	Q15
Ladysmith Av., Kilb.	43	C15
Ladywell St. G4	36	X12
Laggan Rd. G43	63	U17
Laggan Rd., Bish.	11	Y7
Laggan Ter., Renf.	17	L10
Laidlaw Gdns., Udd.	57	GG15
Laidlaw St. G5	35	V13
Laigh Kirk La., Pais.	46	K14
Causeyside St.		
Laigh Possil Rd. G23	21	V8
Balmore Rd.		
Laighcartside St., John.	44	E14
Laighlands Rd. G71	69	HH19
Laighmuir St., Udd.	69	GG17
Laighpark Harbour, Pais.	30	K12
Lainshaw Dr. G45	63	V19
Laird Pl. G40	52	X14
Lairds Gate, Both.	69	GG17
Lairds Hill, Cumb.	70	NN3
Lairg Dr., Blan.	68	FF19
Lamb St. G22	21	V9
Lambhill St. G41	34	T13
Lamerton Dr. G52	32	P13
Lamerton Rd., Cumb.	71	QQ3
Lamington Rd. G52	48	P14
Lamlash Cres. G33	38	BB12
Lammermoor Av. G52	49	Q14
Lammermoor Dr., Cumb.	70	NN4
Lammermuir Dr., Pais.	46	K16
Lamont Rd. G21	23	Y9
Lanark St. G1	36	W13
Lancaster Cres. G12	20	T10
Lancaster Cres. La. G12	20	S9
Clevedon Rd.		
Lancaster Rd., Bish.	11	Y6
Lancaster Ter. G12	20	T10
Westbourne Gdns. W.		
Lancaster Ter. La. G12	20	T10
Westbourne Gdns. W.		
Lancefield Quay G3	35	U12
Lancefield St. G3	35	U12
Landemer Dr. G73	64	X17
Landressy St. G40	52	X14
Lanfine Rd., Pais.	47	L14
Lang Av., Renf.	31	M11
Lang St., Pais.	47	L14
Langa St. G20	21	U8
Langbank St. G5	51	V14
Eglinton St.		
Langbar Cres. G33	39	DD12
Langbar Path G33	39	CC12
Langcraigs Dr., Pais.	58	J17
Langcraigs Ter., Pais.	58	J17
Langcroft Dr. G72	67	CC18
Langcroft Pl. G51	33	Q12

Name		
Langcroft Rd. G51	33	Q12
Langcroft Ter. G51	33	Q12
Langdale Av. G33	24	AA10
Langdale Av., Cumb.	70	MM3
Langdale St. G33	24	AA10
Langford Av. G53	60	P18
Langford Dr. G53	60	P18
Langford Pl. G53	60	P18
Langford Dr.		
Langhill Dr., Cumb.	70	MM2
Langholm Ct., Chr.	15	HH7
Heathfield Av.		
Langholm Dr., Linw.	28	F13
Langlands Av. G51	33	Q12
Langlands Dr. G51	33	Q12
Langlands Path G51	33	R12
Langlands Rd. G51	33	Q12
Langlands Rd. G51	34	S12
Langlea Av. G72	65	Z18
Langlea Gro. G72	66	AA18
Langlea Rd. G72	66	AA18
Langley Av. G13	18	P8
Langmuir Rd., Bail.	41	HH13
Langmuir Way, Bail.	41	HH13
Langmuirhead Rd., Lenz.	24	BB8
Langness Rd. G33	38	BB12
Langrig Rd. G21	23	Y10
Langshot St. G51	34	T13
Langside Av. G41	51	U15
Langside Dr. G43	63	U17
Langside Dr. G78	42	B15
Langside Gdns. G42	51	V16
Langside La. G42	51	V15
Langside Pk. G78	42	B15
Langside Pl. G41	51	U16
Langside Rd. G42	51	V16
Langside Rd., Both.	69	HH19
Langside St., Clyde.	6	N5
Langstile Pl. G52	32	N13
Langstile Rd. G52	32	N13
Langton Cres. G53	49	Q15
Langton Cres., Barr.	59	M19
Langton Gdns., Bail.	55	DD14
Langton Rd. G53	49	Q15
Langtree Av., Giff.	62	S19
Lanrig Pl., Chr.	26	FF8
Lanrig Rd., Chr.	26	FF8
Lansbury Gdns., Pais.	30	J12
Cowdie St.		
Lansdowne Cres. G20	35	U11
Lansdowne Cres. La. G12	21	U10
Great Western Rd.		
Lansdowne Dr., Cumb.	70	NN2
Lanton Dr. G52	32	P13
Lanton Rd. G43	63	U17
Lappin St., Clyde.	17	M8
Larch Av., Bish.	23	Y8
Larch Av., Lenz.	13	CC5
Larch Ct., Cumb.	71	QQ2
Larch Cres., Lenz.	13	CC5
Larch Gro. G67	71	RR2
Larch Pl., John.	44	E16
Larch Rd. G41	50	S14
Larch Rd., Cumb.	71	QQ2
Larches, The, Chr.	15	HH6
Larchfield Av. G14	18	P10
Larchfield Dr. G73	65	Y18
Larchfield Pl. G14	18	P10
Larchfield Rd. G69	15	GG7
Larchfield Rd., Bear.	7	R7
Larchgrove Av. G32	39	CC13
Larchgrove Pl. G32	39	CC12
Larchgrove Rd.		
Larchgrove Rd. G32	39	CC12
Larchwood Ter., Barr.	60	N19
Largie Rd. G43	63	U17
Largo Pl. G51	33	R12
Largs St. G31	37	Y12
Larkfield Rd., Lenz.	13	DD5
Larkfield St. G42	51	V15
Cathcart Rd.		
Larkin Gdns., Pais.	30	J12
Lasswade St. G14	18	N9
Latherton Dr. G20	20	T9
Latherton Pl. G20	20	T9
Latherton Dr.		
Latimer Gdns. G52	48	P14
Lauder Dr. G73	65	Z17
Lauder Dr., Linw.	28	E13
Lauder Gdns., Blan.	68	FF19
Lauder St. G5	51	V14
Eglinton St.		
Lauderdale Gdns. G12	20	S10
Laundry La. G33	25	CC9
Laurel Av., Dalm.	4	J6
Laurel Av., Lenz.	13	CC5
Laurel Bk. Rd., Chr.	26	EE8
Laurel Gdns., Udd.	57	GG16
Laurel Pl. G11	34	S11
Laurel St. G11	34	S11
Laurel Wk. G73	65	Z18
Laurel Way, Barr.	59	L18
Graham St.		
Laurence Dr., Bear.	7	Q5
Laurie Ct., Udd.	57	HH16
Hillcrest Rd.		
Laurieston La. G51	34	T13
Paisley Rd.		
Laurieston Rd. G5	36	W13
Laurieston Way G73	65	Y18
Laverock Ter., Chr.	15	GG7
Laverockhall St. G21	22	X10
Law St. G40	37	Y13
Lawers Rd. G43	62	S17
Lawers Rd., Bear.	7	Q5
Lawers Rd., Renf.	31	M11
Lawhill Av. G44	64	W18
Lawmoor Av. G5	52	W14
Lawmoor La. G5	36	W13
Ballater St.		
Lawmoor Pl. G5	52	W15
Lawmoor Av.		
Lawmoor Rd. G5	52	W14
Lawmoor St. G5	52	W14
Lawn St., Pais.	30	K13
Lawrence Av., Giff.	62	T19
Lawrence St. G11	34	T11
Lawrie St. G11	34	S11
Lawside Dr. G53	49	Q16
Laxford Av. G44	63	V18
Laxton Dr., Lenz.	13	DD6
Leabank Av., Pais.	46	K16
Leadburn Rd. G21	23	Z10
Rye Rd.		
Leadburn St. G32	38	AA12
Leader St. G33	37	Z11
Leander Cres., Renf.	32	N11
Leckethill St. G21	22	X10
Springburn Rd.		
Leckie St. G43	50	T16
Ledaig Pl. G31	37	Z12
Ledaig St. G31	37	Z12
Ledard Rd. G42	51	U16
Ledcameroch Cres., Bear.	7	Q6
Ledcameroch Pk., Bear.	7	Q6
Ledcameroch Rd.		
Ledcameroch Rd., Bear.	7	Q6
Ledgowan Pl. G20	20	T8
Ledi Dr., Bear.	7	Q5
Ledi Rd. G43	62	T17
Ledmore Dr. G15	9	N6
Lednock Rd. G33	25	CC9
Lednock Rd. G52	32	P13
Lee Av. G33	38	AA11
Lee Cres., Bish.	22	X8
Leebank Dr. G44	63	U19
Leefield Av. G44	63	U19
Leehill Rd. G21	22	X8
Leeside Rd. G21	22	X8
Leewood Dr. G44	63	U19
Leicester Av. G12	20	S9
Leighton St. G20	21	U9
Leitchland Rd. G78	44	F16
Leitchs Ct. G1	36	W13
Trongate		
Leith St. G33	37	Z12
Leithland Av. G53	48	P16
Leithland Rd. G53	48	P15
Lendale La., Bish.	11	Y6
Lendel Pl. G51	35	U13
Paisley Rd. W.		
Lenhall Dr. G45	64	X19
Lenhall Ter. G45	64	X19
Lennox Av. G14	19	Q10
Lennox Cres., Bish.	22	X8
Lennox Dr., Bear.	7	R5
Lennox La. W. G14	19	Q10
Lennox Av.		
Lennox Pl. G14	19	Q10
Scotstoun St.		
Lennox Pl., Dalm.	4	K6
Swindon St.		
Lennox Rd., Cumb.	70	NN3
Lennox St. G20	20	T8
Maryhill Rd.		
Lennox Ter., Pais.	31	L12
Lennox Vw., Clyde.	5	L6
Granville St.		
Lentran St. G34	40	FF12
Leny St. G20	21	V10
Lenzie Dr. G21	22	X9
Lenzie Rd. G33	25	CC9
Lenzie St. G21	22	X9
Lenziemill Rd., Cumb.	71	PP4
Lerwick St. G4	35	V11
Dobbies Ln.		
Leslie Rd. G41	51	U15
Leslie St. G41	51	U14
Lesmuir Dr. G14	18	P9
Lesmuir Pl. G14	18	N9
Letham Ct. G43	63	U17
Letham Dr. G43	63	U17
Letham Dr. G64	23	Z8
Letham Gra., Cumb.	70	NN2
Lethamhill Cres. G33	38	AA11
Lethamhill Pl. G33	38	AA11
Lethamhill Rd. G33	38	AA11
Letherby Dr. G44	51	V16
Lethington Av. G41	51	U16
Letterfearn Dr. G23	9	U7
Letterickhills Cres. G72	67	DD18
Lettoch St. G51	34	S13
Leven Av., Bish.	11	Y7
Leven Ct., Barr.	59	L17
Leven Dr., Bear.	7	R6
Leven Sq., Renf.	17	L10
Leven St. G41	51	U14
Leven Vw., Clyde.	5	L6
Radnor St.		
Leven Way, Pais.	45	G15
Levern Cres., Barr.	59	L19
Levern Gdns., Barr.	59	L18
Chappel St.		
Levernside Av., Barr.	59	L19
Levernside Cres. G53	48	P15
Levernside Rd. G53	48	P15
Lewis Av., Renf.	31	M11
Lewis Ct., Kilb.	42	B15
Lewis Cres., Old K.	4	J5
Lewis Gdns., Bear.	6	P5
Lewis Gdns., Old K.	4	J5
Lewis Cres.		
Lewis Gro., Old K.	4	J5
Lewiston Dr. G23	8	T7
Lewiston Rd.		
Lewiston Pl. G23	8	T7
Lewiston Rd.		
Lewiston Rd. G23	8	T7
Lexwell Av., John.	44	F14
Lexwell Rd., Pais.	45	G15
Leyden Ct. G20	21	U9
Leyden St.		
Leyden Gdns. G20	21	U9
Leyden St.		
Leyden St. G20	21	U9
Leys, The, Bish.	11	Y7
Liberton St. G33	37	Z12
Liberty Av., Bail.	41	HH13
Libo Av. G53	49	Q15
Liddale Way G73	52	X16
Liddel Rd., Cumb.	70	NN3
Liddell St. G32	55	CC15
Liddesdale Av., Pais.	44	F16

Liddesdale Pl. G22	22	W8
Liddesdale Sq.		
Liddesdale Rd. G22	22	W8
Liddesdale Sq. G22	22	W8
Liddesdale Ter. G22	22	X8
Liff Gdns., Bish.	23	Z8
Liff Pl. G34	40	FF11
Lightburn Pl. G32	38	BB12
Lightburn Rd. G72	67	CC18
Lilac Av., Dalm.	4	K6
Lilac Gdns., Bish.	23	Y8
Lilac Pl., John.	44	E15
Lily St. G40	53	Y14
Lilybank Av. G72	67	CC18
Lilybank Av., Chr.	26	FF8
Lilybank Gdns. G12	34	T11
Lilybank Gdns. La. G12	20	T10
Great George St.		
Lilybank Ter. G12	20	T10
Great George St.		
Lilybank Ter. La. G12	20	T10
Great George St.		
Lilyburn Pl. G15	6	N5
Lime Gro., Blan.	68	FF19
Lime Gro., Lenz.	13	CC5
Lime St. G14	19	Q10
Limecraigs Cres., Pais.	46	J16
Limecraigs Rd., Pais.	46	J16
Limeside Av. G73	53	Y16
Limeside Gdns. G73	53	Z16
Calderwood Rd.		
Limetree Av., Udd.	57	HH16
Limetree Dr., Dalm.	5	L6
Limeview Av., Pais.	45	H16
Limeview Cres., Pais.	45	H16
Limeview Rd., Pais.	45	H16
Limeview Av.		
Limeview Way, Pais.	45	H16
Limeview Av.		
Linacre Dr. G32	39	CC13
Linacre Gdns. G32	39	CC13
Linbank Av. G53	49	Q16
Linburn Pl. G52	32	P13
Linburn Rd. G52	32	N12
Linclive Link Rd., Linw.	29	G13
Linclive Ter., Linw.	28	F13
Lincoln Av. G13	18	P9
Lincoln Av., Udd.	57	GG15
Lindams, Udd.	69	GG17
Linden Dr., Clyde.	5	L5
Linden St. G13	19	R8
Lindores Av. G73	53	Y16
Lindores St. G42	51	V16
Somerville Dr.		
Lindrick Dr. G23	9	U7
Lindsay Dr. G12	20	S9
Lindsay Pl. G12	20	S9
Lindsay Pl., Lenz.	13	CC6
Lindsaybeg Rd., Lenz.	13	DD6
Linfern Rd. G12	20	T10
Links Rd. G32	55	CC14
Links Rd. G44	64	W18
Linkwood Av. G15	6	N6
Kinfauns Dr.		
Linkwood Cres. G15	6	N6
Linkwood Dr. G15	6	N6
Linkwood Pl. G15	6	N6
Kinfauns Dr.		
Linlithgow Gdns. G32	39	CC13
Linn Cres., Pais.	46	J16
Linn Dr. G44	63	U18
Linnet Av., John.	43	C16
Linnhe Av. G44	63	V18
Linnhe Av., Bish.	11	Y7
Linnhe Dr., Barr.	59	L17
Linnhe Pl., Blan.	68	FF19
Linnhead Dr. G53	60	P17
Linnhead Pl. G14	18	P10
Linnpark Av. G44	63	U19
Linnpark Ct. G44	63	U19
Linnpark Gdns., John.	44	E15
Lunn Brae		
Linside Av., Pais.	47	L14
Lintfield Ln., Udd.	69	HH17
Myers Cres.		
Linthaugh Rd. G53	48	P15
Linthouse Bldgs. G51	33	R12
Lintlaw, Blan.	68	FF19
Lintlaw Dr. G52	33	Q13
Linton St. G33	38	AA12
Linwell Cres., Pais.	46	J16
Linwood Ct. G44	63	V17
Bowling Grn. Rd.		
Linwood Moss Rd., Linw.	28	F13
Linwood Rd., John.	28	F13
Linwood Ter. G12	21	U10
Glasgow St.		
Lismore Av., Renf.	31	M11
Lismore Dr., Pais.	46	J16
Lismore Gdns., John.	43	C15
Lismore Pl., Chr.	15	HH6
Altnacreag Gdns.		
Lismore Rd. G12	20	S10
Lister Rd. G52	32	P12
Lister St. G4	36	W11
Lithgow Cres., Pais.	47	L15
Little Dovehill G1	36	W13
Little Holm, Dalm.	4	K6
Little St. G3	35	U12
Littlehill St. G21	22	X10
Edgefauld Rd.		
Littleton Dr. G23	8	T7
Rothes Dr.		
Livingstone Av. G52	32	P12
Livingstone Cres., Blan.	68	FF19
Livingstone St. G21	22	W10
Keppochhill Rd.		
Livingstone St., Clyde.	5	M7
Lloyd Av. G32	54	BB15
Lloyd St. G31	37	Y12
Lloyd St. G73	53	Y15
Loanbank Quad. G51	34	S12
Loancroft Av., Bail.	56	FF14
Loancroft Gdns., Udd.	69	GG17
Loancroft Pl., Bail.	56	EE14
Loanend Cotts. G72	67	DD19
Loanfoot Av. G13	18	P8
Loanhead Av., Linw.	28	E13
Loanhead Av., Renf.	17	M10
Loanhead La., Linw.	28	E13
Loanhead Rd.		
Loanhead Rd., Linw.	28	E13
Loanhead St. G32	38	AA12
Lobnitz Av., Renf.	17	M10
Loch Achray St. G32	55	CC14
Loch Katrine St. G32	55	CC14
Loch Laidon St. G32	55	CC14
Loch Voil St. G32	55	CC14
Lochaber Dr. G73	65	Z18
Lochaber Rd., Bear.	8	S7
Lochaline Av. G78	45	H15
Lochaline Dr. G44	63	V18
Lochalsh Dr., Pais.	45	H15
Lochalsh Pl., Blan.	68	EE19
Lochar Cres. G53	49	Q15
Lochard Dr., Pais.	45	H15
Lochay St. G32	55	CC14
Lochbrae Dr. G73	65	Z18
Lochbridge Rd. G33	40	EE12
Lochbroom Dr., Pais.	45	H15
Lochburn Cres. G20	21	U8
Lochburn Gro. G20	21	U8
Cadder Rd.		
Lochburn Pas. G20	21	U8
Lochburn Rd. G20	20	T9
Lochdochart Path G34	40	FF12
Lochdochart Rd.		
Lochdochart Rd. G34	40	FF12
Lochearn Cres., Pais.	45	H15
Lochearnhead Rd. G33	25	CC9
Lochend Av., Gart.	27	GG8
Lochend Cres., Bear.	7	Q6
Lochend Dr., Bear.	7	Q6
Lochend Rd. G34	40	EE11
Lochend Rd., Bear.	7	R6
Lochend Rd., Gart.	27	GG8
Locher Rd., Kilb.	42	A14
Lochfauld Rd. G23	9	V7
Lochfield Cres., Pais.	46	K15
Lochfield Dr., Pais.	47	L15
Lochfield Rd., Pais.	46	K15
Lochgilp St. G20	20	T8
Lochgoin Av. G15	6	N6
Lochgreen St. G33	24	AA10
Lochhead Av., Linw.	28	E13
Lochiel La. G73	65	Z18
Lochiel Rd., Thorn.	61	R18
Lochinver Cres., Pais.	45	H15
Lochinver Dr. G44	63	V18
Lochinver Gro. G72	67	CC17
Andrew Sillars Av.		
Lochlea Av., Clyde.	5	M6
Lochlea Rd. G43	62	T17
Lochlea Rd., Cumb.	71	QQ2
Lochleven La. G42	51	V16
Battlefield Rd.		
Lochleven Rd. G42	51	V16
Lochlibo Av. G13	18	N9
Lochlibo Cres., Barr.	59	L19
Lochlibo Rd., Barr.	59	L19
Lochlibo Ter., Barr.	59	L19
Lochmaben Rd. G52	48	N14
Lochmaddy Av. G44	63	V18
Lochside, Bear.	7	R6
Drymen Rd.		
Lochside, Gart.	27	GG9
Lochside St. G41	51	U15
Minard Rd.		
Lochview Cotts., Gart.	27	GG10
Lochview Cres. G33	24	AA10
Lochview Dr. G33	24	AA10
Lochview Gdns. G33	24	AA10
Lochview Pl. G33	24	AA10
Lochview Rd., Bear.	7	R6
Lochview Ter., Gart.	27	GG9
Lochwood St. G33	38	AA11
Lochy Av., Renf.	32	N11
Lochy Gdns., Bish.	11	Y7
Lockerbie Av. G43	63	U17
Lockhart Av. G72	67	CC17
Lockhart Dr. G72	67	CC17
Lockhart St. G21	37	Y11
Locksley Av. G13	19	Q8
Locksley Rd., Pais.	45	G15
Logan Dr., Cumb.	70	MM2
Logan Dr., Pais.	30	J13
Logan St. G5	52	W15
Logan Twr. G72	67	DD18
Claude Av.		
Loganswell Dr. G46	61	Q19
Loganswell Gdns. G46	61	R19
Loganswell Pl. G46	61	R19
Loganswell Rd. G46	61	R19
Logie St. G51	34	S12
Lomax St. G33	37	Z12
Lomond Av., Renf.	31	L11
Lomond Ct., Barr.	59	M19
Lomond Cres., Pais.	46	J16
Lomond Dr., Barr.	59	L18
Lomond Dr., Udd.	69	HH18
Lomond Gdns., John.	44	F15
Lomond Pl. G33	25	CC10
Lomond Rd., Bear.	7	R7
Lomond Rd., Bish.	10	X6
Lomond Rd., Lenz.	13	CC5
Lomond Rd., Udd.	57	GG15
Lomond St. G22	21	V9
Lomond Vw., Clyde.	5	L6
Granville St.		
London Arc. G1	36	W13
London Rd.		
London La. G1	36	W13
London Rd.		
London Rd. G1	36	W13
London St., Renf.	17	M9
Long Row, Bail.	40	FF13
Longay Pl. G22	22	W8
Longay St. G22	22	W8
Longcroft Dr., Renf.	17	M10
Longdale Rd., Chr.	15	GG7
Longden St., Clyde.	17	M8
Longford St. G33	37	Z12
Longlee, Bail.	56	EE14
Longmeadow, John.	43	C15
Longstone Rd. G33	38	BB12

Longwill Ter., Cumb.	71	PP2	Lye Brae, Cumb.	71	PP3	Mainhill Dr., Bail.	40	FF13
Lonmay Rd. G33	39	CC12	Lyle Ter., Pais.	46	K15	Mainhill Pl., Bail.	40	FF13
Lonsdale Av., Giff.	62	T18	Lymburn St. G3	34	T12	Mainhill Rd., Bail.	41	GG13
Loom St. G40	36	X13	Lyndale Pl. G20	20	T8	Mains Av., Giff.	62	S19
Stevenson St.			Lyndale Rd. G20	20	T8	Mains Dr., Renf.	4	J7
Loom Wk., Kilb.	42	B14	Lyndhurst Gdns. G20	21	U10	Mains Hill, Renf.	4	J7
Shuttle St.			Lyne Cft., Bish.	11	Y6	Mains Holm, Renf.	4	J7
Lora Dr. G52	49	R14	Lyne Dr. G23	9	U7	Mains River, Renf.	4	J7
Loretto Pl. G33	38	AA12	Lynedoch Cres. G3	35	U11	Mains Wd., Renf.	4	J7
Loretto St. G33	38	AA12	Lynedoch Pl. G3	35	U11	Mainscroft, Renf.	4	J7
Lorne Av., Chr.	26	FF8	Lynedoch St. G3	35	U11	Mair St. G51	35	U13
Lorne Cres., Bish.	11	Z7	Lynedoch Ter. G3	35	U11	Maitland Pl., Renf.	31	L11
Lorne Dr., Linw.	28	E13	Lynn Gdns. G12	20	T10	Maitland St. G4	35	V11
Lorne Rd. G52	32	N12	*Great George St.*			Malcolm St. G31	37	Z13
Lorne St. G51	34	T13	Lynn Wk., Udd.	69	HH17	Malin Pl. G33	38	AA12
Lorne Ter. G72	66	AA18	*Flax Rd.*			Mallaig Path G51	33	Q12
Lorraine Gdns. G12	20	T10	Lynnhurst, Udd.	57	GG16	Mallaig Pl. G51	33	Q12
Kensington Rd.			Lynton Av., Giff.	62	S19	Mallaig Rd. G51	33	Q12
Lorraine Rd. G12	20	T10	Lyon Cross Av., Barr.	59	M19	Mallard Rd., Clyde.	5	L5
Loskin Dr. G22	21	V8	Lyon Rd., Pais.	45	G15	Malloch Cres., John.	44	E15
Lossie Cres., Renf.	32	N11	Lyoncross Cres., Barr.	59	M18	Malloch St. G20	21	U9
Lossie St. G33	37	Z11	Lyoncross Rd. G53	48	P15	Malta St., Clyde.	17	M8
Lothian Cres., Pais.	46	J15	Lytham Dr. G23	9	U7	Maltbarns St. G20	21	V10
Lothian Gdns. G20	21	U10	Lytham Meadows, Both.	69	GG19	Malvern Ct. G31	37	Y13
Lothian St. G52	32	N12				Malvern Way, Pais.	30	J12
Loudon Gdns., John.	44	E14				Mambeg Dr. G51	33	R12
Loudon Rd. G33	24	BB9	Macbeth Pl. G31	53	Z14	Mamore Pl. G43	62	T17
Loudon Ter. G12	20	T10	*Macbeth St.*			Mamore St. G43	62	T17
Observatory Rd.			Macbeth St. G31	53	Z14	Manchester Dr. G12	20	S9
Lounsdale Cres., Pais.	45	H15	Macdonald St. G73	53	Y16	Manitoba Pl. G31	37	Y13
Lounsdale Dr., Pais.	45	H15	*Greenhill Rd.*			*Janefield St.*		
Lounsdale Pl. G14	18	P10	Macdougal St. G43	50	T16	Mannering Ct. G41	50	T16
Lounsdale Rd., Pais.	45	H15	Macdowall St., John.	43	D14	*Pollokshaws Rd.*		
Lourdes Av. G52	49	Q14	Macdowall St., Pais.	30	J13	Mannering Rd. G41	50	T16
Lovat Pl. G73	65	Z18	Macduff Pl. G31	53	Z14	Mannering Rd., Pais.	45	G16
Lovat St. G4	36	W11	Macduff St. G31	53	Z14	Mannofield, Bear.	7	Q6
Love St., Pais.	30	K13	Mace Rd. G13	7	Q7	*Chesters Rd.*		
Low Barholm, Kilb.	42	B15	Macfarlane Rd., Bear.	7	R7	Manor Rd. G14	19	R10
Low Cres., Clyde.	18	N8	Machrie Dr. G45	64	X18	Manor Rd. G15	6	N7
Low Parksail, Renf.	16	J8	Machrie Rd. G45	64	X18	Manor Rd., Gart.	27	GG9
Low Rd., Pais.	46	J14	Machrie St. G45	64	X18	Manor Rd., Pais.	45	G15
Lower Bourtree Dr. G73	65	Z18	Mackean St., Pais.	30	J13	Manor Way G73	65	Y18
Lower English Bldgs.	51	V14	Mackeith St. G40	52	X14	Manse Av., Bear.	7	R5
G42			Mackenchnie St. G51	34	S12	Manse Av., Both.	69	HH19
Lower Millgate, Udd.	57	GG16	Mackenzie Dr., John.	42	B16	Manse Brae G44	63	V17
Lowndes La., Pais.	30	K13	Mackie St. G4	22	W10	Manse St., Barr.	59	M18
New Sneddon St.			*Borron St.*			Manse Rd. G32	55	CC14
Lowndes St., Barr.	59	M19	Mackiesmill Rd., John.	44	F16	Manse Rd., Bail.	41	GG13
Lowther Ter. G12	20	T10	Mackinlay St. G5	51	V14	Manse Rd., Bear.	7	R5
Loyne Dr., Renf.	32	N11	Maclay Av., Kilb.	42	B15	Manse St., Renf.	17	M10
Morriston Cres.			Maclean St. G41	35	U13	Mansefield Av. G72	66	BB18
Luath St. G51	34	S12	Maclean St. G51	34	T13	Mansefield Dr., Udd.	69	HH17
Lubas Av. G42	52	W16	Maclean St., Clyde.	18	N8	Mansefield St. G11	34	T11
Lubas Pl. G42	52	W16	*Wood Quad.*			Mansel St. G21	22	X9
Lubnaig Rd. G43	63	U17	Maclehose Rd., Cumb.	71	QQ2	Mansewood Rd. G43	62	S17
Luckingsford Av., Renf.	16	J8	Maclellan St. G41	34	T13	Mansfield Rd. G52	32	N12
Luckingsford Dr., Renf.	16	J8	Madison Av. G44	63	V17	Mansion Ct. G72	66	BB17
Luckingsford Rd., Renf.	16	J8	Madison La. G44	63	V17	Mansion St. G22	22	W9
Lucy Brae, Udd.	57	GG16	*Carmunnock Rd.*			Mansion St. G72	66	BB17
Ludovic Sq., John.	43	D14	Madras Pl. G40	52	X14	Mansionhouse Av. G32	55	CC16
Luffness Gdns. G32	54	BB15	*Madras St.*			Mansionhouse Dr. G32	39	CC13
Lugar Dr. G52	49	R14	Madras St. G40	52	X14	Mansionhouse Gdns.	51	U16
Lugar Pl. G44	64	X17	Mafeking St. G51	34	S13	G41		
Luggiebank Pl., Bail.	57	HH14	Magdalen Way, Pais.	44	F16	*Mansionhouse Rd.*		
Luing Rd. G52	33	R13	Magnus Cres. G44	63	V18	Mansionhouse Gro. G32	55	DD14
Lumloch St. G21	23	Y10	Mahon Ct., Chr.	15	GG7	Mansionhouse Rd. G32	55	DD14
Lumsden La. G3	34	T12	Maida St. G43	50	S16	Mansionhouse Rd. G41	51	U16
Lumsden St.			Maidland Rd. G53	49	Q16	Mansionhouse Rd. G42	51	U16
Lumsden St. G3	34	T12	Mailerbeg Gdns., Chr.	15	GG6	Mansionhouse Rd., Pais.	31	L13
Lunan Dr., Bish.	23	Z8	Mailing Av., Bish.	11	Y7	Maple Dr., Dalm.	4	K5
Lunan Pl. G51	33	R12	Main Rd., John.	44	F14	Maple Dr., John.	44	E16
Luncarty Pl. G32	54	BB14	Main Rd., Pais.	46	J14	Maple Dr., Lenz.	12	BB5
Luncarty St. G32	54	BB14	Main St. G40	52	X14	Maple Rd. G41	50	S14
Lunderston Dr. G53	48	P16	Main St. G72	66	BB17	Mar Gdns. G73	65	Z18
Lundie Gdns., Bish.	23	Z8	Main St. G73	53	Y16	March La. G41	51	U15
Lundie St. G32	54	AA14	Main St., Bail.	56	EE14	*Nithsdale Dr.*		
Lunn Brae, John.	43	D15	Main St., Barr.	59	L19	March St. G41	51	U15
Luss Rd. G51	33	R12	Main St., Both.	69	HH19	Marchfield, Bish.	10	X6
Lusset Vw., Clyde.	5	L6	Main St., Chr.	14	FF7	Marchfield Av., Pais.	30	J12
Radnor St.			Main St., Cumb.	71	PP1	Marchglen Pl. G51	33	Q12
Lusshill Ter., Udd.	56	EE15	Main St., Thorn.	61	R18	*Mallaig Rd.*		
Lyall Pl. G21	22	W10	Main St., Udd.	69	GG17	Marchmont Gdns., Bish.	10	X6
Keppochhill Rd.			Mainhead Ter., Cumb.	71	PP1	Marchmont Ter. G12	20	T10
Lyall St. G21	22	W10	*Roadside*			*Observatory Rd.*		
Lybster Cres. G73	65	Z18	Mainhill Av., Bail.	40	FF13	Maree Dr. G52	49	R14

Name	No.	Grid
Maree Gdns., Bish.	11	Y7
Maree Rd., Pais.	45	H15
Marfield St. G32	38	AA13
Margaret St. G1	36	W12
Martha St.		
Margarette Bldgs. G44	63	V17
Clarkston Rd.		
Marguerite Av., Lenz.	13	CC5
Marguerite Dr., Lenz.	13	CC5
Marguerite Gdns., Lenz.	13	CC5
Marguerite Gdns., Udd.	69	HH18
Marguerite Gro., Lenz.	13	CC5
Marine Cres. G51	35	U13
Marine Gdns. G51	35	U13
Mariscat Rd. G41	51	U15
Marjory Dr., Pais.	31	L12
Marjory Rd., Renf.	31	L11
Market St. G40	36	X13
Markinch St. G5	35	V13
West St.		
Marlborough Av. G11	19	R10
Marlinford Rd., Renf.	18	P10
Marlow St. G41	51	U14
Marlow Ter. G41	35	U13
Seaward St.		
Marmion Pl., Cumb.	70	NN4
Marmion Rd., Cumb.	70	NN4
Marmion Rd., Pais.	45	G16
Marmion St. G20	21	U10
Marne St. G31	37	Y12
Marnock Ter., Pais.	47	L15
Marnock Way, Chr.	15	GG7
Braeside Av.		
Marr St. G51	34	S12
Marshalls La., Pais.	46	K14
Mart St. G1	36	W13
Martha St. G1	36	W12
Martin Cres., Bail.	40	FF13
Martin St. G40	52	X14
Martlet Dr., John.	43	C16
Martyr St. G4	36	X12
Martyrs Pl. G64	23	Y8
Marwick St. G31	37	Y12
Marwood Av., Chr.	14	EE5
Mary St. G4	35	V11
Mary St., John.	44	E14
Mary St., Pais.	46	K15
Maryhill Rd., Bear.	8	S7
Maryland Dr. G52	33	R13
Maryland Gdns. G52	33	R13
Marys La., Renf.	17	M10
Maryston Pl. G33	37	Z11
Maryston St. G33	37	Z11
Maryview Gdns., Udd.	56	FF15
Edinburgh Rd.		
Maryville Av., Giff.	62	T19
Maryville Vw., Udd.	56	FF15
Marywood Sq. G41	51	U15
Masonfield Av., Cumb.	70	MM3
Masterton St. G21	22	W10
Mathieson La. G5	52	W14
Mathieson St.		
Mathieson Rd. G73	53	Z15
Mathieson St. G5	52	W14
Mathieson St., Pais.	31	L13
Matilda Rd. G41	51	U14
Mauchline St. G5	51	V14
Maukinfauld Ct. G31	54	AA14
Maukinfauld Rd. G32	54	AA14
Mauldslie St. G40	53	Y14
Maule Dr. G11	34	S11
Mavis Bk., Bish.	22	X8
Mavisbank Gdns. G51	35	U13
Mavisbank Rd. G51	34	S12
Govan Rd.		
Mavisbank Ter., Pais.	46	K14
Maxton Av., Barr.	59	L18
Maxton Gro., Barr.	59	L18
Maxton Ter. G72	66	AA18
Maxwell Av. G41	51	U14
Maxwell Av., Bail.	56	EE14
Maxwell Av., Bear.	7	R7
Maxwell Dr. G41	50	T14
Maxwell Dr., Bail.	40	EE13
Maxwell Gdns. G41	50	T14
Maxwell Gro. G41	50	T14
Maxwell Oval G41	51	U14
Maxwell Pl. G41	51	V14
Maxwell Rd. G41	51	U14
Maxwell Sq. G41	51	U14
Maxwell St. G1	36	W13
Maxwell St., Bail.	56	EE14
Maxwell St., Dalm.	4	K6
Maxwell St., Pais.	30	K13
Maxwellton Rd. G78	45	H14
Maxwellton St., Pais.	46	J14
Maxwelton Rd. G33	37	Z11
May Rd., Pais.	46	K16
May Ter. G42	51	V16
Prospecthill Rd.		
May Ter., Giff.	62	T18
Maybank La. G42	51	V15
Victoria Rd.		
Maybank St. G42	51	V15
Mayberry Cres. G32	39	CC13
Mayberry Gdns. G32	39	CC13
Maybole St. G53	60	N17
Mayfield St. G20	21	U9
McAlpine St. G2	35	V13
McArthur St. G43	50	T16
Pleasance St.		
McArthur St., Clyde.	17	M9
McAslin Ct. G4	36	W12
McAslin St. G4	36	X12
McCallum Av. G73	53	Y16
McClue Av., Renf.	17	L10
McClue Rd., Renf.	17	L10
McCracken Av., Renf.	31	L11
McCreery St., Clyde.	17	M8
McCulloch St. G41	51	U14
McDonald Av., John.	43	D15
McDonald Cres., Clyde.	17	M8
McEwan St. G31	37	Z13
McFarlane St. G4	36	X13
McFarlane St., Pais.	30	J12
McGhee St., Clyde.	5	L6
McGown St., Pais.	30	J13
McGregor Av., Renf.	31	L11
Porterfield Rd.		
McGregor Rd., Cumb.	70	NN3
McGregor St. G51	33	R13
McGregor St., Clyde.	17	M8
McIntosh Ct. G31	36	X12
McIntosh St.		
McIntosh St. G31	36	X12
McIntyre Pl., Pais.	46	J15
McIntyre St. G3	35	U12
McIntyre Ter. G72	66	BB17
McIver St. G72	67	CC17
McKay Cres., John.	44	E15
McKenzie Av., Clyde.	5	L6
McKenzie St., Pais.	30	J13
McKerrel St., Pais.	31	L13
McLaren Av., Renf.	31	M11
Newmains Rd.		
McLaurin Cres., John.	43	C15
McLean Pl., Pais.	30	J12
McLean Sq. G51	34	T13
McLean St., Clyde.	18	N8
Wood Quad.		
McLennan St. G42	51	V16
McLeod St. G4	36	X12
McNair St. G32	38	BB13
McNeil St. G5	52	W14
McNeill Av., Clyde.	6	N7
McPhail St. G40	52	X14
McPhater St. G4	35	V11
Dunblane St.		
McPherson Dr., Udd.	69	HH18
Wordsworth Way		
McPherson St. G1	36	W13
High St.		
McTaggart Rd., Cumb.	70	NN4
Meadow La., Renf.	17	M9
Meadow Rd. G11	34	S11
Meadow Vw., Cumb.	71	QQ2
Meadowbank La., Udd.	69	GG17
Meadowburn, Bish.	11	Y6
Meadowburn Av. G66	13	DD5
Meadowhead Av., Chr.	15	GG7
Meadowpark St. G31	37	Y12
Meadowside Av., John.	44	F15
Meadowside St. G11	34	S11
Meadowside St., Renf.	17	M9
Meadowwell St. G32	38	BB13
Meadside Av. G78	42	B14
Meadside Rd., Kilb.	42	B14
Mears Way, Bish.	11	Z7
Medlar Rd., Cumb.	71	QQ3
Medwin St. G72	67	DD17
Mill Rd.		
Medwyn St. G14	19	Q10
Meek Pl. G72	66	BB17
Meetinghouse La., Pais.	30	K13
Moss St.		
Megan Gate G40	52	X14
Megan St.		
Megan St. G40	52	X14
Meikle Av., Renf.	31	M11
Meikle Rd. G53	49	Q16
Meiklerig Cres. G53	49	Q16
Meikleriggs Dr., Pais.	45	H15
Meiklewood Rd. G51	33	Q13
Melbourne Av., Dalm.	4	J5
Melbourne Ct., Giff.	62	T18
Melbourne St. G31	36	X13
Meldon Pl. G51	33	R12
Meldrum Gdns. G41	50	T15
Meldrum St., Clyde.	18	N8
Melford Av., Giff.	62	T19
Melford Way, Pais.	31	L12
Knock Way		
Melfort Av. G41	50	S14
Melfort Av., Clyde.	5	L6
Melfort Gdns., John.	43	C15
Milliken Pk. Rd.		
Mellerstain Dr. G14	18	N9
Melness Pl. G51	33	Q12
Mallaig Rd.		
Melrose Av. G73	53	Y16
Melrose Av., Bail.	41	GG13
Melrose Av., Linw.	28	E13
Melrose Av., Pais.	45	H15
Melrose Ct. G73	53	Y16
Dunard Rd.		
Melrose Gdns. G20	21	U10
Melrose Gdns., Udd.	57	GG15
Lincoln Av.		
Melrose Pl., Blan.	68	FF19
Melrose St. G4	35	V11
Queens Cres.		
Melvaig Pl. G20	20	T9
Melvick Pl. G51	33	Q12
Mallaig Rd.		
Melville Ct. G1	36	W12
Brunswick St.		
Melville Gdns., Bish.	11	Y7
Melville St. G41	51	U14
Memel St. G21	22	X9
Memus Av. G52	49	Q14
Mennock Dr., Bish.	11	Y6
Menock Rd. G44	63	V17
Menteith Av., Bish.	11	Y7
Menteith Dr. G73	65	Z19
Menteith Pl. G73	65	Z19
Menzies Dr. G21	23	Y9
Menzies Pl. G21	23	Y9
Menzies Rd. G21	23	Y9
Merchant La. G1	36	W13
Clyde St.		
Merchants Clo., Pais.	42	B14
Church St.		
Merchiston St. G32	38	AA12
Merkland Ct. G11	34	S11
Vine St.		
Merkland St. G11	34	S11
Merksworth Way, Pais.	30	J12
Mosslands Rd.		
Merlewood Av. G71	69	HH18
Merlin Way, Pais.	31	L12
Merlinford Av., Renf.	18	N10
Merlinford Cres., Renf.	18	N10
Merlinford Dr., Renf.	18	N10
Merlinford Way, Renf.	18	N10
Merrick Gdns. G51	34	S13

Name	Page	Grid
Merrick Ter., Udd.	57	HH16
Merrick Way G73	65	Y18
Merryburn Av., Giff.	62	T17
Merrycrest Av., Giff.	62	T18
Merrycroft Av., Giff.	62	T18
Merryland Pl. G51	34	T12
Merryland St. G51	34	S12
Merrylee Cres., Giff.	62	T17
Merrylee Pk. Av., Giff.	62	T18
Merrylee Pk. La., Giff.	62	T18
Merrylee Pk. Ms., Giff.	62	T18
Merrylee Rd. G43	62	T17
Merryton Av. G15	6	P6
Merryton Av., Giff.	62	T18
Merryton Pl. G15	6	P6
Merryvale Av., Giff.	62	T18
Merryvale Pl., Giff.	62	T17
Merton Dr. G52	32	P13
Meryon Gdns. G32	55	CC15
Meryon Rd. G32	55	CC15
Methil St. G14	19	Q10
Methuen Rd., Renf.	31	L11
Methven Av., Bear.	8	S5
Methven St. G31	53	Z14
Methven St., Dalm.	4	K6
Metropole La. G1	35	V13
Howard St.		
Michillen Rd., Bear.	8	T5
Micklehouse Oval, Bail.	40	EE13
Micklehouse Rd.		
Micklehouse Pl., Bail.	40	EE13
Micklehouse Rd.		
Micklehouse Rd., Bail.	40	EE13
Micklehouse Wynd, Bail.	40	EE13
Micklehouse Rd.		
Mid Cotts., Gart.	26	FF10
Midcroft, Bish.	10	X6
Midcroft Av. G44	64	W17
Middlemuir Av., Lenz.	13	CC5
Middlemuir Rd., Lenz.	13	CC5
Middlerigg Rd., Cumb.	70	MM3
Middlesex St. G41	35	U13
Middleton Cres., Pais.	30	J13
Middleton Rd., Linw.	28	F12
Middleton St. G51	34	T13
Midland St. G1	35	V13
Midlem Dr. G52	33	Q13
Midlem Oval G52	33	Q13
Midlock St. G51	34	T13
Midlothian Dr. G41	50	T15
Midton Cotts., Chr.	15	HH7
Midton St. G21	22	X10
Midwharf St. G4	36	W11
Migvie Pl. G20	20	T9
Wyndford Rd.		
Milan St. G41	51	V14
Milford St. G33	38	BB12
Mill Ct. G73	53	Y16
Mill Cres. G40	52	X14
Mill Pl., Linw.	28	E13
Mill River, Lenz.	13	CC6
Mill Rd. G72	67	CC18
Mill Rd., Barr.	59	L18
Mill Rd., Both.	69	HH19
Mill Rd., Clyde.	17	M8
Mill Rd. Gdns. G40	36	X13
Mill St. G40	52	X14
Mill St. G73	53	Y16
Mill St., Pais.	46	K14
Mill Vennel, Renf.	18	N10
High St.		
Millands Av., Blan.	68	FF19
Millar St., Pais.	30	K13
Millar Ter. G73	53	Y15
Millarbank St. G21	22	X10
Millarston Av., Pais.	45	H14
Millarston Dr., Pais.	45	H14
Millbeg Cres. G33	39	DD13
Millbeg Pl. G33	39	DD13
Millbrae Ct. G42	51	U16
Millbrae Rd.		
Millbrae Cres. G13	17	M8
Millbrae Cres. G42	51	U16
Millbrae Rd. G42	51	U16
Millbrix Av. G14	18	P9
Millburn Av. G73	65	Y17
Millburn Av., Clyde.	18	N8
Millburn Av., Renf.	18	N10
Millburn Dr., Renf.	17	M10
Millburn Rd., Renf.	17	M10
Millburn St. G21	37	Y11
Millburn Way, Renf.	18	N10
Millcroft Rd. G73	52	X15
Millcroft Rd., Cumb.	71	PP3
Miller St. G1	36	W12
Miller St., Bail.	56	EE14
Miller St., Clyde.	5	L7
Miller St., John.	44	E14
Millerfield Pl. G40	53	Y14
Millerfield Rd. G40	53	Y14
Millers Pl., Lenz.	13	CC6
Millersneuk Av., Lenz.	13	CC6
Millersneuk Cres. G33	24	BB9
Millersneuk Dr., Lenz.	13	CC6
Millerston St. G31	37	Y13
Millford Dr., Linw.	28	E13
Millgate, Udd.	57	GG16
Millgate Av., Udd.	57	GG16
Millholm Rd. G44	63	V18
Millhouse Cres. G20	20	T8
Millhouse Dr. G20	20	T8
Milliken Dr., Kilb.	43	C15
Milliken Pk. Rd., Kilb.	43	C15
Millpond Dr. G40	36	X13
Millport Av. G44	52	W16
Millroad Dr. G40	36	X13
Millroad St. G40	36	X13
Millview Pl. G53	60	P18
Millwood St. G41	51	U16
Milnbank St. G31	37	Y12
Milncroft Rd. G33	38	BB11
Milner Rd. G13	19	R9
Milngavie Rd., Bear.	7	R6
Milnpark Gdns. G41	35	U13
Milnpark St. G41	35	U13
Milovaig St. G23	8	T7
Milrig Rd. G73	52	X16
Milton Av. G72	66	AA17
Milton Douglas Rd., Clyde.	5	L5
Milton Dr., Bish.	22	X8
Milton Gdns., Udd.	57	GG16
Milton Mains Rd., Dalm.	5	L5
Milton St. G4	35	V11
Milverton Av., Bear.	7	Q5
Milverton Rd., Giff.	62	S19
Minard Rd. G41	51	U15
Minard Way, Udd.	57	HH16
Newton Dr.		
Minerva St. G3	35	U12
Minerva Way G3	35	U12
Mingarry La. G20	20	T10
Clouston St.		
Mingary St. G20	21	U10
Mingulay Cres. G22	22	W8
Mingulay Pl. G22	22	X8
Mingulay St. G22	22	W8
Minmoir Rd. G53	48	N16
Minstrel Rd. G13	7	Q7
Minto Av. G73	65	Z18
Minto Cres. G52	33	R13
Minto St. G52	33	R13
Mireton St. G22	21	V9
Mirrlees Dr. G12	20	T10
Mirrlees La. G12	20	T10
Redlands Rd.		
Mitchell Av. G72	67	DD17
Mitchell Av., Renf.	31	L11
Mitchell Dr. G73	65	Y17
Mitchell La. G1	35	V12
Buchanan St.		
Mitchell Rd., Cumb.	71	PP3
Mitchell St. G1	35	V12
Mitchell St., Coat.	57	HH14
Mitchellhill Rd. G45	64	X19
Mitchison Rd., Cumb.	71	PP2
Mitre Ct. G14	19	Q10
Mitre Rd.		
Mitre La. G14	19	R10
Mitre La. W. G14	19	R10
Mitre La.		
Mitre Rd. G14	19	R10
Moat Av. G13	19	Q8
Mochrum Rd. G43	63	U17
Moffat Pl., Blan.	68	FF19
Moffat St. G5	52	W14
Mogarth Av., Pais.	45	H16
Amochrie Rd.		
Moidart Av., Renf.	17	L10
Moidart Ct., Barr.	59	M17
Moidart Cres. G52	33	R13
Moidart Rd.		
Moidart Pl. G52	33	R13
Moidart Rd.		
Moidart Rd. G52	33	R13
Moir La. G1	36	W13
Moir St.		
Moir St. G1	36	W13
Molendinar St. G1	36	W13
Mollinsburn St. G21	22	X10
Monach Rd. G33	39	CC12
Monachie Gdns., Bish.	11	Z7
Muirhead Way		
Monart Pl. G20	21	U10
Caithness St.		
Moncrieff Av., Lenz.	13	CC5
Moncrieff Gdns., Lenz.	13	CC5
Moncrieff Pl. G4	35	V11
North Woodside Rd.		
Moncrieff St. G4	35	V11
Braid Sq.		
Moncur St. G40	36	X13
Moness Dr. G52	49	R14
Monica Gdns. G53	61	Q19
Monifieth Av. G52	49	Q14
Monikie Gdns., Bish.	11	Z7
Muirhead Way		
Monkcastle Dr. G73	66	BB17
Monkland Av., Lenz.	13	CC5
Monkland Vw., Udd.	57	HH15
Lincoln Av.		
Monkland Vw. Cres., Bail.	41	HH13
Monksbridge Av. G13	7	Q7
Monkscroft Av. G11	20	S10
Monkscroft Ct. G11	34	S11
Monkscroft Gdns. G11	20	S10
Monkscroft Av.		
Monkton Dr. G15	6	P7
Monmouth Av. G12	20	S9
Monreith Av., Bear.	7	Q7
Monreith Rd. G43	62	T17
Monreith Rd. E. G44	63	V17
Monroe Dr., Udd.	57	GG15
Monroe Pl., Udd.	57	GG15
Montague La. G12	20	S10
Montague St. G4	35	U11
Montague Ter. G12	20	S10
Hyndland Rd.		
Montclair Pl., Linw.	28	E13
Monteith Dr., Clark.	63	V19
Monteith Pl. G40	36	X13
Monteith Row G40	36	X13
Monteith Row La. G40	36	X13
Monteith Pl.		
Montford Av. G44	52	W16
Montgomerie Gdns. G14	19	Q10
Lennox Av.		
Montgomery Av., Pais.	31	L12
Montgomery Dr., Giff.	62	T19
Montgomery Dr., Kilb.	42	B14
Meadside Av.		
Montgomery La. G42	51	V16
Somerville Dr.		
Montgomery Rd., Pais.	31	L12
Montgomery St. G42	52	X14
London Rd.		
Montgomery St. G72	67	DD17
Mill Rd.		
Montrave St. G52	49	Q14
Montrave St. G73	53	Y15
Montreal Ho., Dalm.	4	J5
Perth Cres.		
Montron Dr. G15	6	P7
Moraine Av.		

Murrin Av., Bish.	11	Z7
Murroes Rd. G51	33	Q12
Muslin St. G40	52	X14
Mybster Pl. G51	33	Q12
Mybster Rd. G51	33	Q12
Myers Cres., Udd.	69	HH17
Myres Rd. G53	49	Q16
Myreside Pl. G32	37	Z13
Myreside St. G32	37	Z13
Myrie Gdns., Bish.	11	Y7
Myroch Pl. G34	40	FF11
Myrtle Av., Lenz.	13	CC5
Myrtle Hill La. G42	52	W16
Myrtle Hill Vw. G42	52	W16
Myrtle Pk. G42	52	W15
Myrtle Pl. G42	52	W16
Myrtle Rd., Dalm.	4	J6
Myrtle Rd., Udd.	57	HH16
Myrtle Sq., Bish.	23	Y8
Myrtle St., Blan.	68	FF19
Myrtle Wk. G72	66	AA17
Naburn St. G5	52	W14
Nairn Av., Blan.	68	FF19
Nairn Gdns., Bear.	7	Q6
Nairn Pl., Dalm.	4	K6
Dumbarton Rd.		
Nairn St. G3	34	T11
Nairn St., Dalm.	4	K6
Nairn Way, Cumb.	71	PP1
Nairnside Rd. G21	23	Z8
Naismith St. G32	55	CC16
Nansen St. G20	21	V10
Napier Ct., Old K.	4	J5
Freelands Rd.		
Napier Dr. G51	34	S12
Napier Gdns., Linw.	28	F13
Napier Pl. G51	34	S12
Napier Pl., Old K.	4	J5
Old Dalnottar Rd.		
Napier Rd. G51	34	S12
Napier Rd. G52	32	N11
Napier St. G51	34	T12
Napier St., Clyde.	17	M8
Napier St., Linw.	28	F13
Napier Ter. G51	34	S12
Napiershall La. G20	35	U11
Napiershall St.		
Napiershall Pl. G20	35	U11
Napiershall St.		
Napiershall St. G20	35	U11
Naseby Av. G11	19	R10
Nasmyth Rd. G52	32	P12
Nasmyth Rd. N. G52	32	P12
Nasmyth Rd. S. G52	32	P12
National Bk. La. G2	35	V12
St. Vincent St.		
Navar Pl., Pais.	47	L15
Naver St. G33	38	AA11
Neil St., Renf.	17	M9
Neilsland Oval G53	49	Q16
Neilsland St. G53	49	Q15
Neilston Av. G53	61	Q17
Neilston Rd., Barr.	59	L19
Neilston Rd., Pais.	46	K14
Neilvaig Dr. G73	65	Z18
Nelson Mandela Pl. G1	36	W12
Buchanan St.		
Nelson Pl., Bail.	56	EE14
Nelson St. G5	35	V13
Nelson St., Bail.	56	EE14
Nelson Ter. G12	21	U10
Glasgow St.		
Neptune St. G51	34	S12
Nerston Av. G53	49	Q16
Ness Av., John.	43	C16
Ness Dr., Blan.	69	GG19
Ness Gdns., Bish.	11	Y7
Ness Rd., Renf.	17	L10
Ness St. G33	38	AA11
Netham St. G51	34	S12
Nether Auldhouse Rd.	62	S17
G43		
Netherburn Av. G44	63	U19
Netherby Dr. G41	50	T14
Nethercairn Rd. G43	62	T18
Nethercliffe Av. G44	63	U19
Nethercommon	30	K12
Harbour, Pais.	30	K12
Nethercraig Cotts., Pais.	58	J17
Glenfield Rd.		
Nethercraigs Dr., Pais.	46	J16
Nethercraigs Rd., Pais.	45	H16
Netherdale Dr., Pais.	48	N14
Netherfield St. G31	37	Z13
Netherhill Av. G44	63	U19
Netherhill Cres., Pais.	31	L13
Netherhill Rd., Chr.	15	GG7
Netherhill Rd., Pais.	30	K13
Netherhouse Av., Lenz.	13	DD6
Netherhouse Pl., Bail.	41	GG12
Netherhouse Rd., Bail.	40	FF12
Netherlee Rd. G44	63	U18
Netherpark Av. G44	63	U19
Netherplace Cres. G53	48	P16
Netherplace Rd. G53	48	P16
Netherton Ct. G45	64	X19
Netherton Dr., Barr.	60	N19
Netherton Rd. G13	19	R8
Netherton St. G13	19	R8
Crow Rd.		
Nethervale Av. G44	63	U19
Netherview Rd. G44	63	V19
Netherway G44	63	U19
Nethy Way, Renf.	32	N11
Teith Av.		
Neuk Way G32	55	CC16
Nevis Rd. G43	62	S17
Nevis Rd., Bear.	6	P5
Nevis Rd., Renf.	31	L11
New City Rd. G4	35	V11
New Edinburgh Rd.,	57	GG16
Udd.		
New Inchinnan Rd., Pais.	30	K12
New Kirk Pl., Bear.	7	R5
New Kirk Rd.		
New Kirk Rd., Bear.	7	R5
New Rd. G72	67	DD18
New Sneddon St., Pais.	30	K13
New St., Clyde.	5	L5
New St., Kilb.	42	B14
New St., Pais.	46	K14
New Wynd G1	36	W13
Newark Dr. G41	50	T14
Newark Dr., Pais.	46	J16
Newbattle Ct. G32	54	BB15
Newbattle Gdns. G32	54	BB15
Newbattle Pl. G32	54	BB15
Newbattle Rd. G32	54	BB15
Newbold Av. G21	22	X8
Newburgh St. G43	50	T16
Newcastleton Dr. G23	9	U7
Newcroft Dr. G44	64	W17
Newfield Pl. G73	52	X16
Newfield Pl., Thorn.	61	R19
Rouken Glen Rd.		
Newfield Sq. G53	60	P17
Newhall St. G40	52	X14
Newhaven Rd. G33	38	BB12
Newhaven St. G32	38	BB12
Newhills Rd. G33	39	DD12
Newington St. G32	38	AA13
Newlands Gdns., John.	44	F15
Renshaw Rd.		
Newlands Rd. G43	63	U17
Newlands Rd., Udd.	57	GG16
Newlandsfield Rd. G43	50	T16
Newluce Dr. G32	55	CC14
Newmains Rd., Renf.	31	L11
Newmill Rd. G21	23	Z9
Newnham Rd., Pais.	48	N14
Newpark Ct. G72	54	BB16
Newshot Ct., Clyde.	17	M8
Clydeholm Ter.		
Newshot Dr., Renf.	4	J7
Newstead Gdns. G23	9	U7
Newton Av. G72	67	CC17
Newton Av., Barr.	59	M19
Newton Av., John.	45	G14
Newton Av., Pais.	31	L12
Newton Brae G72	67	DD17
Newton Dr., John.	45	G14
Newton Dr., Udd.	57	HH16
Newton Fm. Rd. G72	55	DD16
Newton Pl. G3	35	U11
Newton Rd., Lenz.	13	DD6
Newton Sta. Rd. G72	67	DD17
Newton St., Pais.	46	J14
Newton Ter. G3	35	U12
Sauchiehall St.		
Newton Ter. La. G3	35	U11
Elderslie St.		
Newtongrange Av. G32	54	BB15
Newtongrange Gdns.	54	BB15
G32		
Newtyle Pl., Bish.	11	Z7
Newtyle Rd., Pais.	47	M14
Nicholas St. G1	36	W12
Nicholson Ct. G33	25	CC9
Nicholson La. G5	35	V13
Nicholson St.		
Nicholson St. G5	35	V13
Niddrie Rd. G42	51	U15
Niddrie Sq. G42	51	U15
Niddry St., Pais.	30	K13
Nigel Gdns. G41	50	T15
Nigg Pl. G34	40	EE12
Nightingale La., John.	43	C16
Nimmo Dr. G51	33	R12
Nisbet St. G31	37	Z13
Nith Av., Pais.	45	G15
Nith Dr., Renf.	32	N11
Nith Pl., John.	43	C16
Nith St. G33	37	Z11
Nithsdale Cres., Bear.	7	Q5
Nithsdale Dr. G41	51	U15
Nithsdale Pl. G41	51	U14
Shields Rd.		
Nithsdale Rd. G41	50	S14
Nithsdale St. G41	51	U15
Nitshill Rd. G53	60	N17
Niven St. G20	20	T9
Noldrum Av. G32	55	CC16
Noldrum Gdns. G32	55	CC16
Norbreck Dr., Giff.	62	T18
Norby Rd. G11	19	R10
Norfield Dr. G44	51	V16
Norfolk Ct. G5	35	V13
Norfolk Cres., Bish.	10	X6
Norfolk La. G5	35	V13
Norfolk St.		
Norfolk St. G5	35	V13
Norham St. G41	51	U15
Norman St. G40	52	X14
Norse La. N. G14	19	Q10
Ormiston Av.		
Norse La. S. G14	19	Q10
Verona Av.		
Norse Rd. G14	19	Q10
North Av. G72	66	AA17
North Av., Clyde.	5	L7
North Bk. Pl., Clyde.	17	M8
North Bk. St.		
North Bk. St., Clyde.	17	M8
North Brae Pl. G13	18	P8
North British Rd., Udd.	69	GG17
North Canalbank St. G4	36	W11
North Carbrain Rd.,	70	NN4
Cumb.		
North Claremont St. G3	35	U11
North Corsebar Av.,	46	J15
Pais.		
North Ct. La. G1	36	W12
Buchanan St.		
North Cft. St., Pais.	30	K13
North Deanpark Av.,	69	HH18
Udd.		
North Douglas St.,	17	M8
Clyde.		
North Dr. G1	36	W13
North Dr., Linw.	28	E13
North Elgin St., Clyde.	17	M8
North Erskine Pk., Bear.	7	Q5
North Frederick St. G1	36	W12

Street	Page	Grid
North Gardner St. G11	20	S10
North Gra. Rd., Bear.	7	R5
North Greenhill Rd., Pais.	30	J12
North Hanover Pl. G4	36	W11
North Hanover St. G1	36	W12
North Iverton Pk. Rd., John.	44	E14
North Lo. Rd., Renf.	17	M10
North Moraine La. G15	7	Q7
Moraine Av.		
North Pk. Av., Thorn.	61	R18
North Pl. G3	35	U12
North St.		
North Portland St. G1	36	W12
North Queen St. G2	36	W12
George Sq.		
North Rd., John.	43	D15
North Spiers Wf. G4	35	V11
North St. G3	35	U12
North St., Clyde.	5	L7
Dumbarton Rd.		
North St., Pais.	30	K13
North Vw., Bear.	7	Q7
North Wallace St. G4	36	W11
North Way, Blan.	68	FF19
North Woodside Rd. G20	21	U10
Northampton Dr. G12	20	S9
Northampton La. G12	20	S9
Northampton Dr.		
Northbank Av. G72	67	CC17
Northbank St. G72	67	CC17
Northcroft Rd. G21	22	X10
Northcroft Rd., Chr.	15	GG7
Northgate Quad. G21	23	Z8
Northgate Rd. G21	23	Z8
Northinch St. G14	33	Q11
Northland Dr. G14	19	Q9
Northland La. G14	19	Q10
Northland Dr.		
Northmuir Rd. G15	6	P6
Northpark St. G20	21	U10
Northpark Ter. G12	21	U10
Hamilton Dr.		
Northumberland St. G20	21	U10
Norval St. G11	34	S11
Norwich Dr. G12	20	S9
Norwood, Bear.	7	R6
Norwood Dr., Giff.	62	S19
Norwood Ter. G12	35	U11
Southpark Av.		
Norwood Ter., Udd.	57	HH16
Nottingham Av. G12	20	S9
Nottingham La. G12	20	S9
Northampton Dr.		
Novar Dr. G12	20	S10
Novar Gdns., Bish.	10	X7
Numrow St., Clyde.	4	K5
Nuneaton St. G40	53	Y14
Nurseries Rd., Bail.	39	DD13
Nursery La. G41	51	U15
Nursery St. G41	51	U15
Pollokshaws Rd.		
Nursery St. La. G41	51	U15
Nithsdale Dr.		
Nutberry Ct. G42	51	V15
Oak Cres., Bail.	56	EE14
Oak Dr. G72	67	CC18
Oak Dr., Lenz.	12	BB5
Oak Pl., Bish.	11	Y7
Oak Rd., Dalm.	4	K5
Oak Rd., Pais.	47	L15
Oak St. G2	35	V12
Cadogan St.		
Oakbank Dr., Barr.	60	N19
Oakbank La. G20	21	V10
Oakbank Ter. G20	21	V10
Oakdene Av., Udd.	57	HH16
Oakfield Av. G12	35	U11
Oakfield Ter. G12	35	U11
Oakfield Av.		
Oakhill Av., Bail.	55	DD14
Oakley Dr. G44	63	U18
Oakley Ter. G31	36	X12
Oaks, The, John.	43	C15
Oakshaw Sch. Brae, Pais.	30	J13
Oakshaw St., Pais.	30	J13
Oakshawhead, Pais.	30	J13
Oakwood Av., Pais.	45	H15
Oatfield St. G21	23	Y10
Oban Ct. G22	21	U10
Oban Dr. G20	21	U10
Observatory La. G12	20	T10
Observatory Rd.		
Observatory Rd. G12	20	T10
Ochil Dr., Barr.	59	M19
Ochil Dr., Pais.	46	K16
Ochil Pl. G32	54	BB14
Ochil Rd., Bish.	11	Z7
Ochil Rd., Renf.	31	L11
Ochil St. G32	54	BB14
Ochiltree Av. G13	19	R8
Ogilvie Pl. G31	54	AA14
Ogilvie St. G31	53	Z14
Old Bothwell Rd., Both.	69	HH19
Old Castle Rd. G44	63	V17
Old Dalmarnock Rd. G40	52	X14
Old Dalnottar Rd., Old K.	4	J5
Old Dumbarton Rd. G3	34	T11
Old Edinburgh Rd., Udd.	57	GG15
Old Gartcosh Rd., Gart.	27	GG9
Old Glasgow Rd., Udd.	56	FF16
Old Govan Rd., Renf.	18	N10
Old Greenock Rd., Renf.	16	J8
Old Manse Rd. G32	39	CC13
Old Mill Rd. G72	67	CC17
Old Mill Rd., Both.	69	HH19
Old Mill Rd., Clyde.	5	L5
Old Mill Rd., Udd.	69	GG17
Old Renfrew Rd., Renf.	32	P11
Old Rd., John.	44	F14
Old Roundknowe Rd., Udd.	56	FF15
Old Rutherglen Rd. G5	52	W14
Old Shettleston Rd. G32	38	AA13
Old Sneddon St., Pais.	30	K13
Old St., Clyde.	4	K5
Old Wd. Rd., Bail.	56	EE14
Old Wynd G1	36	W13
Oldhall Rd., Pais.	31	M13
Olifard Av., Both.	69	HH18
Oliphant Cres., Pais.	45	G16
Olive St. G33	23	Z10
Olrig Ter. G41	51	U14
Shields Rd.		
Olympia St. G40	36	X13
Onslow Dr. G31	37	Y12
Onslow Rd., Clyde.	5	M7
Onslow Sq. G31	37	Y12
Onslow Dr.		
Oran Gdns. G20	21	U9
Oran Gate G20	21	U10
Oran Pl. G20	21	U9
Oran St. G20	21	U9
Oransay Cres., Bear.	8	S6
Orbiston Gdns. G32	38	BB13
Balintore St.		
Orcades Dr. G44	63	V18
Orchard Av. G17	69	HH19
Orchard Ct. G32	54	BB16
Orchard Ct., Thorn.	62	S18
Orchard Dr. G73	52	X16
Orchard Dr., Giff.	62	S18
Orchard Gro., Giff.	62	S18
Orchard Pk., Giff.	62	T18
Orchard Pk. Av., Thorn.	62	S18
Orchard Sq., Pais.	46	K14
Orchard St., Pais.	46	K14
Orchard St., Renf.	17	M10
Orchardfield, Lenz.	13	CC6
Orchy Ct., Clyde.	5	M5
Orchy Cres., Bear.	7	Q7
Orchy Cres., Pais.	45	G15
Orchy Dr., Clark.	63	U19
Orchy Gdns., Clark.	63	U19
Orchy St. G44	63	V17
Oregon Pl. G5	52	W14
Orion Way G72	66	BB17
Orkney Pl. G51	34	S12
Orkney St.		
Orkney St. G51	34	S12
Orleans Av. G14	19	R10
Orleans La. G14	19	R10
Ormiston Av. G14	19	Q10
Ormiston La. G14	19	Q10
Ormiston Av.		
Ormiston La. S. G14	19	Q10
Ormiston Av.		
Ormonde Av. G44	63	U18
Ormonde Ct. G44	63	U18
Ormonde Cres. G44	63	U18
Ormonde Dr. G44	63	U18
Ornsay St. G22	22	W8
Orr Pl. G40	36	X13
Orr Sq., Pais.	30	K13
Orr St. G40	36	X13
Orr St., Pais.	30	K13
Orton St. G51	34	S13
Orwell St. G21	22	X10
Osborn Ter. G51	34	S13
Copland Rd.		
Osborne St. G1	36	W13
Osborne St., Clyde.	5	L6
Osborne Vill. G44	63	V17
Holmhead Rd.		
Osprey Dr., Udd.	57	HH16
Ossian Av., Pais.	32	N13
Auchmannoch Av.		
Ossian Rd. G43	63	U17
Oswald La. G1	35	V13
Oswald St.		
Oswald St. G1	35	V13
Otago La. G12	35	U11
Otago St.		
Otago La. N. G12	35	U11
Otago St.		
Otago St. G12	35	U11
Ottawa Cres., Dalm.	4	J6
Otter La. G11	34	S11
Castlebank St.		
Otterburn Dr., Giff.	62	T19
Otterswick Pl. G33	39	CC11
Oval, The, Clark.	63	U19
Overbrae Pl. G15	6	N5
Overdale Av. G42	51	U16
Overdale Gdns. G42	51	U16
Overdale St. G42	51	U16
Overdale Vills. G42	51	U16
Overdale St.		
Overlea Av. G73	65	Z17
Overnewton Pl. G3	34	T12
Kelvinhaugh St.		
Overnewton Sq. G3	34	T12
Overnewton St. G3	34	T11
Overton Cres., John.	44	E14
Overton Rd. G72	67	CC18
Overton Rd., John.	44	E15
Overton St. G72	67	CC18
Overtoun Ct., Dalm.	4	K6
Dunswin Av.		
Overtoun Dr. G73	53	Y16
Overtoun Dr., Dalm.	4	K6
Overtoun Rd., Dalm.	4	K6
Overtown Av. G53	60	P17
Overtown St. G31	37	Y13
Overwood Dr. G44	64	W17
Oxford Dr., Linw.	28	E13
Oxford La. G5	35	V13
Oxford Rd., Renf.	17	M10
Oxford St. G5	35	V13
Oxton Dr. G52	32	P13
Paisley Ct., Barr.	59	L18
Paisley Rd.		
Paisley Rd. G5	35	U13
Paisley Rd., Barr.	59	L18
Paisley Rd., Renf.	31	L11
Paisley Rd. W. G52	48	P14
Palace St. G31	53	Z14
Paladin Av. G13	19	Q8

Name		
Palermo St. G21	22	X10
Palmer Av. G13	7	Q7
Palmerston Pl. G3	34	T12
Kelvinhaugh St.		
Palmerston Pl., John.	43	C16
Pandora Way, Udd.	57	HH16
Hillcrest Rd.		
Panmure St. G20	21	V10
Park Av. G3	35	U11
Park Av., Barr.	59	L19
Park Av., Bish.	11	Y6
Park Av., John.	44	F15
Park Av., Pais.	46	J15
Park Brae, Renf.	16	J8
Park Dr.		
Park Circ. G3	35	U11
Park Circ. La. G3	35	U11
Lynedoch Pl.		
Park Circ. Pl. G3	35	U11
Park Ct., Bish.	11	Y6
Park Ct., Dalm.	4	K6
Little Holm		
Park Ct., Giff.	62	S18
Belmont Dr.		
Park Ct., Giff.	62	S19
Park Cres., Bear.	6	P5
Park Cres., Bish.	11	Y6
Park Cres., Renf.	16	J8
Park Dr. G3	35	U11
Park Dr. G73	53	Y16
Park Dr., Renf.	16	J8
Park Gdns. G3	35	U11
Park Gdns., Kilb.	42	B14
Park Gdns. La. G3	35	U11
Clifton St.		
Park Gate G3	35	U11
Park Gro., Renf.	16	J8
Park La. G40	36	X13
Park La., Pais.	30	K13
Netherhill Rd.		
Park Pl. G20	20	T8
Fingal St.		
Park Quad. G3	35	U11
Park Ridge, Renf.	16	J8
Park Dr.		
Park Rd. G4	35	U11
Park Rd., Bail.	41	GG13
Park Rd., Bish.	11	Y7
Park Rd., Chr.	26	FF8
Park Rd., Dalm.	4	K6
Park Rd., Giff.	62	T19
Park Rd., John.	43	D15
Park Rd., Pais.	46	J15
Park Rd., Renf.	16	J8
Park St. S. G3	35	U11
Park Ter. G3	35	U11
Park Ter. G42	51	U15
Queens Dr.		
Park Ter., Giff.	62	T19
Park Top, Renf.	16	J8
Park Way, Cumb.	71	PP2
Park Winding, Renf.	16	J8
Parkburn Av., Lenz.	13	CC5
Parker St. G14	33	R11
Parkgrove Av., Giff.	62	T18
Parkgrove Ct., Giff.	62	T18
Parkgrove Ter. G3	35	U11
Parkgrove Ter. La. G3	35	U12
Derby St.		
Parkhall Rd., Dalm.	4	K6
Parkhall Ter., Dalm.	4	K5
Parkhead Cross G31	37	Z13
Parkhill Dr. G73	53	Y16
Parkhill Rd. G43	50	T16
Parkholm La. G5	35	U13
Paisley Rd.		
Parkhouse Path G53	60	P18
Parkhouse Rd. G53	60	N18
Parklands Rd. G44	63	U18
Parklea, Bish.	10	X6
Midcroft		
Parkneuk Rd. G43	62	T18
Parksail, Renf.	16	J8
Parksail Dr., Renf.	16	J8
Parkvale Av., Renf.	16	J8
Parkvale Cres., Renf.	16	J8
Parkvale Av.		
Parkvale Dr., Renf.	16	J8
Parkvale Av.		
Parkvale Gdns., Renf.	16	J8
Parkvale Av.		
Parkvale Pl., Renf.	16	J8
Parkvale Av.		
Parkvale Way, Renf.	16	J8
Parkvale Av.		
Parkview G78	42	B14
Parkview, Pais.	46	J15
Parkview Av., Lenz.	13	CC5
Parkview Ct., Lenz.	13	CC5
Parkview Dr. G33	25	DD9
Parliament Rd. G21	36	X12
Parnie St. G1	36	W13
Parson St. G4	36	X12
Parsonage Row G1	36	W12
Parsonage Sq. G1	36	W12
Partick Bri. St. G11	34	T11
Partickhill Av. G11	20	S10
Partickhill Ct. G11	20	S10
Partickhill Av.		
Partickhill Rd. G11	20	S10
Paterson St. G5	35	V13
Pathead Gdns. G33	24	AA9
Patna St. G40	53	Y14
Paton St. G31	37	Y12
Patrick St., Pais.	46	K14
Patterton Dr., Barr.	59	M19
Pattison St., Dalm.	4	K6
Payne St. G4	36	W11
Peacock Av., Pais.	45	G15
Peacock Dr.		
Peacock Dr., Pais.	45	G14
Pearce St. G51	34	S12
Pearson Dr., Renf.	31	M11
Pearson Pl., Linw.	28	E13
Peat Pl. G53	60	P17
Peat Rd. G53	60	P17
Peathill Av., Chr.	26	EE8
Peathill St. G21	22	W10
Peel Glen Rd., Bear.	6	P5
Peel La. G11	34	S11
Burgh Hall St.		
Peel Pl., Both.	69	HH18
Peel St. G11	34	S11
Peel Vw., Clyde.	5	M6
Kirkoswald Dr.		
Peirshill St. G32	38	AA12
Pembroke St. G3	35	U12
Pencaitland Dr. G32	54	BB14
Falside Rd.		
Pencaitland Gro. G32	54	BB14
Falside Rd.		
Pencaitland Pl. G23	9	U7
Pendeen Cres. G33	39	DD13
Pendeen Pl. G33	39	DD13
Pendeen Rd. G33	39	DD13
Pendicle Cres., Bear.	7	Q6
Pendicle Rd., Bear.	7	Q6
Penicuik St. G32	37	Z13
Penilee Rd., Pais.	32	N13
Penilee Ter. G52	32	N12
Peninver Dr. G51	33	R12
Penman Av. G73	52	X16
Pennan Pl. G14	18	P9
Penneld Rd. G52	32	N13
Penrith Av., Giff.	62	T19
Penrith Dr. G12	20	S9
Penryn Gdns. G32	55	CC14
Penston Rd. G33	39	CC12
Pentland Ct., Barr.	59	L19
Pentland Cres., Pais.	46	J16
Pentland Dr., Barr.	59	M19
Pentland Dr., Bish.	11	Z7
Pentland Dr., Linw.	28	E13
Pentland Dr., Renf.	31	L12
Pentland Pl. G40	52	X14
Pentland Rd. G43	62	T17
Pentland Rd., Chr.	26	FF8
Penzance Way, Chr.	15	GG6
Peockland Gdns., John.	44	E14
Peockland Pl., John.	44	E14
Percy Dr., Giff.	62	T19
Percy Rd., Renf.	31	L12
Percy St. G51	34	T13
Perran Gdns., Chr.	15	GG7
Perth Cres., Dalm.	4	J5
Perth St. G3	35	U12
Argyle St.		
Peters Ct. G20	20	T8
Maryhill Rd.		
Petershill Ct. G21	23	Y10
Petershill Dr. G21	23	Y10
Petershill Pl. G21	23	Y10
Petershill Rd. G21	22	X10
Petition Pl., Udd.	69	HH17
Pettigrew St. G32	38	BB13
Peveril Av. G41	50	T15
Peveril Av. G73	65	Z17
Pharonhill St. G31	38	AA13
Quarrybrae St.		
Phoenix Pk. Ter. G4	35	V11
Corn St.		
Phoenix Pl., John.	44	F14
Phoenix Rd. G4	35	V11
Great Western Rd.		
Piccadilly St. G3	35	U12
Pikeman Av. G13	19	Q9
Pikeman Rd. G13	19	Q9
Pilmuir Av. G44	63	U18
Pilrig St. G32	38	AA12
Pilton Rd. G15	6	P6
Pine Cres., John.	44	E15
Pine Gro., Udd.	57	HH16
Douglas Cres.		
Pine Pl. G5	52	W14
Pine Pl., Cumb.	71	RR2
Pine Rd., Cumb.	71	RR2
Pine Rd., Dalm.	4	J6
Pine St., Pais.	47	L15
Pinelands, Bish.	11	Y6
Pinewood Av., Lenz.	12	BB5
Pinewood Ct., Lenz.	12	BB5
Pinewood Pl., Kirk.	12	BB5
Pinewood Pl., Lenz.	12	BB5
Pinewood Sq. G15	6	N6
Pinkerton Av. G73	52	X16
Pinkston Dr. G21	36	W11
Pinkston Rd. G21	22	W10
Pinmore Path G53	60	N17
Pinmore Pl. G53	60	N17
Pinmore St. G53	60	N17
Pinwherry Dr. G33	24	AA9
Pinwherry Pl., Udd.	69	HH18
Hume Dr.		
Pirn St. G40	52	X14
Pitcairn St. G31	54	AA14
Pitcaple Dr. G43	62	S17
Pitlochry Dr. G52	48	P14
Pitmedden Rd., Bish.	11	Z7
Pitmilly Rd. G15	7	Q6
Pitreavie Pl. G33	39	CC11
Pitt St. G2	35	V12
Pladda Rd., Renf.	31	M11
Plane Tree Pl., John.	44	E15
Planetree Rd., Dalm.	5	L5
Planetrees Av., Pais.	46	K15
Carriagehill Dr.		
Plant St. G31	37	Z13
Plantation Pk. Gdns. G51	34	T13
Plantation Pl. G51	35	U13
Govan Rd.		
Plantation Sq. G51	35	U13
Playfair St. G40	53	Y14
Pleaknowe Cres., Chr.	15	GG7
Pleamuir Pl., Cumb.	70	MM3
Plean St. G14	18	P9
Pleasance La. G43	50	T16
Pleasance St. G43	50	T16
Plover Pl., John.	43	C16
Pollock Dr., Bish.	10	X7
Pollock Rd., Bear.	8	S6
Pollokshaws Rd. G43	50	S16
Polmadie Av. G42	52	W15
Polmadie Rd. G5	52	W15
Polmadie St. G42	52	W15

Polnoon Av. G13	18	P9		Prospecthill Rd. G42	51	V16		Queenslie St. G33	37	Z11
Polson Cres., Pais.	46	J15		Prospecthill Sq. G42	52	W16		Quendale Dr. G32	54	AA14
Polson Dr., John.	43	D15		Provan Rd. G33	37	Z11		Quentin St. G41	51	U15
Polwarth Gdns. G12	20	S10		Provand Hall Cres.,	56	EE14		Quinton Gdns., Bail.	40	EE13
Novar Dr.				*Bail.*						
Polwarth La. G12	20	S10		Provanhill Pl. G21	36	X11				
Novar Dr.				Provanmill Pl. G33	23	Z10		Raasay Dr., Pais.	46	J16
Polwarth St. G12	20	S10		*Provanmill Rd.*				Raasay Pl. G22	22	W8
Poplar Av. G11	19	R10		Provanmill Rd. G33	23	Z10		Raasay St. G22	22	W8
Poplar Av., John.	44	E15		Purdon St. G11	34	S11		Rachan St. G34	40	FF11
Poplar Cotts. G14	18	N9		Pykestone Rd. G33	39	CC11		Radnor St. G3	35	U12
Dumbarton Rd.								*Argyle St.*		
Poplar Dr., Dalm.	4	K5						Radnor St., Clyde.	5	L6
Poplar Dr., Lenz.	12	BB5		Quadrant Rd. G43	63	U17		Raeberry St. G20	21	U10
Poplar Pl., Blan.	68	FF19		Quarrelton Rd., John.	43	D15		Raeswood Dr. G53	48	N16
Poplar Rd. G41	34	S13		Quarry Av. G72	67	DD18		Raeswood Gdns. G53	48	N16
Urrdale Rd.				Quarry Pl. G72	66	AA17		Raeswood Pl. G53	48	N16
Poplin St. G40	52	X14		Quarry Rd., Barr.	59	L18		Raeswood Rd. G53	48	N16
Porchester St. G33	39	CC11		Quarry Rd., Pais.	46	K15		Raglan St. G4	35	V11
Port Dundas Pl. G2	36	W12		Quarry St., John.	43	D14		Raith Av. G44	64	W18
Port Dundas Rd. G4	36	W11		Quarrybank, John.	43	C15		Raithburn Av. G45	64	W18
Port St. G3	35	U12		Quarrybrae St. G31	38	AA13		Raithburn Rd. G45	64	W18
Portal Rd. G13	19	Q8		Quarryknowe G73	52	X16		Ralston Av., Pais.	48	N14
Porterfield Rd., Renf.	31	L11		Quarryknowe St. G31	38	AA13		Ralston Ct. G52	48	N14
Portman Pl. G12	35	U11		Quarrywood Av. G21	23	Z10		Ralston Dr. G52	48	N14
Cowan St.				Quarrywood Rd. G21	23	Z10		Ralston Path G52	48	N14
Portman St. G41	35	U13		Quay Rd. G73	53	Y15		*Ralston Dr.*		
Portmarnock Dr. G23	20	T8		Quay Rd. N. G73	53	Y15		Ralston Pl. G52	48	N14
Portreath Rd., Chr.	15	GG6		Quebec Ho., Dalm.	4	J5		Ralston Rd., Bear.	7	R5
Portsoy Av. G13	18	N8		*Perth Cres.*				Ralston St., Barr.	59	M19
Portsoy Pl. G13	18	N8		Queen Arc. G2	35	V12		Ralston St., Pais.	47	L14
Portugal La. G5	35	V13		*Renfrew St.*				*Seedhill Rd.*		
Bedford St.				Queen Elizabeth Av. G52	32	N12		Ram St. G32	38	AA13
Portugal St. G5	35	V13		Queen Elizabeth Sq. G5	52	W14		Rampart Av. G13	18	P8
Norfolk Ct.				Queen Margaret Ct. G20	21	U10		Ramsay Av., John.	43	D15
Possil Cross G22	21	V10		Queen Margaret Cres.	21	U10		Ramsay Cres., John.	42	B16
Possil Rd. G4	21	V10		G12				Ramsay Pl., John.	43	D15
Post La., Renf.	17	M10		*Hamilton Dr.*				Ramsay St., Dalm.	4	K6
Potassels Rd., Chr.	26	FF8		Queen Margaret Dr. G12	20	T10		Ranald Gdns. G73	65	Z18
Potter Clo. G32	54	AA14		Queen Margaret Dr. G20	21	U10		Randolph Av., Clark.	63	U19
Potter Pl.				Queen Margaret Rd.	21	U10		Randolph Dr., Clark.	63	U19
Potter Gro. G32	54	AA14		G20				Randolph Gdns., Clark.	63	U19
Potter Pl.				Queen Mary Av. G42	51	V15		Randolph Rd. G11	19	R10
Potter Pl. G32	54	AA14		Queen Mary Av., Clyde.	5	M7		Randolph Ter. G72	66	BB17
Potter St. G32	54	AA14		Queen Mary St. G40	52	X14		*Hamilton Rd.*		
Potterhill Av., Pais.	46	K16		Queen Sq. G41	51	U15		Ranfurley Rd. G52	32	N13
Potterhill Rd. G53	48	P15		Queen St. G1	36	W12		Rankine Pl., John.	43	D14
Powburn Cres., Udd.	56	FF16		Queen St. G73	53	Y16		*Rankine St.*		
Powfoot St. G31	37	Z13		Queen St., Pais.	46	J14		Rankine St., John.	43	D14
Powrie St. G33	25	CC10		Queen St., Renf.	17	M10		Rankines La., Renf.	17	M10
Preston Pl. G42	51	V15		Queen Victoria Dr. G14	19	Q10		*Manse St.*		
Prestwick St. G53	60	P17		Queen Victoria Gate G13	19	Q9		Rannoch Av., Bish.	11	Y7
Priesthill Av. G53	61	Q17		Queenbank Av., Gart.	27	GG8		Rannoch Dr., Bear.	8	S7
Priesthill Cres. G53	61	Q17		Queens Av. G72	66	BB17		Rannoch Dr., Renf.	17	M10
Priesthill Rd. G53	60	P17		Queens Cres. G4	35	V11		Rannoch Gdns., Bish.	11	Y7
Primrose Ct. G14	19	Q10		Queens Cres., Bail.	41	GG13		Rannoch Pl., Pais.	47	L14
Primrose St. G14	19	Q10		Queens Cross G20	21	U10		Rannoch Rd., John.	43	D15
Prince Albert Rd. G12	20	S10		Queens Dr. G42	51	U15		Rannoch Rd., Udd.	57	GG15
Prince Edward St. G42	51	V15		Queens Dr., Cumb.	70	NN1		Rannoch St. G44	63	V17
Prince of Wales Gdns.	20	T8		Queens Dr. La. G42	51	V15		Ranza Pl. G33	23	Z10
G20				Queens Gdns. G12	20	T10		Raploch Av. G14	18	P10
Prince of Wales Ter. G12	20	T10		*Victoria Cres. Rd.*				Ratford St. G51	34	S12
Byres Rd.				Queens Pk. Av. G42	51	V15		Rathlin St. G51	34	S12
Princes Gdns. G12	20	S10		Queens Pl. G12	20	T10		Ratho Dr. G21	22	X9
Princes Gate G73	53	Y16		Queens Rd., John.	44	F15		Rattray St. G32	54	AA14
Greenbank St.				Queensborough Gdns.	20	S10		Ravel Row G31	37	Z13
Princes Pl. G12	20	T10		G12				Ravelston Rd., Bear.	7	R7
Princes Sq. G1	36	W12		Queensby Av., Bail.	40	EE13		Ravelston St. G32	37	Z13
Princes Sq., Barr.	59	M18		*Queensby Rd.*				Ravens Ct., Bish.	22	X8
Princes St. G73	53	Y16		Queensby Dr., Bail.	40	EE13		*Lennox Cres.*		
Princes Ter. G12	20	T10		*Queensby Rd.*				Ravenscliffe Dr., Giff.	62	S18
Princess Cres., Pais.	31	L13		Queensby Pl., Bail.	40	EE13		Ravenscraig Av., Pais.	46	J15
Priory Av., Pais.	31	L12		*Queensby Rd.*				Ravenscraig Dr. G53	60	P17
Priory Cotts., Blan.	68	FF19		Queensby Rd., Bail.	40	EE13		Ravenscraig Ter. G53	61	Q17
Priory Dr., Udd.	56	FF16		Queensferry St. G5	52	X15		Ravenshall Rd. G41	50	T16
Priory Pl. G13	19	Q8		*Rosebery St.*				Ravenstone Rd., Giff.	62	T18
Priory Rd. G13	19	Q8		Queenshill St. G21	22	X10		Ravenswood Av. G78	45	G16
Prosen St. G32	54	AA14		Queensland Ct. G52	33	Q13		Ravenswood Dr. G41	50	T15
Prospect Av. G72	66	AA17		Queensland Dr. G52	33	Q13		Ravenswood Rd., Bail.	40	FF13
Prospect Av., Udd.	57	GG16		Queensland Gdns. G52	33	Q13		Rayne Pl. G15	6	P6
Prospect Rd. G43	50	T16		Queensland La. E. G52	32	P13		Red Rd. G21	23	Y10
Prospecthill Circ. G42	52	W15		*Kingsland Dr.*				Red Rd. Ct. G21	23	Y10
Prospecthill Cres. G42	52	X16		Queensland La. W. G52	33	Q13		Redan St. G40	36	X13
Prospecthill Dr. G42	52	W16		*Queensland Dr.*				Redcastle Sq. G33	39	CC11
Prospecthill Pl. G42	52	X16		Queenslie Ind. Est. G33	39	CC12		Redford St. G33	37	Z12

Redgate Pl. G14	18	P10	Richmond Dr. G73	53	Z16	Rockbank St. G40	37	Y13
Redhill Rd., Cumb.	70	MM2	Richmond Dr., Bish.	11	Y6	Rockcliffe St. G40	52	X14
Redhurst Cres., Pais.	45	H16	Richmond Dr., Linw.	28	E12	Rockfield Pl. G21	23	Z9
Redhurst Way, Pais.	45	H16	Richmond Gdns., Chr.	14	EE7	Rockfield Rd. G21	23	Z9
Redlands La. G12	20	T10	Richmond Gro. G73	53	Z16	Rockmount Av., Barr.	59	M19
Kirklee Rd.			Richmond Pl. G73	53	Z16	Rockmount Av., Thorn.	62	S18
Redlands Rd. G12	20	T10	Richmond St. G1	36	W12	Rockwell Av., Pais.	46	J16
Redlands Ter. G12	20	T10	Richmond St., Clyde.	5	M7	Rodger Dr. G73	65	Y17
Redlands Ter. La. G12	20	T10	Riddell St., Clyde.	5	M6	Rodger Pl., Ruth.	65	Y17
Julian Av.			Riddon Av. G13	18	N8	Rodil Av. G44	64	W18
Redlawood Pl. G72	68	EE17	Riddrie Cres. G33	38	AA12	Rodney St. G4	35	V11
Redlawood Rd.			Riddrie Knowes G33	38	AA12	Roebank Dr., Barr.	59	M19
Redlawood Rd. G72	68	EE17	Riddrie Ter. G33	23	Z10	Roebank St. G31	37	Y12
Redmoss St. G22	21	V9	*Provanmill Rd.*			Roffey Pk. Rd., Pais.	31	M13
Rednock St. G22	22	W10	Riddrievale Ct. G33	38	AA11	Rogart St. G40	36	X13
Redpath Dr. G52	32	P13	Riddrievale St. G33	38	AA11	Rogerfield Rd., Bail.	40	FF12
Redwood Dr. G21	23	Y10	Rigby St. G32	37	Z13	Rokeby Ter. G12	20	T10
Foresthall Dr.			Rigg Pl. G33	39	DD12	*Great Western Rd.*		
Redwood Pl., Lenz.	12	BB5	Rigghead Av., Cumb.	71	PP1	Roman Av. G15	6	P7
Redwood Rd., Cumb.	71	QQ3	Riggside Rd. G33	39	CC11	Roman Av., Bear.	7	R5
Reelick Av. G13	18	N8	Riggside St. G33	39	CC11	Roman Ct., Bear.	7	R5
Reelick Quad. G13	18	N8	Riglands Way, Renf.	17	M10	Roman Dr., Bear.	7	R5
Regent Moray St. G3	34	T11	Riglaw Pl. G13	18	P8	Roman Gdns., Bear.	7	R5
Regent Pk. Sq. G41	51	U15	Rigmuir Rd. G51	33	Q13	Roman Rd., Bear.	7	R5
Regent Pk. Ter. G41	51	U15	Rimsdale St. G40	37	Y13	Roman Rd., Clyde.	5	L5
Pollokshaws Rd.			Ringford St. G21	22	X10	Romney Av. G44	64	W17
Regent Pl., Dalm.	4	K6	Ripon Dr. G12	20	S9	Rona St. G21	37	Y11
Regent Sq., Lenz.	13	CC6	Risk St. G40	36	X13	Rona Ter. G72	66	AA18
Regent St., Dalm.	4	K6	Risk St., Dalm.	4	K6	Ronaldsay Dr., Bish.	11	Z7
Regent St., Pais.	31	L13	Ristol Rd. G13	19	Q9	Ronaldsay Pl., Cumb.	70	MM4
Regents Gate, Both.	69	GG18	*Anniesland Rd.*			Ronaldsay St. G22	22	W8
Regwood St. G41	50	T16	Ritchie Cres., John.	44	F14	Ronay St. G22	22	W8
Reid Av., Bear.	8	S5	Ritchie Pk., John.	44	E14	Rooksdell Av., Pais.	46	J15
Reid Av., Linw.	28	E13	Ritchie St. G5	51	V14	Rose Cotts. G13	19	R9
Reid Pl. G40	52	X14	River Rd. G32	54	BB16	*Crow Rd.*		
Muslin St.			River Rd. G41	51	U16	Rose Dale, Bish.	23	Y8
Reid St. G40	52	X14	*Mansionhouse Rd.*			Rose Knowe G73	52	X15
Reid St. G73	53	Y16	Riverbank St. G43	50	T16	Rose St. G3	35	V12
Reidhouse St. G21	22	X10	Riverford Rd. G43	50	T16	Rosebank Av., Blan.	69	GG19
Muir St.			Riverford Rd. G73	53	Z15	Rosebank Dr. G72	67	CC18
Reids Row, Bail.	56	FF14	Riversdale Cotts. G14	18	N9	Rosebank Ter., Bail.	57	GG14
Reidvale St. G31	36	X13	*Dumbarton Rd.*			Roseberg Pl., Clyde.	5	L7
Renfield St. G2	35	V12	Riversdale La. G14	18	N9	*Kilbowie Rd.*		
Renfield St., Renf.	17	M10	*Dumbarton Rd.*			Rosebery Pl., Clyde.	5	L7
Renfrew Ct. G2	35	V12	Riverside Ct. G44	63	V19	*Miller St.*		
Renfrew St.			Riverside Pk. G44	63	V19	Rosebery St. G5	52	X15
Renfrew La. G2	35	V12	*Linnpark Av.*			Rosedale Av. G78	44	F16
Renfield St.			Riverside Pl. G72	67	DD17	Rosedale Dr., Bail.	56	EE14
Renfrew Rd. G51	32	P11	Riverside Rd. G43	51	U16	Rosedale Gdns. G20	20	T8
Renfrew Rd., Pais.	30	K13	Riverview Av. G5	35	V13	Rosefield Gdns., Udd.	57	GG16
Renfrew Rd., Renf.	32	P11	*West St.*			Roselea Gdns. G13	19	R8
Renfrew St. G3	35	V11	Riverview Dr. G5	35	V13	Roselea Pl., Blan.	68	FF19
Rennies Rd., Renf.	16	J8	Riverview Gdns. G5	35	V13	Rosemont Meadows,	69	GG19
Renshaw Dr. G52	32	P13	Riverview Pl. G5	35	V13	Both.		
Renshaw Rd., John.	44	F15	Roaden Av., Pais.	45	G16	Rosemount, Cumb.	70	NN1
Renton St. G4	36	W11	Roaden Rd., Pais.	45	G16	Rosemount Cres. G21	37	Y11
Renwick St. G41	35	U13	Roadside, Cumb.	71	PP1	Rosemount St. G21	36	X11
Scotland St.			Robb St. G21	22	X10	Rosemount Ter. G51	35	U13
Residdl Rd. G33	25	DD9	Robert Burns Av.,	5	M6	*Paisley Rd. W.*		
Reston Dr. G52	32	P13	Clyde.			Rosevale Rd., Bear.	7	R6
Reuther Av. G73	53	Y16	Robert St. G51	34	S12	Rosevale St. G11	34	S11
Revoch Dr. G13	18	P8	Robert Templeton Dr.	67	CC17	Rosewood Av., Pais.	45	H15
Rhannan Rd. G44	63	V17	G72			Rosewood St. G13	19	R8
Rhannan Ter. G44	63	V17	Roberton Av. G41	50	T15	Roslea Dr. G31	37	Y12
Rhindhouse Pl., Bail.	40	FF13	Roberts St., Dalm.	4	K6	Roslyn Dr., Bail.	41	GG13
Rhindhouse Rd., Bail.	40	FF13	Robertson La. G2	35	V12	Rosneath St. G51	34	S12
Swinton Av.			*Robertson St.*			Ross Av., Renf.	31	L11
Rhindmuir Av., Bail.	40	FF13	Robertson St. G2	35	V12	Ross Hall Pl., Renf.	17	M10
Rhindmuir Dr., Bail.	40	FF13	Robertson St., Barr.	59	L18	Ross St. G40	36	W13
Rhindmuir Gro., Bail.	40	FF13	Robertson Ter., Bail.	40	FF13	Ross St., Pais.	47	L14
Rhindmuir Rd., Bail.	40	FF13	*Edinburgh Rd.*			Rossendale Rd. G43	50	T16
Rhindmuir Vw., Bail.	40	FF13	Robin Way G32	55	CC16	Rosshall Av., Pais.	47	M14
Rhinds St., Coat.	57	HH14	Robroyston Av. G33	24	AA10	Rosshill Av. G52	32	N13
Rhinsdale Cres., Bail.	40	FF13	Robroyston Rd. G33	24	AA9	Rosshill Rd. G52	32	N13
Rhumhor Gdns., John.	43	C15	Robslee Cres., Thorn.	62	S18	Rossie Cres., Bish.	23	Z8
Rhymer St. G21	36	X11	Robslee Dr., Giff.	62	S18	Rosslea Dr., Giff.	62	T19
Rhymie Rd. G32	55	CC14	Robslee Rd., Thorn.	62	S19	Rosslyn Av. G73	53	Y16
Rhynie Dr. G51	34	S13	Robson Gro. G42	51	V15	Rosslyn Rd., Bear.	6	P5
Riccarton St. G42	52	W15	Rock Dr. G78	42	B15	Rosslyn Ter. G12	20	T10
Riccartsbar Av., Pais.	46	J14	Rock St. G4	21	V10	*Horslethill Rd.*		
Richard St. G2	35	V12	Rockall Dr. G44	64	W18	Rostan Rd. G43	62	T17
Cadogan St.			Rockbank Pl. G40	37	Y13	Rosyth Rd. G5	52	X15
Richard St., Renf.	17	M10	*Broad St.*			Rosyth St. G5	52	X15
Richmond Ct. G73	53	Z16	Rockbank Pl., Clyde.	5	L5	Rotherwick Dr., Pais.	48	N14
Richmond Dr. G72	66	AA17	*Glasgow Rd.*			Rotherwood Av. G13	7	Q7

131

Street	No.	Grid
Rotherwood Av., Pais.	45	G16
Rotherwood La. G13	7	Q7
Rotherwood Av.		
Rotherwood Pl. G13	19	Q8
Rothes Dr. G23	8	T7
Rothes Pl. G23	8	T7
Rottenrow G4	36	W12
Rottenrow E. G4	36	W12
Roual Ter., Pais.	31	L13
Greenlaw Av.		
Rouken Glen Rd., Thorn.	61	R19
Roukenburn St. G46	61	R18
Roundhill Dr., John.	45	G14
Rowallan Gdns. G11	20	S10
Rowallan La. G11	20	S10
Churchill Dr.		
Rowallan La. E. G11	20	S10
Churchill Dr.		
Rowallan Rd., Thorn.	61	R19
Rowallan Ter. G33	24	BB10
Rowan Av., Renf.	17	M10
Rowan Cres., Lenz.	13	CC5
Rowan Dr., Dalm.	4	K6
Rowan Gdns. G41	50	S14
Rowan Gdns. G71	69	HH18
Rowan Gate, Pais.	46	K15
Rowan Pl. G72	67	CC17
Caledonian Circuit		
Rowan Rd. G41	50	S14
Rowan Rd., Cumb.	71	QQ2
Rowan Rd., Linw.	28	E12
Rowan St., Pais.	46	K15
Rowand Av., Giff.	62	T19
Rowandale Av., Bail.	56	EE14
Rowanlea Av. G78	45	G16
Rowanlea Dr., Giff.	62	T18
Rowanpark Dr., Barr.	59	L17
Rowans, The, Bish.	10	X7
Rowans Gdns., Both.	69	HH18
Rowantree Av. G73	65	Y17
Rowantree Gdns. G73	65	Y17
Rowantree Rd., John.	43	D15
Rowchester St. G40	37	Y13
Rowena Av. G13	7	Q7
Roxburgh La. G12	20	T10
Saltoun St.		
Roxburgh Rd., Pais.	44	F16
Roxburgh St. G12	20	T10
Roy St. G21	22	W10
Royal Bk. Pl. G1	36	W12
Buchanan St.		
Royal Cres. G3	35	U11
Royal Cres. G42	51	V15
Royal Ex. Bldgs. G1	36	W12
Royal Ex. Sq.		
Royal Ex. Ct. G1	36	W12
Queen St.		
Royal Ex. Sq. G1	36	W12
Campbell St.		
Royal Inch Cres., Renf.	17	M9
Royal Inch Ter., Renf.	17	M9
Royal Ter. G3	35	U11
Royal Ter. G42	51	V15
Queens Dr.		
Royal Ter. La. G3	35	U11
North Claremont St.		
Royston Rd. G21	36	X11
Royston Sq. G21	36	X11
Roystonhill G21	36	X11
Rozelle Av. G15	6	P6
Rubislaw Dr., Bear.	7	R6
Ruby St. G40	53	Y14
Ruchazie Pl. G33	38	AA12
Ruchazie Rd. G32	38	AA13
Ruchill Pl. G20	21	U9
Ruchill St. G20	21	U9
Ruel St. G44	51	V16
Rufflees Av., Barr.	59	M18
Rugby Av. G13	18	P8
Rullion Pl. G33	38	AA12
Rumford St. G40	52	X14
Rupert St. G4	35	U11
Rushyhill St. G21	23	Y10
Cockmuir St.		
Ruskin La. G12	21	U10
Ruskin Pl. G12	20	T10
Great Western Rd.		
Ruskin Sq., Bish.	11	Y7
Ruskin Ter. G12	21	U10
Ruskin Ter. G73	53	Y15
Russel Pl., Linw.	28	E13
Gilmerton Rd.		
Russell Cres., Bail.	56	FF14
Russell Dr., Bear.	7	R5
Russell St. G11	34	S11
Vine St.		
Russell St., John.	44	E14
Russell St., Pais.	30	J12
Rutherford Av., Chr.	14	EE5
Chryston Rd.		
Rutherford La. G2	35	V12
Hope St.		
Rutherglen Rd. G5	36	W13
Ruthven Av., Giff.	62	T19
Ruthven La. G12	20	T10
Byres Rd.		
Ruthven Pl., Bish.	23	Z8
Ruthven St. G12	20	T10
Rutland Cres. G51	35	U13
Rutland La. G51	35	U13
Govan Rd.		
Rutland Pl. G51	35	U13
Ryan Rd., Bish.	11	Y7
Ryan Way G73	65	Z18
Rye Cres. G21	23	Z9
Rye Rd. G21	23	Z9
Rye Way, Pais.	45	G15
Ryebank Rd. G21	23	Z9
Ryecroft Dr., Bail.	40	EE13
Ryedale Pl. G15	6	P6
Ryefield Av., John.	43	C15
Ryefield Pl., John.	43	C15
Ryefield Rd. G21	23	Y9
Ryehill Gdns. G21	23	Z9
Ryehill Pl. G21	23	Z9
Ryehill Rd. G21	23	Z9
Ryemount Rd. G21	23	Z9
Ryeside Rd. G21	23	Y9
Rylands Dr. G32	55	DD14
Rylands Gdns. G32	55	DD14
Rylees Cres. G52	32	N12
Rylees Pl. G52	32	N13
Rylees Rd. G52	32	N13
Ryvra Rd. G13	19	Q9
Sackville Av. G13	19	R9
Sackville La. G13	19	R9
Sackville Av.		
Saddell Rd. G15	6	P6
St. Abbs Dr., Pais.	45	H15
St. Andrews Av., Pais.	10	X7
St. Andrews Av., Both.	69	HH19
St. Andrews Cres. G41	51	U14
St. Andrews Cres., Pais.	30	J11
St. Andrews Cross G41	51	V14
St. Andrews Dr. G41	50	T15
St. Andrews Dr., Pais.	30	K11
St. Andrews Dr. W., Pais.	30	J11
St. Andrews La. G1	36	W13
Gallowgate		
St. Andrews Rd. G41	51	U14
St. Andrews Rd., Renf.	31	M11
St. Andrews Sq. G1	36	W13
St. Andrews St. G1	36	W13
St. Anns Dr., Giff.	62	T19
St. Blanes Dr. G73	64	X17
St. Boswells Cres., Pais.	45	H15
St. Brides Rd. G43	50	T16
St. Bride's Way, Udd.	69	HH18
St. Catherines Rd., Giff.	62	T19
St. Clair Av., Giff.	62	T18
St. Clair St. G20	35	U11
Woodside Rd.		
St. Conval Pl. G43	50	S16
Shawbridge St.		
St. Cyrus Gdns., Bish.	11	Z7
St. Cyrus Rd., Bish.	11	Y7
St. Enoch Sq. G1	35	V13
St. Enoch Wynd G2	35	V12
Argyle St.		
St. Fillans Rd. G33	25	CC9
St. Georges Cross G3	35	V11
St. Georges Pl. G20	35	V11
St. Georges Rd.		
St. Georges Rd. G3	35	V11
St. Germains, Bear.	7	R6
St. Helena Cres., Clyde.	5	M5
St. Ives Rd., Chr.	15	GG6
St. James Av., Pais.	29	H12
St. James Pl., Pais.	30	K13
Love St.		
St. James Rd. G4	36	W12
St. James St., Pais.	30	K13
St. Johns Ct. G41	51	U14
St. Johns Quad. G41	51	U14
St. Johns Rd. G41	51	U14
St. Johns Ter. G12	35	U11
Southpark Av.		
St. Josephs Pl. G40	36	X13
Abercromby St.		
St. Kenneth Dr. G51	33	R12
St. Kilda Dr. G14	19	R10
St. Leonards Dr., Giff.	62	T18
St. Margarets Pl. G1	36	W13
Bridgegate		
St. Mark Gdns. G32	38	AA13
St. Mark St.		
St. Mark St. G32	38	AA13
St. Marnock St. G40	37	Y13
St. Marys La. G2	35	V12
West Nile St.		
St. Marys Rd., Bish.	10	X7
St. Mirren St., Pais.	46	K14
St. Monance St. G21	22	X9
St. Mungo Av. G4	36	W12
St. Mungo Pl. G4	36	W12
St. Mungo St., Bish.	22	X8
St. Mungos Rd. G67	70	NN3
St. Ninian St. G5	36	W13
St. Ninians Cres., Pais.	46	K15
Rowan St.		
St. Ninians Rd., Pais.	46	K15
St. Peters La. G2	35	V12
Blythswood St.		
St. Peters St. G4	35	V11
St. Ronans Dr. G41	50	T15
St. Ronans Dr. G73	65	Z17
St. Stephens Av. G73	65	Z18
St. Stephens Cres. G73	66	AA18
St. Valleyfield St. G21	22	X10
Ayr St.		
St. Vincent Cres. G3	34	T12
St. Vincent Cres. La. G3	35	U12
Corunna St.		
St. Vincent La. G2	35	V12
Hope St.		
St. Vincent Pl. G1	36	W12
St. Vincent St. G2	35	U12
St. Vincent Ter. G3	35	U12
Salamanca St. G31	37	Z13
Salen St. G52	33	R13
Salisbury Pl. G12	20	T10
Great Western Rd.		
Salisbury Pl., Dalm.	4	K5
Salisbury St. G5	51	V14
Salkeld St. G5	51	V14
Salmona St. G22	21	V10
Saltaire Av., Udd.	69	HH17
Salterland Rd. G53	60	N17
Saltmarket G1	36	W13
Saltmarket Pl. G1	36	W13
King St.		
Saltoun Gdns. G12	20	T10
Roxburgh St.		
Saltoun La. G12	20	T10
Ruthven St.		
Saltoun St. G12	20	T10
Salvia St. G72	66	AA17
Sanda St. G20	21	U10
Sandaig Rd. G33	39	DD13
Sandbank Av. G20	20	T9
Sandbank St. G20	20	T9
Sandbank Ter. G20	20	T8

Sandeman St. G11	33	R11
Sandend Rd. G53	48	P16
Sanderling Pl., John.	43	C16
Sandfield St. G20	21	U9
Maryhill Rd.		
Sandford Gdns., Bail.	56	EE14
Scott St.		
Sandgate Av. G32	55	CC14
Sandhaven Rd. G53	48	P16
Sandholes, Pais.	46	J14
Sandholm Pl. G14	18	N9
Sandholm Ter. G14	18	N9
Sandiefauld St. G5	52	W14
Sandielands Av., Renf.	16	J8
Sandilands St. G32	38	BB13
Sandmill St. G21	37	Y11
Sandra Rd., Bish.	11	Z7
Sandringham Dr., John.	44	E16
Glamis Av.		
Sandringham La. G12	20	T10
Kersland St.		
Sandwood Cres. G52	32	P13
Sandwood Rd.		
Sandwood Path G52	32	P13
Sandwood Rd. G52	32	P13
Sandy La. G11	34	S11
Crawford St.		
Sandy Rd. G11	34	S11
Sandy Rd., Renf.	31	M11
Sandyford Pl. G3	35	U12
Sandyford Pl. La. G3	35	U11
Elderslie St.		
Sandyford Rd., Renf.	31	L12
Sandyford St. G3	34	T12
Sandyhills Cres. G32	54	BB14
Sandyhills Dr. G32	54	BB14
Sandyhills Gro. G32	55	CC15
Hamilton Rd.		
Sandyhills Pl. G32	54	BB14
Sandyhills Rd. G32	54	BB14
Sandyknowes Rd., Cumb.	71	PP4
Sanguhar Gdns., Blan.	68	EE19
Sanilands St. G32	38	BB13
Annick St.		
Sannox Gdns. G31	37	Y12
Saracen Gdns. G22	22	W9
Saracen Head La. G1	36	W13
Gallowgate		
Saracen St. G22	22	W10
Sardinia La. G12	20	T10
Great George St.		
Sardinia Ter. G12	20	T10
Cecil St.		
Saucel Lonend, Pais.	46	K14
Saucel St., Pais.	46	K14
Saucelhill Ter., Pais.	46	K14
Sauchenhall Rd., Chr.	15	GG5
Sauchiehall La. G3	35	V12
Sauchiehall St.		
Sauchiehall St. G3	35	U12
Saughs Av. G33	24	AA9
Saughs Dr. G33	24	AA9
Saughs Gate G33	24	AA9
Saughs Pl. G33	24	AA9
Saughs Rd. G33	24	AA9
Saughton St. G32	38	AA12
Savoy Arc. G40	52	X14
Main St.		
Savoy St. G40	52	X14
Sawfield Pl. G4	35	V11
Garscube Rd.		
Sawmill Rd. G11	33	R11
South St.		
Sawmillfield St. G4	35	V11
Saxon Rd. G13	19	Q8
Scadlock Rd., Pais.	29	H13
Scalpay Pl. G22	22	W8
Scalpay St. G22	22	W8
Scapa Pl. G23	21	U8
Scapa St. G40	53	Y14
Springfield Rd.		
Scaraway Dr. G22	22	W8
Scaraway Pl. G22	22	W8
Scaraway St. G22	22	W8
Scaraway Ter. G22	22	W8

Scarba Dr. G43	62	S17
Scarrell Dr. G45	65	Y18
Scarrell Rd. G45	65	Y18
Scarrell Ter. G45	65	Y18
Schaw Ct., Bear.	7	Q5
Schaw Dr., Bear.	7	R5
Schaw Rd., Pais.	31	L13
Schipka Pas. G1	36	W13
Gallowgate		
School Av. G72	66	BB17
School Rd. G33	25	DD9
School Rd., Pais.	32	N13
School Wynd, Pais.	30	K13
Scioncroft Av. G73	53	Z16
Scone St. G21	22	W10
Sconser St. G23	9	U7
Scorton Gdns., Bail.	55	DD14
Scotland St. G5	35	U13
Scotland St. W. G41	34	T13
Scotsblair Av., Lenz.	13	CC5
Scotsburn Rd. G21	23	Z10
Scotstoun Mill Rd. G11	34	T11
Partick Bri. St.		
Scotstoun Pl. G14	19	Q10
Scotstoun St.		
Scotstoun St. G14	19	Q10
Scott Av., John.	43	D16
Scott Dr., Bear.	7	Q5
Scott Rd. G52	32	N12
Scott St. G3	35	V11
Scott St., Bail.	56	EE14
Scott St., Dalm.	4	K6
Scotts Rd., Pais.	47	M14
Sea Path G53	60	N17
Sea Pl. G53	60	N17
Seafar Rd., Cumb.	70	NN4
Seafield Dr. G73	65	Z18
Seaforth Cres., Barr.	59	L18
Seaforth La., Chr.	15	HH7
Burnbrae Av.		
Seaforth Rd. G52	32	P12
Seaforth Rd., Clyde.	5	L7
Seaforth Rd. N. G52	32	P12
Seaforth Rd. S. G52	32	P12
Seagrove St. G32	37	Z13
Seamill St. G53	60	N17
Seamore St. G20	35	U11
Seath Rd. G73	53	Y15
Seath St. G42	52	W15
Seaward La. G41	35	U13
Seaward St.		
Seaward St. G41	35	U13
Second Av. G33	24	BB9
Second Av. G44	63	V17
Second Av., Bear.	8	S6
Second Av., Clyde.	5	L6
Second Av., Lenz.	13	CC7
Second Av., Renf.	31	M11
Second Av., Udd.	57	GG15
Second Gdns. G41	50	S14
Second St., Udd.	57	GG16
Seedhill, Pais.	46	K14
Seedhill Rd., Pais.	46	K14
Seggielea La. G13	19	Q9
Helensburgh Dr.		
Seggielea Rd. G13	19	Q9
Seil Dr. G44	64	W18
Selborne Pl. G13	19	R9
Selborne Rd.		
Selborne Pl. La. G13	19	R9
Selborne Rd.		
Selborne Rd. G13	19	R9
Selby Gdns. G32	39	DD13
Selkirk Av. G52	49	Q14
Selkirk Av., Pais.	45	H15
Selkirk Dr. G73	53	Z16
Sella Rd., Bish.	11	Z7
Selvieland Rd. G52	32	N13
Semple Pl., Linw.	28	E12
Seton Ter. G31	36	X12
Settle Gdns., Bail.	55	DD14
Seven Sisters, Lenz.	13	DD5
Seventh Av., Udd.	57	GG16
Seyton Av., Giff.	62	T19
Shaftesbury St., Dalm.	4	K7

Shafton Pl. G13	19	R8
Shafton Rd. G13	19	R8
Shaftsbury St. G3	35	U12
Shakespeare Av., Clyde.	4	K6
Shakespeare St. G20	21	U9
Shamrock Cotts. G13	19	R9
Crow Rd.		
Shamrock St. G4	35	V11
Shandon St. G51	34	T12
Govan Rd.		
Shandwick St. G34	40	EE12
Shanks Av., Barr.	59	M19
Shanks Cres., John.	43	D15
Shanks St. G20	21	U9
Shannon St. G20	21	U9
Shapinsay St. G22	22	W8
Sharp St. G51	34	S12
Sharrocks St. G51	34	T13
Clifford St.		
Shaw Pl., Linw.	28	E13
Shaw St. G51	34	S12
Shawbridge St. G43	50	T16
Shawfield Dr. G5	52	X15
Shawfield Rd. G5	52	X15
Shawhill Rd. G43	50	T16
Shawholm Cres. G43	50	S16
Shawlands Arc. G41	51	U16
Shawlands Sq. G41	51	U16
Shawmoss Rd. G41	50	T15
Shawpark St. G20	21	U9
Shearer La. G5	35	U13
Shearer Pl. G51	35	U13
Sheddons Pl. G32	38	AA13
Sheepburn Rd., Udd.	57	GG16
Sheila St. G33	24	AA10
Sheldrake Pl., John.	43	C16
Shelley Ct. G12	20	S9
Shelley Rd.		
Shelley Dr., Clyde.	5	L6
Shelley Dr., Udd.	69	HH18
Shelley Rd. G12	19	R9
Sheppard St. G21	22	X10
Cowlairs Rd.		
Sherbrooke Av. G41	50	T14
Sherbrooke Dr. G41	50	T14
Sherburn Gdns., Bail.	55	DD14
Sheriff Pk. Av. G73	53	Y16
Sherwood Av., Pais.	31	L13
Sherwood Av., Udd.	69	HH17
Sherwood Dr. G46	62	S18
Sherwood Pl. G15	6	P6
Shetland Dr. G44	64	W18
Shettleston Rd. G31	37	Z13
Shettleston Sheddings	38	AA13
G31		
Shiel Ct., Barr.	59	L17
Shiel Rd., Bish.	11	Y7
Shieldaig Dr. G73	65	Y18
Shieldaig Rd. G22	21	V8
Shieldbridge Gdns. G23	9	U7
Shieldburn Rd. G51	33	Q12
Shieldhall Gdns. G51	33	Q12
Shieldhall Rd. G51	33	Q12
Shields Rd. G41	35	U13
Shilford Av. G13	18	P8
Shillay St. G22	22	X8
Shilton Dr. G53	60	P17
Shinwell Av., Clyde.	5	M7
Shipbank La. G1	36	W13
Clyde St.		
Shiskine Dr. G20	20	T8
Shiskine Pl. G20	20	T8
Shiskine St.		
Shiskine St. G20	20	T8
Shore St. G40	52	X15
Shortbridge St. G20	21	U9
Shanks St.		
Shortroods Av., Pais.	30	K12
Shortroods Cres., Pais.	30	K12
Shortroods Rd., Pais.	30	J12
Shotts St. G33	39	CC12
Shuna Pl. G20	21	U9
Shuna St. G20	21	U9
Shuttle La. G1	36	W12
George St.		

133

Location	Page	Grid
Shuttle St. G1	36	W12
Shuttle St., Kilb.	42	B14
Shuttle St., Pais.	46	K14
Sidelaw Av., Barr.	59	M19
Ochil Dr.		
Sidland Rd. G21	23	Z9
Sidlaw Rd., Bear.	6	P5
Sielga Pl. G34	40	EE12
Siemens Pl. G21	37	Y11
Siemens St. G21	37	Y11
Sievewright St. G73	53	Z15
Hunter Rd.		
Silk St., Pais.	30	K13
Silkin Av., Clyde.	5	M7
Silverburn St. G33	38	AA12
Silverdale St. G31	53	Z14
Silverfir St. G5	52	W14
Silvergrove St. G40	36	X13
Silverwells, Both.	69	HH19
Silverwells Cres., Both.	69	HH19
Simons Cres., Renf.	17	M9
Simpson Ct., Udd.	69	GG17
Simpson St. G20	21	U10
Simshill Rd. G44	63	V18
Sinclair Av., Bear.	7	R5
Sinclair Dr. G42	51	U16
Sinclair St., Clyde.	17	M8
Singer Rd., Dalm.	4	K6
Singer St., Clyde.	5	L6
Sir Michael Pl., Pais.	46	J14
Sixth Av., Renf.	31	M11
Sixth St., Udd.	57	GG15
Skaethorn Rd. G20	20	S8
Skaterig La. G13	19	R9
Skaterigg Rd. G13	19	R9
Crow Rd.		
Skelbo Path G34	40	FF11
Auchengill Rd.		
Skelbo Pl. G34	40	FF11
Skene Rd. G51	34	S13
Skerray Quad. G22	22	W8
Skerray St. G22	22	W8
Skerryvore Pl. G33	38	BB12
Skerryvore Rd. G33	38	BB12
Skibo Dr. G46	61	R18
Skibo La. G46	61	R18
Skipness Dr. G51	33	R12
Skirsa Ct. G23	21	V8
Skirsa Pl. G23	21	U8
Skirsa Sq. G23	21	U8
Skirsa St. G23	21	U8
Skirving St. G41	51	U16
Skye Av. G67	31	M11
Skye Ct., Cumb.	70	MM4
Skye Cres., Old K.	4	J5
Skye Cres., Pais.	46	J16
Skye Dr., Cumb.	70	MM4
Skye Dr., Old K.	4	J5
Skye Gdns., Bear.	6	P5
Skye Pl., Cumb.	70	MM4
Skye Rd. G73	65	Z18
Skye Rd., Cumb.	70	MM4
Skye St. G20	20	T8
Bantaskin St.		
Slakiewood Av., Gart.	27	GG8
Slatefield St. G31	37	Y13
Sleads St. G41	35	U13
Sloy St. G22	22	W10
Smeaton St. G20	21	U9
Smith Cres., Clyde.	5	L5
Smith St. G14	33	R11
Smith Ter. G73	53	Y15
Smithhills St., Pais.	30	K13
Smiths La., Pais.	30	K13
Smithy Ends, Cumb.	71	PP1
Smithycroft Rd. G33	38	AA11
Snaefell Av. G73	65	Z18
Snaefell Cres. G73	65	Z17
Society St. G31	37	Y13
Soho St. G40	37	Y13
Sollas Pl. G13	18	N8
Solway Pl., Chr.	14	FF7
Solway Rd., Bish.	11	Z7
Solway St. G40	52	X15
Somerford Rd., Bear.	7	R7
Somerled Av., Renf.	31	L11
Somerset Pl. G3	35	U11
Somerset Pl. Meuse G3	35	U11
Elderslie St.		
Somervell St. G72	66	AA17
Somerville Dr. G42	51	V16
Somerville St., Clyde.	5	L7
Sorby St. G31	37	Z13
Sorn St. G40	53	Y14
Souter La., Clyde.	5	M6
South Annandale St. G42	51	V15
South Av., Clyde.	5	L7
South Av., Pais.	46	K16
South Av., Renf.	17	M10
South Bk. St., Clyde.	17	M8
South Brook St., Clyde.	4	K6
South Campbell St., Pais.	46	K14
South Carbrain Rd., Cumb.	71	PP4
South Chester St. G32	38	BB13
South Cotts. G14	33	R11
Curle St.		
South Cft. St., Pais.	30	K13
Lawn St.		
South Crosshill Rd., Bish.	11	Y7
South Deanpark Av., Udd.	69	HH19
South Douglas St., Clyde.	17	M8
South Dr., Linw.	28	E13
South Elgin Pl., Clyde.	17	M8
South Elgin St.		
South Elgin St., Clyde.	17	M8
South Erskin Pk., Bear.	7	Q5
South Ex. Ct. G1	36	W12
Queen St.		
South Frederick St. G1	36	W12
South Hill Av. G73	65	Z17
South Moraine La. G15	7	Q7
Moraine Av.		
South Muirhead Rd., Cumb.	71	PP3
South Pk. Dr., Pais.	46	K15
South Portland St. G5	35	V13
South Scott St., Bail.	56	EE14
South Spiers Wf. G4	35	V11
South St. G14	18	P10
South Vesalius St. G32	38	BB13
South Vw., Blan.	68	FF19
South Vw., Dalm.	4	K6
South Vw., Lenz.	13	CC7
Gadloch Av.		
South Wardpark Ct., Cumb.	71	QQ1
Wardpark Rd.		
South Wardpark Pl., Cumb.	71	QQ1
South William St., John.	43	D15
South Woodside Rd. G4	35	U11
Southampton Dr. G12	20	S9
Southbank St. G31	37	Z13
Sorby St.		
Southbrae Av. G13	18	P8
Southbrae Dr. G13	19	Q9
Southbrae La. G13	19	R9
Milner Rd.		
Southcroft Rd. G73	52	X15
Southcroft St. G51	34	S12
Southdeen Av. G15	6	P6
Southdeen Rd. G15	6	P6
Southend Rd., Clyde.	5	L5
Southern Av. G73	65	Y17
Southerness Dr., Cumb.	71	PP1
Dornoch Way		
Southesk Av., Bish.	10	X7
Southesk Gdns., Bish.	10	X6
Southfield Av., Pais.	46	K16
Southfield Cres. G53	49	Q16
Southfield Rd., Cumb.	70	MM3
Southinch Av. G14	18	N9
Southinch La. G14	18	N9
Tweedvale Av.		
Southlea Av. G46	62	S16
Southlock St. G21	22	X10
Southmuir Pl. G20	20	T9
Southpark Av. G12	34	T11
Southpark La. G12	21	U10
Glasgow St.		
Southpark Ter. G12	35	U11
Southpark Av.		
Southview Ct. G64	22	X8
Southview Dr., Bear.	7	Q5
Southview Pl., Gart.	27	GG9
Southview Ter. G21	22	X8
Southwold Rd., Pais.	32	N13
Southwood Dr. G44	64	W17
Spateston Rd., John.	43	C16
Spean St. G44	51	V16
Speirs Pl., Linw.	28	E12
Speirs Rd., John.	44	E14
Speirshall Clo. G14	18	N9
Speirshall Ter. G14	18	N9
Spence St. G20	20	T8
Spencer Dr. G78	44	F16
Spencer St. G13	19	R8
Spencer St., Clyde.	5	L6
Spey Av., Pais.	45	G15
Spey Dr., Renf.	32	N11
Almond Av.		
Spey Pl., John.	43	C16
Spey Rd., Bear.	7	Q7
Spey St. G33	38	AA12
Spiers Rd., Bear.	8	S6
Spiersbridge Av., Thorn.	61	R18
Spiersbridge La. G46	61	R18
Spiersbridge Rd., Thorn.	61	R19
Spiersbridge Ter. G46	61	R18
Spindlehowe Rd., Udd.	69	GG17
Spingburn Way G21	22	X10
Spinner Gdns., Pais.	45	H14
Spinners Row, John.	43	C15
Spittal Rd. G73	64	X18
Spittal Ter. G72	68	EE19
Spoutmouth G1	36	W13
Spring La. G5	52	W14
Lawmoor St.		
Springbank Rd., Pais.	30	J12
Springbank St. G20	21	U10
Springbank Ter., Pais.	30	J12
Springboig Av. G32	39	CC13
Springboig Rd. G32	39	CC12
Springburn Rd. G21	22	X9
Springburn Way G21	22	X10
Springcroft Av., Bail.	40	EE13
Springcroft Dr., Bail.	40	EE13
Springcroft Rd., Bail.	40	EE13
Springfield Av., Bish.	23	Y8
Springfield Av., Pais.	47	M14
Springfield Av., Udd.	69	GG17
Springfield Ct. G1	36	W12
Springfield Cres., Bish.	23	Y8
Springfield Cres., Both.	69	GG17
Springfield Dr., Barr.	60	N19
Springfield Pk., John.	44	E15
Springfield Pk. Rd. G73	65	Z17
Springfield Quay G51	35	U13
Springfield Rd. G40	53	Y14
Springfield Rd., Bish.	11	Y7
Springfield Rd., Cumb.	71	PP2
Springfield Sq., Bish.	23	Y8
Springhill Gdns. G41	51	U15
Springhill Rd., Bail.	39	DD13
Springhill Rd., Barr.	59	L19
Springkell Av. G41	50	T14
Springkell Dr. G41	50	S14
Springkell Gdns. G41	50	T15
Springkell Gate G41	50	T15
Springside Pl. G15	6	P6
Springvale Ter. G21	22	X10
Hillkirk Pl.		
Spruce Av., John.	44	E15
Spruce Dr., Lenz.	12	BB5
Spruce Rd., Cumb.	71	QQ2
Spruce St. G22	22	W9
Spynie Pl., Bish.	11	Z7
Squire St. G14	33	R11
Staffa Av., Renf.	31	M11

Street	Page	Grid
Staffa Dr., Pais.	46	K16
Staffa Rd. G72	66	AA18
Staffa St. G31	37	Y12
Staffa Ter. G72	66	AA18
Staffin Dr. G23	8	T7
Staffin St. G23	9	U7
Stafford St. G4	36	W11
Stag St. G51	34	T12
Stair St. G20	21	U10
Stamford St. G40	37	Y13
Stamperland Gdns., Clark.	63	U19
Stanalane St. G46	61	R18
Standburn Rd. G21	23	Z8
Stanely Av., Pais.	45	H15
Stanely Ct., Pais.	45	H15
Stanely Cres., Pais.	45	H16
Stanely Dr., Pais.	46	J15
Stanely Rd., Pais.	46	J15
Stanford St., Clyde.	5	M7
Stanhope Dr. G73	65	Z17
Stanley Dr., Bish.	11	Y6
Stanley Pl., Blan.	68	FF19
Stanley St. G41	35	U13
Stanley St. La. G41	35	U13
Milnpark St.		
Stanmore Rd. G42	51	V16
Stark Av., Clyde.	4	K5
Startpoint St. G33	38	BB12
Station Rd. G20	20	T8
Station Rd. G33	24	BB9
Station Rd., Bail.	56	FF14
Station Rd., Bear.	7	Q6
Station Rd., Blan.	69	GG19
Station Rd., Both.	69	HH19
Station Rd., Chr.	26	FF9
Station Rd., Giff.	62	T18
Fenwick Rd.		
Station Rd., Kilb.	42	B15
Station Rd., Pais.	45	H14
Station Rd., Renf.	17	M10
Station Rd., Step.	25	CC9
Station Rd., Udd.	69	GG17
Station Way, Udd.	69	HH17
Mansefield Dr.		
Station Wynd G78	42	B15
Steel St. G1	36	W13
Steeple St., Kilb.	42	B14
Stenton St. G32	38	AA12
Stepford Path G33	40	EE12
Stepford Rd.		
Stepford Pl. G33	39	DD12
Stepford Rd. G33	39	DD12
Stephen Cres., Bail.	39	DD13
Stephenson St. G52	32	N12
Stepps Rd. G33	39	CC11
Stepps Rd., Lenz.	13	DD7
Steppshill Ter. G33	25	CC9
Stevbrae, Lenz.	13	DD5
Stevenson St. G40	36	X13
Stevenson St., Dalm.	4	K6
Stevenson St., Pais.	46	K14
Stewart Av., Renf.	31	L11
Stewart Ct., Barr.	59	M18
Stewart Dr.		
Stewart Dr., Bail.	41	HH13
Coatbridge Rd.		
Stewart Dr., Clyde.	5	L5
Stewart Rd., Pais.	46	K16
Stewart St. G4	35	V11
Stewart St., Barr.	59	M18
Stewart St., Dalm.	4	K6
Stewarton Dr. G72	66	AA17
Stewarton Rd., Thorn.	61	R19
Stewartville St. G11	34	S11
Stirling Av., Bear.	7	R7
Stirling Dr. G73	65	Y17
Stirling Dr., Bear.	7	Q5
Stirling Dr., Bish.	10	X6
Stirling Dr., John.	43	C15
Stirling Dr., Linw.	28	E13
Stirling Fauld Pl. G5	35	V13
Stirling Gdns., Bish.	10	X6
Stirling Rd. G4	36	W12
Stirling St., Cumb.	71	PP2
Stirling Way, Renf.	31	M11
York Way		
Stirrat St. G20	20	T9
Stirrat St., Pais.	29	H12
Stobcross Rd. G3	35	U12
Stobhill Rd. G21	22	X8
Stobs Dr., Barr.	59	L17
Stobs Pl. G34	40	FF11
Stock Av., Pais.	46	K15
Stock St., Pais.	46	K15
Stockholm Cres., Pais.	46	K14
Stockwell Pl. G1	36	W13
Stockwell St. G1	36	W13
Stoddard Sq., John.	44	F14
Glenpatrick Rd.		
Stonefield Av. G12	20	T9
Stonefield Av., Pais.	46	K15
Stonefield Cres., Pais.	46	K15
Stonefield Dr., Pais.	46	K15
Stonelaw Dr. G73	53	Y16
Stonelaw Rd. G73	53	Y16
Stoneside Dr. G43	62	S17
Stoneside Sq. G43	62	S17
Stoney Brae, Pais.	30	K13
Stoneyetts Cotts., Chr.	15	GG6
Stoneyetts Rd., Chr.	15	GG7
Stony Brae, Pais.	46	K16
Stonyhurst St. G22	21	V10
Stonylee Rd., Cumb.	71	PP3
Storie St., Pais.	46	K14
Stormyland Way, Barr.	59	M19
Stornoway St. G22	22	W8
Stow Brae, Pais.	46	K14
Stow St., Pais.	46	K14
Strachur St. G22	21	V8
Straiton St. G32	38	AA12
Stranka Av., Pais.	46	J14
Stranraer Dr. G15	7	Q7
Moraine Av.		
Stratford St. G20	21	U9
Strathallan La. G12	34	T11
Highburgh Rd.		
Strathallan Ter. G12	34	T11
Caledon St.		
Strathallon Pl. G73	65	Z18
Ranald Gdns.		
Strathbran St. G31	53	Z14
Strathcarron Pl. G20	20	T9
Glenfinnan Rd.		
Strathcarron Rd., Pais.	47	L15
Strathclyde Dr. G73	53	Y16
Strathclyde Path, Udd.	69	GG17
Strathclyde St. G40	53	Y15
Strathclyde Vw. G71	69	HH19
Strathcona Dr. G13	19	R8
Strathcona Gdns. G13	20	S8
Strathcona Pl. G73	65	Z18
Strathcona St. G13	19	R9
Strathdee Av., Clyde.	5	L5
Strathdee Rd. G44	63	U19
Strathdon Av. G44	63	U19
Strathdon Av., Pais.	46	J15
Strathdon Dr. G44	63	U19
Strathendrick Dr. G44	63	U18
Strathmore Av., Blan.	68	FF19
Strathmore Av., Pais.	47	M14
Strathmore Gdns. G12	35	U11
Gibson St.		
Strathmore Gdns. G73	65	Z18
Strathmore Rd. G22	21	V8
Strathord Pl., Chr.	15	HH6
Strathord St. G32	54	BB14
Strathtay Av. G44	63	U19
Strathview Gdns., Bear.	7	Q6
Strathview Gro. G44	63	U19
Strathview Pk. G44	63	U19
Strathy Pl. G20	20	T9
Glenfinnan Rd.		
Strathyre Gdns., Bear.	8	S5
Strathyre Gdns., Chr.	15	HH7
Heathfield Av.		
Strathyre St. G41	51	U16
Stratton Dr., Giff.	62	S19
Strauss Av., Clyde.	6	N7
Stravanan Av. G45	64	W19
Stravanan Rd. G45	64	W19
Stravanan St. G45	64	W19
Strenabey Av. G73	65	Z18
Striven Gdns. G20	21	U10
Stroma St. G21	37	Y11
Stromness St. G5	51	V14
Strone Rd. G33	38	BB12
Stronend St. G22	21	V9
Stronsay Pl., Bish.	11	Z7
Stronsay St. G21	37	Y11
Stronvar Dr. G14	18	P10
Stronvar La. G14	18	P10
Larchfield Av.		
Strowan Cres. G32	54	BB14
Strowan St. G32	54	BB14
Struan Av., Giff.	62	S18
Struan Gdns. G44	63	V17
Struan Rd. G44	63	V17
Struie St. G34	40	EE12
Stuart Av. G73	65	Y17
Stuart Dr., Bish.	22	X8
Succoth St. G13	19	R8
Suffolk St. G40	36	X13
Kent St.		
Sugworth Av., Bail.	40	EE13
Sumburgh St. G33	38	AA12
Summer St. G40	36	X13
Summerfield Cotts. G14	33	R11
Smith St.		
Summerfield Pl. G40	53	Y14
Ardenlea St.		
Summerfield St. G40	53	Y15
Summerhill Rd. G15	6	P6
Summerlee Rd., Thorn.	61	R18
Summerlee St. G33	39	CC12
Summertown Rd. G51	34	S12
Sunart Av., Renf.	17	L10
Sunart Gdns., Bish.	11	Y7
Sunart Rd. G52	33	R13
Sunart Rd., Bish.	11	Y7
Sunningdale Rd. G23	20	T8
Sunningdale Wynd, Both.	69	GG18
Sunnybank St. G40	53	Y14
Sunnylaw Dr. G78	45	H15
Sunnylaw St. G22	21	V10
Sunnyside Av., Udd.	69	GG17
Sunnyside Dr. G15	6	P7
Sunnyside Dr., Bail.	41	GG13
Sunnyside Pl. G15	6	P7
Sunnyside Dr.		
Sunnyside Pl., Barr.	59	L19
Sunnyside Rd., Pais.	46	J15
Surrey La. G5	51	V14
Pollokshaws Rd.		
Sussex St. G41	35	U13
Sutcliffe Rd. G13	19	R8
Sutherland Av. G41	50	T14
Sutherland Dr., Giff.	62	T19
Sutherland Rd., Clyde.	5	L7
Sutherland St., Pais.	30	J13
Swan La. G4	36	W11
Swan Pl., John.	43	C16
Swan St. G4	36	W11
Swan St., Clyde.	4	K6
Swanston St. G40	53	Y15
Sween Dr. G44	63	V18
Sweethope Pl., Both.	69	HH18
Swift Pl., John.	43	C16
Swindon St., Dalm.	4	K6
Swinton Av., Bail.	40	FF13
Swinton Cres., Bail.	40	FF13
Swinton Cres., Coat.	57	HH14
Swinton Dr. G52	32	P13
Swinton Gdns., Bail.	40	FF13
Swinton Av.		
Swinton Pl. G52	32	P13
Swinton Rd., Bail.	40	EE13
Swinton Vw., Bail.	40	FF13
Swinton Av.		
Switchback Rd., Bear.	7	R7
Sword St. G31	36	X13
Swordale Path G34	40	EE12
Swordale Pl.		
Swordale Pl. G34	40	EE12
Sycamore Av., John.	44	E15

Street	Page	Grid
Sycamore Av., Lenz.	13	CC5
Sycamore Dr., Dalm.	5	L6
Sydenham La. G12	20	S10
Crown Rd. S.		
Sydenham Rd. G12	20	T10
Sydney Ct. G2	35	V12
Argyle St.		
Sydney St. G31	36	X13
Sydney St., Dalm.	4	J6
Sylvania Way, Clyde.	5	L7
Sylvania Way S., Clyde.	5	L7
Symington Dr., Clyde.	5	L7
Syriam Pl. G21	22	X10
Syriam St.		
Syriam St. G21	22	X10
Tabard Pl. G13	19	Q8
Tabard Pl. N. G13	19	Q8
Tabard Rd.		
Tabard Pl. S. G13	19	Q8
Tabard Rd.		
Tabard Rd. G13	19	Q8
Tabernacle La. G72	66	BB17
Tabernacle St. G72	66	BB17
Tain Pl. G34	40	FF12
Tait Av., Barr.	59	M18
Talbot Dr. G13	18	P9
Talbot Pl. G13	18	P9
Talbot Ter. G13	18	P9
Talbot Ter., Udd.	57	GG16
Talisman Rd. G13	19	Q9
Talisman Rd., Pais.	45	G16
Talla Rd. G52	32	P13
Tallant Rd. G15	6	P6
Tallant Ter. G15	7	Q6
Tallisman, Clyde.	5	M7
Onslow Rd.		
Tambowie St. G13	19	R8
Tamshill St. G20	21	U9
Tamworth St. G40	37	Y13
Rimsdale St.		
Tanar Av., Renf.	32	N11
Tanar Way, Renf.	32	N11
Tandlehill Rd., Kilb.	42	B15
Tanera Av. G44	64	W18
Tanfield Av. G32	39	CC12
Tanfield Pl. G32	39	CC12
Tanfield Av.		
Tankerland Rd. G44	63	V17
Tanna Dr. G52	49	R14
Tannadice Av. G52	49	Q14
Tannahall Rd., Pais.	29	H13
Tannahall Ter., Pais.	29	H13
Tannahill Cres., John.	43	D15
Tannahill Rd. G43	63	U17
Tannoch Dr. G67	71	PP4
Tannoch Pl. G67	71	PP4
Tannock St. G22	21	V10
Tantallon Dr., Pais.	45	H15
Tantallon Rd. G41	51	U16
Tantallon Rd., Bail.	56	EE14
Tanzieknowe Av. G72	66	BB18
Tanzieknowe Dr. G72	66	BB18
Tanzieknowe Pl. G72	66	BB18
Tanzieknowe Rd. G72	66	BB18
Taransay St. G51	34	S12
Tarbert Av., Blan.	68	FF19
Tarbolton Dr., Clyde.	5	M6
Tarbolton Rd. G43	62	T17
Tarbolton Rd., Cumb.	71	PP3
Tarbolton Sq., Clyde.	5	M6
Tarbolton Dr.		
Tarfside Av. G52	49	Q14
Tarfside Gdns. G52	49	Q14
Tarfside Oval G52	49	Q14
Tarland St. G51	33	R13
Tarras Dr., Renf.	32	N11
Tarras Pl. G72	67	CC17
Tassie St. G41	50	T16
Tattershall Rd. G33	39	CC11
Tavistock Dr. G43	62	T17
Tay Av., Pais.	45	G15
Tay Av., Renf.	18	N10
Tay Cres. G33	38	AA11
Tay Cres., Bish.	11	Y7
Tay Pl., John.	43	C16
Tay Rd., Bear.	7	Q7
Tay Rd., Bish.	11	Y7
Taylor Av. G78	42	A14
Taylor Pl. G4	36	W12
Taylor St. G4	36	W12
Taylor St., Clyde.	17	M8
Taymouth St. G32	54	BB14
Taynish Dr. G44	64	W18
Tealing Av. G52	49	Q14
Tealing Cres. G52	49	Q14
Teasel Av. G53	60	P18
Teith Av., Renf.	32	N11
Teith Dr., Bear.	7	Q6
Teith Pl. G72	67	CC17
Teith St. G33	38	AA11
Telford Pl. G67	71	PP4
Telford Rd., Cumb.	71	PP4
Templar Av. G13	7	Q7
Temple Gdns. G13	19	R8
Temple Pl. G13	19	R8
Temple Rd. G13	20	S8
Templeland Av. G53	49	Q15
Templeland Rd. G53	49	Q15
Templeton St. G40	36	X13
Tennant Rd., Pais.	29	H13
Tennant St., Renf.	17	M10
Tennyson Dr. G31	54	AA14
Tern Pl., John.	43	C16
Terrace Pl. G72	67	DD17
Terregles Av. G41	50	T15
Terregles Cres. G41	50	T15
Terregles Dr. G41	50	T15
Teviot Av., Bish.	11	Y6
Teviot Av., Pais.	45	G16
Teviot Cres., Bear.	7	Q7
Teviot St. G3	34	T12
Teviot Ter. G20	21	U10
Sanda St.		
Teviot Ter., John.	43	C16
Thane Rd. G13	19	Q9
Thanes Gate, Both.	69	GG17
Castle Gate		
Tharsis St. G21	36	X11
Third Av. G33	24	BB9
Third Av. G44	51	V16
Third Av., Lenz.	13	CC7
Third Av., Renf.	31	M11
Third St., Udd.	57	GG16
Thirdpart Cres. G13	18	N8
Thistle Bk., Lenz.	13	CC6
Thistle Cotts. G13	19	R9
Crow Rd.		
Thistle St. G5	36	W13
Thistle St., Pais.	46	J15
Thomas Muir Av., Bish.	23	Y8
Thomas St., Pais.	45	H14
Thompson Pl., Clyde.	5	M5
Thomson Av., John.	43	D14
Thomson Dr., Bear.	7	R5
Thomson Gro. G72	54	BB16
Thomson St. G31	37	Y13
Thomson St., John.	43	D15
Thomson St., Renf.	31	M11
Thorn Brae, John.	44	E14
Thorn Dr. G73	65	Z18
Thorn Dr., Bear.	7	Q5
Thorn Rd. G46	62	S17
Thorn Rd., Bear.	7	Q5
Thorn St. G11	34	S11
Dumbarton Rd.		
Thornbank St. G3	34	T11
Yorkhill Par.		
Thornbridge Av. G12	20	T9
Balcarres Av.		
Thornbridge Av., Bail.	40	EE13
Bannercross Dr.		
Thornbridge Gdns., Bail.	40	EE13
Thornbridge Rd., Bail.	40	EE13
Thorncliffe Gdns. G41	51	U15
Thorncliffe La. G41	51	U14
Thorncroft Dr. G44	64	W18
Thornden Cotts. G14	18	N9
Dumbarton Rd.		
Thornden La. G14	18	N9
Dumbarton Rd.		
Thorndene, John.	44	E14
Thornhill, John.	44	E15
Thornhill Av., John.	44	E15
Thornhill Dr. G78	44	E15
Thornhill Path G31	37	Z13
Beattock St.		
Thornhill Path G31	37	Z13
Grier Path		
Thorniewood Gdns., Udd.	57	HH16
Thorniewood Rd., Udd.	57	GG16
Thornlea Dr., Giff.	62	T18
Thornley Av. G13	18	P9
Thornliebank Rd. G46	62	S18
Thornliebank Rd., Thorn.	61	Q19
Thornly Pk. Av., Pais.	46	K16
Thornly Pk. Dr., Pais.	46	K16
Thornly Pk. Rd., Pais.	46	K16
Thornside Rd., John.	44	E14
Thornton La. G20	21	U8
Thornton St. G20	21	U8
Thorntree Way, Udd.	69	HH18
Thornwood Av. G11	34	S11
Thornwood Av., Lenz.	12	BB5
Thornwood Cres. G11	19	Q10
Thornwood Dr.		
Thornwood Dr. G11	33	R11
Thornwood Dr., Pais.	45	H15
Thornwood Gdns. G11	34	S11
Thornwood Pl. G11	20	S10
Thornwood Quad. G11	19	Q10
Thornwood Dr.		
Thornwood Rd. G11	33	R11
Thornwood Ter. G11	33	R11
Thornyburn Dr., Bail.	56	FF14
Thornyburn Pl., Bail.	56	FF14
Three Ell Rd. G51	34	T12
Govan Rd.		
Threestonehill Av. G32	38	BB13
Thrums Av., Bish.	11	Z7
Thrums Gdns., Bish.	11	Z7
Thrush Pl., John.	43	C16
Thrushcraig Cres., Pais.	46	K15
Thurso St. G11	34	T11
Dumbarton Rd.		
Thurston Rd. G52	32	P13
Tibbermore Rd. G11	20	S10
Tillet Oval, Pais.	30	J12
Tillie St. G20	21	U10
Tillycairn Dr. G33	39	CC11
Tilt St. G33	38	AA11
Tintagel Gdns., Chr.	15	GG6
Tinto Dr., Barr.	59	L19
Tinto Rd. G43	62	T17
Tinto Rd., Bear.	6	P5
Tinto Rd., Bish.	11	Z7
Fintry Cres.		
Tinto Sq., Renf.	31	L11
Ochil Rd.		
Tinwald Av. G52	32	N13
Tinwald Path G52	32	P13
Tiree Av., Pais.	46	J16
Tiree Av., Renf.	31	M11
Tiree Ct., Cumb.	70	MM4
Tiree Dr., Cumb.	70	MM4
Tiree Gdns., Bear.	6	P5
Tiree Rd., Cumb.	70	MM4
Tiree St. G21	37	Z11
Tirry Way, Renf.	32	N11
Morriston Cres.		
Titwood Rd. G41	50	T15
Tiverton Av. G32	55	CC14
Tobago Pl. G40	36	X13
Tobago St. G40	36	X13
Tobermory Rd. G73	65	Z18
Todburn Dr., Pais.	46	K16
Todd St. G31	37	Z12
Todholm Rd., Pais.	47	L15
Todholm Ter., Pais.	47	L15
Toll La. G51	34	T13
Paisley Rd. W.		

Street	Page	Ref.
Viking Way, Renf.	31	M11
Vanguard Way		
Villafield Av., Bish.	11	Y6
Villafield Dr., Bish.	11	Y6
Villafield Ln., Bish.	11	Y6
Village Gdns., Both.	69	GG19
Village Rd. G72	67	DD17
Villiers Ct. G31	36	X13
Sword St.		
Vine St. G11	34	S11
Vinegarhill St. G31	37	Y13
Vinicombe La. G12	20	T10
Vinicombe St.		
Vinicombe St. G12	20	T10
Vintner St. G4	36	W11
Violet St., Pais.	47	L14
Virginia Bldgs. G1	36	W12
Virginia St.		
Virginia Ct. G1	36	W12
Virginia St.		
Virginia Pl. G1	36	W12
Virginia St. G1	36	W12
Viscount Av., Renf.	31	M11
Voil Dr. G44	63	V18
Vorlich Ct., Barr.	59	M19
Vulcan St. G21	22	X10
Ayr St.		
Waddel Ct. G5	36	W13
Waddel St. G5	52	W14
Waldemar Rd. G13	19	Q8
Waldo St. G13	19	R8
Walker Ct. G11	34	S11
Walker St.		
Walker Dr., John.	44	E15
Walker Sq. G20	20	T8
Bantaskin St.		
Walker St. G11	34	S11
Walker St., Pais.	46	J14
Walkerburn Rd. G52	48	P14
Walkinshaw Cres., Pais.	29	H13
Ferguslie Pk. Av.		
Walkinshaw Rd., Renf.	16	J10
Walkinshaw St. G40	53	Y14
Walkinshaw St., John.	43	D14
Walkinshaw Way, Pais.	30	J12
Broomdyke Way		
Wallace Av., John.	44	F15
Wallace Pl., Blan.	69	GG19
Wallace Rd., Renf.	31	L11
Wallace St. G5	35	V13
Wallace St. G73	53	Y16
Wallace St., Clyde.	17	L8
Wallace St., Pais.	30	K13
Wallacewell Cres. G21	23	Y9
Wallacewell Pl. G21	23	Y9
Wallacewell Quad. G21	23	Z9
Wallacewell Rd. G21	23	Y9
Wallbrae Rd., Cumb.	71	PP4
Wallneuk, Pais.	30	K13
Incle St.		
Wallneuk Rd., Pais.	30	K13
Walls St. G1	36	W12
Walmer Cres. G51	34	T13
Walmer Ter. G51	34	T13
Paisley Rd. W.		
Walnut Cres. G22	22	W9
Walnut Cres., John.	44	E15
Walnut Dr., Lenz.	12	BB5
Walnut Pl. G22	22	W9
Walnut Rd. G22	22	W9
Walter St. G31	37	Z12
Walton St. G41	51	U16
Walton St., Barr.	59	M18
Wamba Av. G13	19	R8
Wamba Pl. G13	19	R8
Wandilla Av., Clyde.	5	M7
Wanlock St. G51	34	S12
Warden Rd. G13	19	Q8
Wardhill Rd. G21	23	Y9
Wardhouse Rd., Pais.	46	J16
Wardie Path G33	39	DD12
Wardie Pl. G33	40	EE12
Wardie Rd. G33	40	EE12
Wardlaw Av. G73	53	Y16
Wardlaw Dr. G73	53	Y16
Wardlaw Rd., Bear.	7	R7
Wardpark Rd., Cumb.	71	QQ1
Wardrop St. G51	34	S12
Wardrop St., Pais.	46	K14
Ware Path G33	40	EE12
Ware Rd. G33	39	DD12
Warilda Av., Clyde.	5	M7
Warp La. G3	35	U12
Argyle St.		
Warren St. G42	51	V15
Warriston Cres. G33	37	Z12
Warriston Pl. G32	38	BB12
Warriston St. G33	37	Z12
Warroch St. G3	35	U12
Washington Rd., Renf.	30	K12
Washington St. G3	35	V12
Water Brae, Pais.	30	K13
Smithhills St.		
Water Brae, Pais.	46	K14
Forbes Pl.		
Water Rd., Barr.	59	M18
Waterfoot Av. G53	49	Q16
Waterford Rd., Giff.	62	S18
Waterloo La. G2	35	V12
Waterloo St.		
Waterloo St. G2	35	V12
Watermill Av., Lenz.	13	CC6
Waterside La., Kilb.	43	C15
Kilbarchan Rd.		
Waterside St. G5	52	W14
Waterside Ter., Kilb.	43	C15
Kilbarchan Rd.		
Watling St., Udd.	57	GG16
Watson Av. G73	52	X16
Watson Av., Linw.	28	E13
Watson St. G1	36	W13
Watson St., Udd.	69	GG17
Watt Low Av. G73	64	X17
Watt Rd. G52	32	N12
Watt St. G5	35	U13
Waukglen Av. G53	60	P19
Waukglen Cres. G53	61	Q18
Waukglen Dr. G53	60	P18
Waukglen Gdns. G53	60	P19
Waukglen Path G53	60	P18
Waukglen Rd. G53	60	P18
Waulkmill Av., Barr.	59	M18
Waulkmill St., Thorn.	61	R18
Waverley, Clyde.	5	M7
Onslow Rd.		
Waverley Ct., Udd.	69	HH19
Waverley Cres., Cumb.	70	MM4
Waverley Dr. G73	53	Z16
Waverley Gdns. G41	51	U15
Waverley Gdns., John.	44	F15
Waverley Rd., Pais.	45	G16
Waverley St. G41	51	U15
Waverley Ter. G31	37	Y13
Whitevale St.		
Waverley Way, Pais.	45	G16
Waverley Rd.		
Weardale La. G33	39	CC12
Weardale St. G33	39	CC12
Weaver La., Kilb.	42	B14
Glentyan Av.		
Weaver St. G4	36	W12
Weaver Ter., Pais.	47	L14
Weavers Av., Pais.	45	H14
Weavers Rd., Pais.	45	H14
Webster St. G40	53	Y14
Webster St., Clyde.	18	N8
Wedderlea Dr. G52	32	P13
Weensmoor Pl. G53	60	P18
Weensmoor Rd. G53	60	P17
Weeple Dr., Linw.	28	E13
Weighhouse Clo., Pais.	46	J14
Weir Av., Barr.	59	M19
Weir Rd., Linw.	28	E12
Weir St. G5	35	V13
Weir St., Pais.	30	K13
Weirwood Av., Bail.	55	DD14
Weirwood Gdns., Bail.	55	DD14
Welbeck Rd. G53	60	P17
Welfare Av. G72	67	CC18
Well Grn. G43	50	T16
Well Rd., Kilb.	42	B14
Well St. G40	36	X13
Well St., Pais.	30	J13
Wellbank Pl., Udd.	69	GG17
Church St.		
Wellbrae Ter., Chr.	15	GG7
Wellcroft Pl. G5	51	V14
Wellfield Av., Giff.	62	S18
Wellfield St. G21	22	X10
Wellhouse Cres. G33	39	DD12
Wellhouse Path G33	39	DD12
Wellhouse Rd. G33	39	DD12
Wellington La. G2	35	V12
West Campbell St.		
Wellington Pl., Dalm.	4	J6
Wellington Rd., Bish.	11	Z6
Wellington St. G2	35	V12
Wellington St., Pais.	30	J13
Caledonia St.		
Wellington St. E. G31	37	Z13
Wellington Way, Renf.	31	M11
Tiree Av.		
Wellmeadow Rd. G43	62	S17
Wellmeadow St., Pais.	46	J14
Wellpark St. G31	36	X12
Wells St., Clyde.	4	K6
Wellshot Dr. G72	66	AA17
Wellshot Rd. G32	54	AA14
Wellside Dr. G72	67	CC18
Wemyss Gdns., Bail.	56	EE14
Wendur Way, Pais.	30	J12
Abbotsburn Way		
Wenloch Rd., Pais.	46	K15
Wentworth Dr. G23	9	U7
West Av. G33	25	CC9
West Av., Renf.	17	M10
West Av., Udd.	69	HH17
West Brae, Pais.	46	J14
West Campbell St. G2	35	V12
West Campbell St., Pais.	45	H14
West Chapelton Av., Bear.	7	R6
West Chapelton Cres.,	7	R6
Bear.		
West Chapelton Dr., Bear.	7	R6
West Chapelton La., Bear.	7	R6
West Chapelton Av.		
West Coats Rd. G72	66	AA18
West Cotts., Gart.	26	EE10
West Ct., Dalm.	4	K6
Little Holm		
West George La., Udd.	35	V12
West Campbell St.		
West George St. G2	35	V12
West Graham St. G4	35	V11
West Greenhill Pl. G3	35	U12
West Sta., Pais.	45	H14
West Nile St. G2	35	V12
West Lo. Rd., Renf.	17	L10
West Princes St. G4	35	U11
West Regent La. G2	35	V12
Renfield St.		
West Regent St. G2	35	V12
West St. G5	51	V14
West St., Clyde.	18	N8
West St., Kilb.	42	B14
West St., Pais.	46	J14
West Thomson St.,	5	L6
Clyde.		
West Whitby St. G31	53	Z14
Westbank La. G12	35	U11
Gibson St.		
Westbank Quad. G12	35	U11
Gibson St.		
Westbank Ter. G12	35	U11
Gibson St.		
Westbourne Cres., Bear.	7	Q5
Westbourne Dr., Bear.	7	Q5
Westbourne Gdns. La.	20	T10
G12		
Lorraine Rd.		
Westbourne Gdns. N. G12	20	T10
Westbourne Gdns. S.	20	T10
G12		

Name	Map	Grid
Westbourne Gdns. W. G12	20	T10
Westbourne Rd. G12	20	S10
Westbourne Ter. La. G12	20	S10
Westbourne Rd.		
Westbrae Dr. G14	19	R10
Westburn G72	67	DD17
Westburn Av. G72	67	CC17
Westburn Av., Pais.	29	H13
Westburn Cres. G73	52	X16
Westburn Dr. G72	66	BB17
Westburn Fm. Rd. G72	66	BB17
Westburn Rd. G72	68	EE17
Westclyffe St. G41	51	U15
Westend, Bear.	8	S7
Maryhill Rd.		
Westend Pk. St. G3	35	U11
Wester Cleddens Rd., Bish.	11	Y7
Wester Common Dr. G22	21	V10
Wester Common Rd. G22	21	V10
Wester Common Ter. G22	21	V10
Wester Rd. G32	55	CC14
Westerburn St. G32	38	AA12
Westercraigs G31	36	X12
Westergreens Av., Lenz.	13	CC5
Parkburn Av.		
Westerhill Rd., Bish.	11	Y6
Westerhill St. G22	22	W10
Westerhouse Rd. G34	40	EE11
Westerkirk Dr. G23	9	U7
Western Av. G73	52	X16
Western Isles Rd., Old K.	4	J5
Western Rd. G72	66	AA18
Westerton Av., Bear.	19	R8
Westfield Av. G73	52	X16
Westfield Cres., Bear.	7	R7
Westfield Dr. G52	32	P13
Westfield Dr., Bear.	7	R7
Westfield Rd., Thorn.	61	R19
Westfield Vills. G73	52	X16
Westfields, Bish.	10	X6
Westhouse Av. G73	52	X16
Westhouse Gdns. G73	52	X16
Westknowe Gdns. G73	65	Y17
Westland Dr. G14	19	Q10
Westland Dr. La. G14	19	Q10
Westland Dr.		
Westlands, Bish.	10	X6
Westlands Gdns., Pais.	46	J15
Westminster Gdns. G12	20	T10
Kersland St.		
Westminster Ter. G3	35	U12
Claremont St.		
Westmoreland St. G42	51	V15
Westmuir Pl. G73	52	X16
Westmuir St. G31	37	Z13
Westpark Dr., Pais.	29	H13
Westray Circ. G22	22	W9
Westray Ct., Cumb.	70	NN4
Westray Pl. G22	22	W8
Westray Pl., Bish.	11	Z7
Ronaldsay Dr.		
Westray Rd., Cumb.	70	NN4
Westray Sq. G22	22	W8
Westray St. G22	22	W8
Westwood Av., Giff.	62	S18
Westwood Quad., Clyde.	5	M7
Westwood Rd. G43	62	S17
Weymouth Dr. G12	20	S9
Whamflet Av., Bail.	40	FF12
Wheatfield Rd., Bear.	7	Q7
Wheatlands Dr., Kilb.	42	B14
Wheatlands Fm. Rd., Kilb.	42	B14
Whin Dr., Barr.	59	L18
Whin St., Clyde.	5	L6
Whinfield Path G53	60	P18
Whinfield Rd. G53	60	P18
Whinfold Av. G72	54	AA16
Whinhill Av. G53	48	P14
Whinhill Rd., Pais.	47	L15
Whins Rd. G41	50	T15
Whirlow Gdns., Bail.	40	EE13
Whirlow Rd., Bail.	40	EE13
Whistlefield, Bear.	7	R6
Whitacres Path G53	60	P18
Whitacres Pl. G53	60	P18
Whitacres Rd. G53	60	P18
Whitburn St. G32	38	AA12
White St. G11	34	S11
White St., Clyde.	17	M8
Whitecraigs Pl. G23	21	U8
Whitefield Av. G72	66	BB18
Whitefield Rd. G51	34	T13
Whiteford Rd., Pais.	47	L15
Whitehall Ct. G3	35	U12
Whitehall St. G3	35	U12
Whitehaugh Av., Pais.	31	L13
Whitehaugh Cres. G53	60	P18
Whitehaugh Dr., Pais.	31	L13
Whitehaugh Path G53	60	P18
Whitehaugh Rd. G53	60	P18
Whitehill Av. G33	25	CC9
Whitehill Av., Cumb.	70	MM3
Whitehill Fm. Rd. G33	25	CC9
Whitehill Gdns. G31	37	Y12
Garthland Dr.		
Whitehill La., Bear.	7	Q6
Whitehill Rd.		
Whitehill Rd. G33	25	CC8
Whitehill Rd., Bear.	7	Q5
Whitehill St. G31	37	Y12
Whitehurst, Bear.	7	Q5
Whitekirk Pl. G15	6	P7
Whitelaw St. G20	20	T8
Whitelawburn Av. G72	66	AA18
Whitelawburn Rd. G72	66	AA18
Whitelawburn Ter. G72	66	AA18
Whitelaws Ln., Both.	69	HH18
Whiteloans, Udd.	69	HH18
Wordsworth Way		
Whitemoss Av. G44	63	U18
Whitestone Av., Cumb.	70	MM2
Dungoil Av.		
Whitevale St. G31	37	Y13
Whithope Rd. G53	60	N18
Whithope Ter. G53	60	N18
Whitriggs Rd. G53	60	N17
Whitslade St. G34	40	EE11
Whittingehame Dr. G12	19	R9
Whittingehame Gdns. G12	20	S9
Whittliemuir Av. G44	63	U18
Whitton Dr., Giff.	62	T18
Whitton St. G20	20	T8
Whitworth Dr., Clyde.	5	L7
Whitworth St. G20	21	V9
Whyte Av. G72	66	AA17
Wick St. G51	34	S12
Wickets, The, Pais.	47	L14
Wigton St. G4	21	V10
Wigtoun Pl., Cumb.	71	PP2
Wilderness Brae, Cumb.	71	PP2
Wilfred Av. G13	19	Q8
Wilkie Rd., Udd.	69	HH17
Wilkie St. G31	37	Y13
William St. G2	35	V12
William St. G3	35	U12
William St., Clyde.	5	L5
William St., John.	43	D14
William St., Pais.	46	J14
Williamson Pk. W. G44	63	U19
Williamson Pl., John.	44	E15
Williamson St. G31	53	Z14
Williamson St., Clyde.	5	L6
Williamwood Dr. G44	63	U19
Williamwood Pk. G44	63	U19
Willoughby Dr. G13	19	R9
Willow Av., Bish.	23	Y8
Willow Av., John.	44	F15
Hillview Rd.		
Willow Av., Lenz.	13	CC5
Willow Dr., John.	43	D15
Willow La. G32	54	BB15
Willow St. G13	19	R8
Willowbank Cres. G3	35	U11
Willowbank St. G3	35	U11
Willowdale Cres., Bail.	56	EE14
Willowdale Gdns., Bail.	56	EE14
Willowford Rd. G53	60	N18
Wilmot Rd. G13	19	Q9
Wilson Av., Linw.	28	E13
Wilson St. G1	36	W12
Wilson St., Pais.	46	J14
William St.		
Wilson St., Renf.	17	M10
Wilsons Pl., Pais.	46	K14
Seedhill		
Wilton Ct. G20	21	U10
Wilton Cres. G20	21	U10
Wilton Cres. La. G20	21	U10
Wilton Cres.		
Wilton Dr. G20	21	U10
Wilton Gdns. G20	21	U10
Wilton Mans. G20	21	U10
Wilton St.		
Wilton St. G20	21	U10
Wiltonburn Path G53	60	P18
Wiltonburn Rd. G53	60	P18
Wilverton Rd. G13	19	R8
Winchester Dr. G12	20	S9
Windhill Pl. G43	62	T17
Windhill Rd.		
Windhill Rd. G43	62	S17
Windlaw Ct. G45	64	W19
Windlaw Gdns. G44	63	U18
Windlaw Pk. Gdns. G44	63	U18
Windmill Cres. G43	62	S17
Windhill Rd.		
Windmill Pl. G43	62	T17
Windhill Rd.		
Windmillcroft Quay G5	35	V13
Windsor Cres., Clyde.	5	L6
Windsor Cres., John.	44	E15
Windsor Cres., Pais.	31	L13
Windsor Rd., Renf.	31	M11
Windsor St. G20	35	V11
Windsor St. G32	39	CC13
Windsor Ter. G20	35	V11
Windsor Wk., Udd.	57	HH16
Windyedge Cres. G13	19	Q9
Windyedge Pl. G13	19	Q9
Wingfield Gdns., Both.	69	HH19
Blairston Av.		
Winifred St. G33	23	Z10
Winning Ct., Blan.	69	GG19
Ness Dr.		
Winning Row G31	38	AA13
Winton Av., Giff.	62	T19
Winton Dr. G12	20	T9
Winton Gdns., Udd.	57	GG16
Winton La. G12	20	T9
Wirran Pl. G13	18	N8
Wishart St. G4	36	X12
Wisner Ct., Thorn.	61	R18
Wiston St. G72	67	DD17
Woddrop St. G40	53	Y15
Wolseley St. G5	52	W14
Wood Fm. Rd., Giff.	62	S19
Wood La., Bish.	23	Y8
Wood Quad., Clyde.	18	N8
Wood St. G31	37	Y12
Wood St., Pais.	47	L14
Woodbank Cres., John.	43	D15
Woodbank Ter., Gart.	27	GG9
Woodburn Rd. G43	62	T17
Woodburn Rd., Cumb.	70	MM3
Woodcroft Av. G11	19	R10
Woodcroft Ter. G11	19	R10
Crow Rd.		
Woodend, Giff.	62	S19
Milverton Rd.		
Woodend Ct. G32	55	DD15
Woodend Dr. G13	19	R9
Woodend Dr., Pais.	47	M14
Woodend Gdns. G32	55	DD15
Woodend Pl., John.	44	E15
Malloch Cres.		
Woodend Rd. G32	55	CC15
Woodend Rd. G73	65	Y18
Woodfield Av., Bish.	11	Y7

Street	No.	Grid
Woodfoot Path G53	60	P18
Woodfoot Pl. G53	60	P18
Woodfoot Quad. G53	60	P18
Woodfoot Rd. G53	60	P18
Woodford Pl., Linw.	28	E13
Woodford St. G41	51	U16
Woodgreen Av. G44	64	W17
Woodhall St. G40	53	Y15
Woodhead Av. G71	69	HH19
Old Bothwell Rd.		
Woodhead Cres., Udd.	57	GG16
Woodhead Path G53	60	P17
Woodhead Rd. G53	60	N17
Woodhead Rd., Chr.	26	EE9
Woodhead Ter., Chr.	26	EE8
Woodhill Rd. G21	23	Y9
Woodhill Rd., Bish.	11	Y7
Woodholm Av. G44	64	W17
Woodhouse St. G13	19	R8
Woodilee Cotts., Lenz.	13	DD5
Woodilee Rd., Lenz.	13	DD5
Woodland Av., Gart.	27	GG8
Woodland Av., Pais.	46	K16
Woodland Cres. G72	66	BB18
Woodland Vw., Cumb.	71	PP2
Braehead Rd.		
Woodland Way, Cumb.	71	PP2
Woodlands Av., Both.	69	HH18
Woodlands Cres., Both.	69	HH18
Woodlands Cres., Thorn.	61	R18
Woodlands Dr. G4	35	U11
Woodlands Gdns., Udd.	69	GG18
Woodlands Gate G3	35	U11
Woodlands Gate, Thorn.	61	R18
Woodlands Pk., Thorn.	61	R19
Woodlands Rd. G3	35	U11
Woodlands Rd., Thorn.	61	R19
Woodlands Ter. G3	35	U11
Woodlands Ter., Both.	69	HH18
Woodlea Dr., Giff.	62	T18
Woodlinn Av. G44	63	V17
Woodneuk Av., Gart.	27	HH9
Woodneuk Rd. G53	60	P17
Woodneuk Rd., Gart.	27	GG9
Woodrow Circ. G41	50	T14
Woodrow Pl. G41	50	T14
Maxwell Dr.		
Woodrow Rd. G41	50	T14
Woods La., Renf.	17	M10
Woodside Av. G73	53	Z16
Woodside Av., Lenz.	13	CC5
Woodside Av., Thorn.	62	S18
Woodside Cres. G3	35	U11
Woodside Cres., Barr.	59	M19
Woodside Cres., Pais.	46	J14
William St.		
Woodside Pl. G3	35	U11
Woodside Pl. La. G3	35	U11
Elderslie St.		
Woodside Rd. G20	21	U10
Woodside Ter. G3	35	U11
Woodside Ter., Bish.	10	W6
Woodside Ter. La. G3	35	U11
Woodlands Rd.		
Woodstock Av. G41	50	T15
Woodstock Av., Pais.	45	G16
Woodvale Av., Bear.	8	S7
Woodvale Dr., Pais.	29	H13
Woodville St. G51	34	S13
Wordsworth Way, Udd.	69	HH18
Works Av. G72	67	DD17
Wraes Av., Barr.	59	M18
Wren Pl., John.	43	C16
Wright Av., Barr.	59	L19
Wright St., Renf.	31	L11
Wrightlands Cres., Renf.	16	K8
Wykeham Pl. G13	19	Q9
Wykeham Rd. G13	19	Q9
Wynd, The, Cumb.	71	PP1
Wyndford Dr. G20	20	T9
Wyndford Pl. G20	20	T9
Wyndford Rd.		
Wyndford Rd. G20	20	T9
Wyndham St. G12	20	T10
Wynford Ter., Udd.	57	HH16
Dalry Rd.		
Wyper Pl. G40	37	Y13
Gallowgate		
Wyvil Av. G13	7	R7
Wyvis Av. G13	18	N8
Wyvis Pl. G13	18	N8
Wyvis Quad. G13	18	N8
Yair Dr. G52	32	P13
Yarrow Ct., Cumb.	67	CC17
Yarrow Gdns. G20	21	U10
Yarrow Gdns. La. G20	21	U10
Yarrow Gdns.		
Yarrow Rd., Bish.	11	Y6
Yate St. G31	37	Y13
Yetholm St. G14	18	N9
Yew Dr. G21	23	Y10
Foresthall Dr.		
Yew Pl., John.	44	E15
Yoker Ferry Rd. G14	18	N9
Yoker Mill Gdns. G13	18	N8
Yoker Mill Rd. G13	18	N8
Yokerburn Ter., Clyde.	17	M8
York Dr. G73	65	Z17
York La. G2	35	V12
York St.		
York St. G2	35	V13
York St., Clyde.	5	M7
York Way, Renf.	31	M11
Yorkhill La. G3	34	T12
Yorkhill St.		
Yorkhill Par. G3	34	T11
Yorkhill St. G3	34	T12
Young St., Clyde.	5	L6
Young Ter. G21	23	Y10
Zambesi Dr., Blan.	68	FF19
Zena Cres. G33	23	Z10
Zena Pl. G33	23	Z10
Zena St. G33	23	Z10
Zetland Rd. G52	32	N12